CW00536357

The Illustrated History of
EAST COAST
JOINT STOCK

North Eastern Railway R class 4-4-0 No. 1026 at King Edward Bridge Junction, Gateshead, c1910. (*R. J. Purves*)

The Illustrated History of
EAST COAST JOINT STOCK

Ken Hoole

Oxford Publishing Co.

© 1993 The Ken Hoole Trust

All rights reserved. No part of this book may be reproduced or transmitted in any form or by any means, electronic or mechanical, including photocopying, recording or by any information storage or retrieval system, without written permission from the copyright owner.

A catalogue record for this book is available from the British Library.

ISBN 0-86093-430-6

Oxford Publishing Co. is part of the
Haynes Publishing Group PLC
Sparkford, near Yeovil, Somerset, BA22 7JJ

Haynes Publications Inc.
861 Lawrence Drive, Newbury Park, California 91320, USA.

Printed and bound in Great Britain by Butler & Tanner Ltd, Frome and London
Typeset in Times Roman Medium

All photographs are from the Kenneth Taylor collection unless stated otherwise.

Publisher's note:
The publishers would like to thank the Trustees of the Ken Hoole Trust for the valuable assistance given in preparing this book for publication.

Ken Hoole

The name of Ken Hoole is well known to railway enthusiasts. He wrote over 40 books in his own right, shared in the production or editing of a dozen more, wrote numerous articles for magazines and newspapers and also made some broadcasts on radio.

Through this he established his reputation as the leading writer and authority on the long history and operation of railways in the North East of England, and of the North Eastern Railway in particular.

He was one of the few full time professional writers on railway history, his occupation and pleasure for over 30 years until his death in late 1988. His enthusiasm for railways commenced at an early age and was sparked off by the 1925 Stockton & Darlington Railway Centenary Celebrations. It grew during his schooldays when travelling by train every day between his home in Bridlington and school in Hull.

Locomotives and train working became a special interest and he built up meticulous records on the subject, plus an extensive collection of historic photographs. He made painstaking researches through official records and archives, whilst he also knew many prominent railway enthusiasts and professional railwaymen who shared their knowledge.

Ken was one of the founder members of the North Eastern Railway Association, a body created for enthusiasts to foster interest in the railways of the North East. His name is also remembered in the recently opened Ken Hoole Study Centre at Darlington Railway Museum, where his extensive collection of railway archives is now housed.

C. B. Foster,
Trustee, Ken Hoole Trust,
January 1993.

Contents

North Eastern Railway Q class 4-4-0 No. 1875 leaves York for the North in 1898. (*Dr T. Budden*)

1 Introduction

Occasionally, items on East Coast Joint Stock coaches appeared in the railway press prior to 1923, in the *Railway Magazine*, the *Locomotive Magazine & Railway Carriage and Wagon Review* (to give it its full title), and the *Railway Engineer* but, as far as I know, no detailed history of its vehicles has ever appeared.

A long established interest in these fine vehicles, and the availability of ECJS 1903 and 1909 Diagram Books at the British Railways Board Historical Records Office at York meant that at last I could identify the individual vehicles. I also found that the late Guy Hemingway shared my interest and he kindly presented me with a typed copy of his notes compiled from official GN, NE and East Coast minute books. Later, Willie Yeadon of Hull was good enough to present me with a 1909 Diagram Book, while a 1903 Diagram Book was bequeathed to the Library of the North Eastern Railway Association by Valentine Rippon.

Unfortunately there is no cohesion between the 1903 and 1909 Diagram Books and, for instance, although 3rd class dining saloons Nos 313/4/5 are illustrated on page 58 in the 1903 Book, they are on page 30 in the 1909 Book. Both editions refer to 'Plans of the East Coast Joint Stock' and nowhere do they refer to the pages as Diagram Numbers. However, to fit in with the generally accepted practice, and for consistency, the page numbers have been referred to as Diagram Numbers.

Contrary to usual procedure preference has been given to diagrams of ECJS vehicles rather than photographs. The reason for this is because externally the vehicles are generally similar—teak livery with a number of doors and windows—but with no indication of the internal layout, whereas the diagrams show both features. However, it must be remembered that the door and window arrangements often differed on the opposite sides of the same vehicle. This was particularly so with compartment stock; on the corridor side there were usually three or four doors, but on the compartment side there would be a door to each of the seven or eight compartments. Dummy doors were often used on East Coast vehicles, presumably for the sake of appearance.

The majority of the East Coast vehicles were built at Doncaster and followed Great Northern practice, but in 1893 a number of coaches were obtained from various contractors. The specifications for these vehicles were prepared at York by the NER and some GN features were eradicated; the North Eastern commenced to build East Coast stock at York in 1895, and eventually the North British works at Cowlairs (Glasgow) was allowed to build for the fleet.

There is an imbalance in the number of train views used in this volume, with a preponderance of trains hauled by North Eastern locomotives; south of Doncaster it is virtually impossible to tell if a train behind a Great Northern Atlantic was made up of East Coast or Great Northern stock, because of their great similarity. However north of York an East Coast train behind a North Eastern engine would invariably be made up of East Coast vehicles, although there may have been a Great Northern van added for strengthening purposes.

Until quite recently there were a number of former ECJS coach bodies in use as bungalows or holiday chalets, particularly in Yorkshire, but many have now disappeared due to old age and the changes in the social conditions demanding better accommodation. The most intriguing is old ECJS No. 14, built in 1898 and transferred to the North Eastern Area in 1925. At the time of writing the timber skeleton still exists at Humshaugh (formerly Chollerford) on the ex-North British Border Counties line between Hexham and Riccarton Junction.

The two notable Royal Saloons built for the East Coast in 1908, Nos 395 and 396, have both been preserved in the National Collection; No. 395, built at Doncaster, is at the National Railway Museum at York, whereas No. 396, built at York, is on loan to Bressingham. Special Brake Van No. 109 (originally 82), also built at Doncaster in 1908 for use with the Royal Train, has also been preserved at York, together with Corridor 3rd No. 12, built by the NER in 1898. The latter was transferred to the Great Northern Section in 1925 and became No. 41805; it owes its continued existence to the fact that in 1952 it was chosen to be restored to participate in the exhibition marking the centenary of King's Cross station.

The life of the ECJS fleet can be divided into three periods; namely 4-wheel and 6-wheel stock up to 1896, the clerestory roof era 1896–1906, and the elliptical roof era 1906–1922. Most of the bogie vehicles continued to run well into LNER days, and some into the BR period, although not in the East Coast fleet. In the 1920s and 1930s it was possible to ride in former East Coast vehicles on every section of the LNER; whereas pre-1923 replaced vehicles were distributed between the Great Northern, North Eastern and North British, after 1923 they were also used on former Great Central, Great Eastern and Great North of Scotland routes.

How did the East Coast Joint Stock look develop? Certainly there is no doubt about the 6-wheel stock, which clearly showed its Great Northern parentage, and the Gresley stock with its high roof, but what about the distinctive 8-wheel and 12-wheel coaches which appeared between 1894 and 1906? They could owe their origins to the carriage building firm of Craven Bros of Darnall, Sheffield, which built two 12-wheel clerestory roofed dining saloons for the GNR in 1885. The design included a pantry and kitchen, and two saloons, one 13 ft 3 in long seating eight, and the other 19 ft 10½ in long, seating twelve, both with one seat on each side of the centre gangway. Stirling was usually not in favour of bogies but he actually suggested these two coaches for the Leeds service at a cost of £1,800 each. It was said that the order was placed 'outside' because Doncaster was too busy—but I wonder if Doncaster, so long steeped in the tradition of short 6-wheel vehicles, could have built a coach with 12-wheels! The only other bogie vehicles on the East Coast Main Line were the three Pullman sleeping cars, although the MS&LR were using some Craven-built bogie cars on the Manchester service—which ran into King's Cross.

The eight North Eastern designed bogie coaches built for the first dining car trains in 1893 did little to further development, being only 46 ft long with plain roofs, but the Doncaster-built replacements for the four 'too good' 3rd class cars did show signs of progress; these were Nos 188/9, 222/3, 52 ft 6 in long and carried on two 4-wheel bogies.

E. F. Howlden, who had been with the GN for many years, was promoted to Carriage & Wagon Superintendent in 1877, but what prompted his leap to clerestory roofed bogie stock after 16 years of producing mediocre vehicles for the GN and ECJS? Was it because the influence of Stirling was waning due to his age; after all he was 73 in 1893.

Next to appear was the NER-built sleeping car, the first ECJS vehicle to be built at York, and this is where an unresolved problem creeps in. In various publications mention is made of a preliminary design prepared at York in 1894, and an accompanying drawing shows a coach with a clerestory roof, but with the clerestory finishing about 3 ft from each end of the roof. However, when the car appeared as No. 234 in 1895 the interior layout was exactly as in the preliminary design—but was the roof on the actual coach as indicated on the drawing, or did it slope down in the familiar East Coast pattern? There is an official photograph of No. 234 with the clerestory sloping down at the ends—but this was taken some years later and proves nothing.

Certainly the new vehicles (Nos 239–256) built for the three new day trains in 1896 had the clerestory sloping down, and all were carried on two 6-wheel bogies, and it was this series which set the pattern for a decade, but did the inspiration come from the Craven cars of 1885? I suspect that it did. Unfortunately I have been unable to locate a suitable view of one of the Craven cars to illustrate my point, although a drawing based on GN Carriage Dgm. No. 55 appears in F. A. S. Brown's book *From Stirling to Gresley* (OPC 1974), and a distant view of one of the cars appears as an illustration to an article entitled 'The GNR Four-Coupled Engines' by J. F. Vickery in the *Railway Magazine* for May 1904 (Vol. XIV, p. 401). In this photograph the 12-wheel diner is in the centre of a 4-coach set of GN (or ECJS) 6-wheelers, towering above them and virtually twice as long!

Before the appearance of the 1896 East Coast stock, discussions were taking place and on 10th April 1895 it was decided that bogie carriages were the most suitable, but no decision was taken as to whether they should have 'clear stories'. In June Mr Gibb of the NER expressed a preference for saloons with centre gangway, ie 'open' vehicles, for both 1st and 3rd class accommodation, but Mr Stirling proposed that the 3rds be open and the 1sts be compartments. However, it must be remembered that the GN was developing its internal stock along the same lines, particularly for its Leeds services, with four 12-wheel dining cars (Nos 2753/4 1st class with kitchen) and Nos 2755/6 (3rd class with pantry), also built in 1896.

In August 1898 the NER representatives suggested that it was about time that the 10 am services were provided with dining cars, so that the 30 minute meal halt at York could be abolished, and on 11th August this was agreed to by the GN Board. However, it was pointed out that the new facilities could not be introduced until 1st July 1900 as this was the earliest date by which Mr Ivatt could provide the coaches.

The meal halts on the Scotsman trains were withdrawn as planned from 1st August 1900, but although the GN vehicles were ready, not all the NE and NB coaches were available. Perhaps that is why the 'down' 10 am was allowed only ten minutes at York (1.45 pm to 1.55 pm) whereas the 'up' train was allowed 20 minutes (2.15 pm to 2.35 pm)?

When new trains for the 10 am trains were discussed in December 1912 a ten-coach set was proposed, with the dining cars, kitchen car composite coach and van work-

---

NOTICE.

Passengers travelling by the SCOTCH EXPRESS Trains

LEAVING

EDINBURGH & KING'S CROSS

At 10-0 a.m.

ARE ALLOWED

HALF-AN-HOUR at YORK for REFRESHMENTS,

AND BY THE

EXPRESS TRAINS leaving EDINBURGH at 10-15 a.m., KING'S CROSS at 10-35 a.m., and NEWCASTLE at 4-0 p.m.,

TWENTY MINUTES.

HOT DINNERS ARE PROVIDED, at 2s. 6d. EACH,

INCLUDING

SOUPS, JOINTS, VEGETABLES, TART, & CHEESE. NO FEES.

WARNING IS GIVEN in the rooms FIVE MINUTES BEFORE these trains depart.

Notice from NER Timetable for July 1881 when the 10 am from King's Cross and the 10 am from Edinburgh were allowed a half-hour meal halt at York; other trains were allowed 20 minutes.

---

ing through to Aberdeen, but in August 1913 it was decided to terminate the catering vehicles at Edinburgh, with the other vehicles going on to Perth (composite), Glasgow (brake 3rd and composite) and Aberdeen (composite, 3rd and van).

Early in 1914 it was decided to reform the 9.50 am from King's Cross and the 10.10 am from Edinburgh, making up four trains out of the 22 existing coaches and the eleven still to be delivered, although this involved altering the seating arrangements in some coaches.

From the foregoing it will be seen that the ECJS fleet was always closely supervised and that every endeavour was made to provide the most suitable stock for the service, perhaps spurred on by the fact that the two main partners took a great pride in the stock and its working.

The vehicles of the ECJS were numbered in one series between 1 and 396, but the position is complicated by the various renumberings and replacements which took place over the years. This was because of transfers between the three companies and the Joint Stock, or vice versa, and the renewals necessary by old age or accident. New stock was numbered into the list, taking either a blank number where an earlier vehicle had been withdrawn, or at the end of the list. Sometimes the old vehicle continued to run for a few more years, placed on the Duplicate List and carrying a letter 'A' suffix to its number.

It was agreed at an early date that vehicles displaced by new construction should be disposed of to the three companies, and when they reached their new owners the old vehicles were renumbered into that company's stock list. On a few early occasions, where new vehicles could not be provided in time, transfer of vehicles was made from the company having suitable vehicles (usually the Great Northern) to the Joint Stock, involving renumbering into the East Coast list.

On a few occasions a vehicle was transferred from the Joint Stock to one of the partners (usually the North Eastern) and then, after modification, transferred back to the Joint Stock. The coach would be renumbered on both occasions but did not necessarily take up its original number on transfer back to the Joint Stock, probably because that number had already been filled by a new vehicle. It is a coincidence that two such changes involved coaches numbered 196 and 197:

EC 196 Built 1893: transferred to NER in 1896 and renumbered 2647; transferred back to ECJS in 1897 and renumbered 195.

EC 196 Replacement built 1902: transferred to NER in 1904 and renumbered 3498; transferred back to ECJS in 1906 and renumbered 354.

EC 196 Replacement built 1905 and sold to NBR in 1913.

EC 196 Replacement built 1922.

No. 197 was dealt with similarly although it remained in EC stock until 1928 and thus there was no third replacement.

East Coast expresses conveying Joint Stock vehicles—particularly the night trains—were involved in numerous accidents and in some of these, of a more serious nature, five or six vehicles could be damaged beyond repair. Normally a replacement vehicle was built, often of the same type as the original but to an improved design.

In LNER days, when all three companies came under common ownership, the former Joint Stock fleet continued to be operated in the same way, largely restricted to East Coast services, running under the same numbers but with the addition of a letter 'J' suffix to distinguish them from the internal Great Northern, North Eastern and North British stock. The suffix was later replaced by a figure 1 prefix. Transfer from East Coast stock continued to take place as new coaches and vans were produced, but because of the wider scope available redundant coaches were also transferred to the Great Central, Great Eastern and Great North of Scotland sections, which had not previously received displaced East Coast stock. The vehicles were renumbered into each Section's stock. For example:

EC 78 became 78J, 178, and Northern Scottish (GNoS Section) 7819.

EC 93 became 93J, 193, and Southern Area (Great Central Section) 52035.

EC 100 became 100J, 1100, and Southern Area (Great Eastern Section) 6738.

Prior to the 1923 Grouping redundant sleeping cars were usually converted to saloons on transfer from East Coast to company stock, as the latter had no need for such vehicles. However, after Grouping redundant sleeping cars were usually condemned and not distributed to the various Areas. Almost all true ECJS vehicles were withdrawn in the 1920s and 1930s and many ended their days as Service (Departmental) vehicles, although many were sold for use as homes, or holiday chalets, some of which still exist.

The East Coast companies were tardy in introducing dining car trains, and it was not until 1893 that the first train to include such vehicles ran between London and Edinburgh. This facility applied to only one train in each direction and it was not until four years later that it was extended to another pair of trains: even this was a last minute decision and meant that North Eastern cars had to be used as no East Coast vehicles had been built for the service. Even the famous 10 am from King's Cross still made a 20-minute meal halt at York until further dining car trains were introduced in 1900.

Throughout the existence of the Joint Stock the East Coast group was constantly watching what the West Coast companies were doing, and if the West Coast provided facilities which the East Coast did not have then the East Coast followed suit, leading to umbrella and hat racks in East Coast coaches, stuffed backs to third class seats, footwarmers for third class passengers, reduced charges for sleeping berths, the provisions of rugs etc, etc.

The provision of sleeping cars on East Coast services brought about more discussion than any other topic and there were numerous meetings of the East Coast partners to decide on the type of coaches and layout of berths. Mr Stirling of the Great Northern did not like bogie coaches and preferred longitudinal berths, and although the first North Eastern designed bogie sleepers had longitudinal berths a change was soon made to transverse berths; these were an immediate success and set the pattern for all future East Coast sleepers.

For the first 35 years of the partnership the design and provision of East Coast coaching stock was almost wholly the responsibility of the Great Northern Railway. Occasionally the NER was asked to approve a new design proposed by Mr Stirling, and later by Mr Howlden, but the North British seems to have been virtually ignored. There was sometimes disagreement and the NER vetoed a design, but the North Eastern came unstuck when it designed the first East Coast diners for the 1893 trains. Four 1st class and four 3rd class bogie diners were obtained from contractors to work with the 6-wheel kitchen cars—but both 1st class and 3rd class diners seated only 24 passengers and thus both classes could dine in equal comfort. Naturally there was a reluctance to pay 1st class fares when the same facilities were available in the 3rd class! This was immediately recognised and four 3rd class dining cars each seating 42 passengers were ordered from Doncaster, and as soon as they were ready they replaced the NER designed cars, although the latter returned in modified form in 1897.

The next NER venture into East Coast coaches was the first transverse-berth sleeping car built at York in 1895, and henceforward the North Eastern took a greater part in building East Coast vehicles at its York Carriage Works. Such coaches were, of course, usually built to match the Doncaster produced stock, originally with clerestory roofs, but later with the Gresley high pattern roof. In 1905 the North Eastern went its own way and designed some straight-sided stock, both for internal and East Coast use, but these did not find favour and they were not perpetuated.

The North British played only a small part in the design and building of East Coast coaches and it was not until 1901 that Cowlairs built some 12-wheel coaches and a number of 8-wheel vans. However, the NBR was responsible for one of the first sleeping cars used on East Coast services, which was put into use between Glasgow, Edinburgh and London in 1873. A Great Northern sleeper was also introduced in that year and both were purchased in 1876 for inclusion in the East Coast fleet; the North British car was replaced in 1884 and the GN car in 1893. The first sleeping car built to ECJS order was turned out from Doncaster in 1877 and started work on 1st July between London and Glasgow, with another car on the new Perth service. East Coast sleeping cars eventually ran through from London to Aberdeen and Inverness, competing with the West Coast companies, although the two groups eventually worked closer together. This took the form of running the Inverness sleeper in the winter months from Euston, travelling via the West Coast route, on Mondays, Wednesdays and Fridays, and from King's Cross, travelling via the East Coast route, on Tuesdays, Thursdays and Saturdays. In the opposite direction the Tuesday, Thursday and Saturday departures from Inverness were bound for Euston, and the Monday, Wednesday and Friday departures for King's Cross.

The earliest East Coast vehicles ran on four wheels but by 1879 only one was still in use; it was taken over later that year by the Great Northern at a figure of £300. The date at which 6-wheelers were introduced has not been established, but they were getting thin on the ground by 1915, when it was proposed that they should all be withdrawn. However, presumably because of World War I, this was deferred and it was not until 1922 that the last was withdrawn, although some were probably still in existence (but not in stock) on the formation of the LNER on 1st January 1923. Although distributed to the companies most of these 6-wheelers appear to have been scrapped rather than found further use by their new owners.

2 Early History

In November 1855 an agreement was reached between the Great Northern, North Eastern, North British, Edinburgh & Glasow and Scottish Central railway companies, being 'the owners of the main line of railway from London via York to Edinburgh, Stirling and Perth, which is herein called the East Coast Route', and being 'mutually desirous of facilitating the transit of traffic along the said East Coast Route passing south of Edinburgh' and of 'establishing a united system for the working and management of through traffic over and along the railways forming the said East Coast Route or in connection therewith'. The Edinburgh & Glasgow and Scottish Central companies were 'to use their best endeavours. . . with all possible expedition and despatch to collect, receive, forward, carry and deliver over to the North British Railway Company, and by them to the said other Companies, all traffic which may arise or be produced in. . . places lying eastwards or to the north of Larbert (except Edinburgh)'.

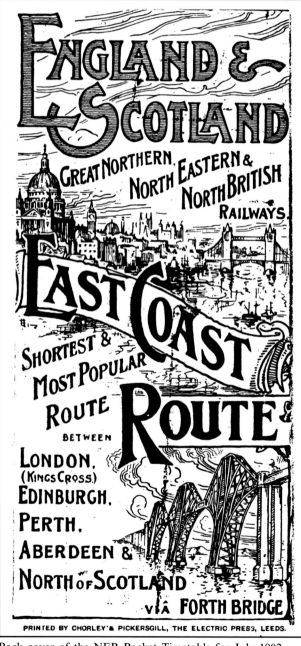

Back cover of the NER Pocket Timetable for July 1902.

However, up to 1860 the East Coast 'Scotch Expresses' were evidently made up of a mixture of carriages provided by the various companies, in such proportions as roughly to balance the mileage earnings. A typical Great Northern 3-compartment coach of the period would be carried on four wheels, 18 ft over headstocks, width 7 ft 4 in, with one central 1st class compartment 6 ft $4\frac{3}{4}$ in wide, and two 2nd class 5 ft 6 in wide. Luggage was carried on the roof, within a low railed enclosure 10 ft long and 7 ft wide, with spaces railed off round the three roof lamps. There were square-cornered sunken panels between the windows, and rounded beadings at the waist and below, also in square-cornered panels. They would probably be built of teak, with a highly polished and varnished finish.

Then, on 15th March 1860 Mr Leith of the Great Northern wrote to his General Manager, Seymour Clarke, 'When at York yesterday with Mr Christison (NER General Passenger Supt.) and Mr McLaren, (NBR General Passenger Supt.) I discovered that both their companies were either renewing or rebuilding additional stock, and I mooted the question of a common East Coast stock of passenger carriages, and these gentlemen seemed to think that the question would now be favourably entertained by their Managers. My proposal you know, is that there should be a common stock of East Coast passenger carriages and break (sic) vans, built at the cost of the three companies and divided on mileage, and that repairs shall be made at Doncaster, Newcastle or Edinburgh as may be agreed, and charged on the same principle. If these carriages earn mileage over other companies' lines; it is to be credited to the three companies in mileage proportion. Our proportion would be about 20 carriages, which our increasing passenger traffic warrants as an addition to our stock.'

On 19th March Seymour Clarke recommended this proposal to the Great Northern Board, and negotiations began between the three companies. By 1st August agreement had been reached as to the number of carriages required to form a stock to be used between London and Edinburgh, and this comprised:

			£
16	1st Class	@ £310 each	= 4,960
6	2nd Class	@ £245 each	= 1,470
10	3rd Class	@ £230 each	= 2,300
10	Composites	@ £300 each	= 3,000
8	Brake Vans	@ £215 each	= 1,720
50			13,450

This total was then divided on a mileage basis:

GN mileage	191	Proposed share	£6,422
NE mileage	151	Proposed share	£5,077
NB mileage	58	Proposed share	£1,950
	400		£13,449

and it was then decided that the coaches should be allocated thus:

GNR: 8 1st; 3 2nd; 5 3rd; 4 compo; 4 brakes
= 24 vehicles £6,425
NER: 4 1st; 1 2nd; 5 3rd; 6 compo; 3 brakes
= 19 vehicles £5,080
NBR: 4 1st; 2 2nd; 1 brake = 7 vehicles £1,945
Total: 50 vehicles £13,450

The scheme was approved by the NER Directors (in principle) and this was conveyed to Seymour Clarke of the GNR in a letter from Capt. O'Brien (General Manager) dated 1st August 1860, suggesting 'It will be necessary, however, that the plans and details of colour and arms be approved by us, as we wish that the distinctive colour of each of our companies' stock should be avoided, and another colour be adopted, so that the public may see at once that they are Joint Stock and not exclusively the property of either of the three companies.'

On the same date Capt. O'Brien wrote to T. K. Rowbotham of the North British Railway, informing him of the latest developments, and stating that the stock 'be used only in the traffic of the three Railway Companies and not of two only; for example the carriages must be put on at the termini only (London or Edinburgh) and not be allowed to stop short at any intermediate point. They may be used for intermediate traffic whilst so running. Secondly, no demurrage or mileage to be charged on the NER, GN or NB. Thirdly, that the Clearing House credit any mileage the carriages may earn north of Edinburgh in mileage proportion to the three companies'. He also suggested that the carriages 'should be designed and built by the GNR, who certainly do their carriage work extremely well'.

The Great Northern directors approved the idea on 1st September 1860 with the comment 'One great benefit to us will be that the stock will be built entirely according to our views, and that we shall cease to have objections raised by the public to ride in carriages (which they find in our express trains) which are provided by other companies'. Seymour Clarke advised Capt. O'Brien of his Board's approval by letter dated 15th September 1860 and agreed that Mr Sturrack (sic) be requested to prepare diagrams 'embracing the most recent improvements, and suggest your Carriage Superintendent be sent to Doncaster, where we have some stock now in hand, in order that he may see the mode in which we are putting our carriages together and the materials we employ. The Carriage Foreman told me that if commenced at once he could ensure the whole of the proposed carriages being at work during June 1861'. In acknowledgement Capt. O'Brien advised the GN General Manager that Mr Fletcher, the NER Locomotive Superintendent, would attend on behalf of the NER.

The North Eastern directors were still pressing for a distinctive livery and on 15th September decided that 'The arms and lettering should be red instead of blue, so that they may be easily distinguished from the rest of the stock', and later suggested that if a carriage had three compartments then the arms and name of one of the companies should be placed on each compartment! This was not approved, although many years later the East Coast coaches carried three separate arms—England, Scotland and the ECJS.

The actual cost of the vehicles was slightly above the estimate and came out at £14,018 5s 5d and in August 1861 the North Eastern paid the Great Northern £5,280 11s 11d for their share of 19 vehicles.

The livery adopted was varnished teak, with gold lettering shaded red. This, and the general arrangement of the panelling and beading, continued (except for a few vehicles built at York in 1905) throughout the Joint Stock's existence. All that can be stated with certainty about the numbering is that Nos 1 to 16 were 3-compartment 1sts, though the luggage brakes were probably Nos

45–50. There is nothing to suggest that the Joint Stock ever followed the GN practice, discontinued about 1870, of having separate numerical lists for the different types of carriage. It seems likely that five of the ten composites had two 1st and one 2nd class compartments, and the other five had two 2nds and one 1st.

In February 1863 it was pointed out that there were too many 1st class coaches and that of the 16 available only two were in daily use during the winter months and eight during the summer. After some discussion it was decided to transfer four ECJS 1st class (Nos 13–16) to the Great Northern in exchange for four composites, which took the same ECJS numbers.

In February 1864 Mr Leith of the North British suggested that as the West Coast consortium covered the route from London to Aberdeen the companies in the north of Scotland should be admitted to the East Coast partnership, which extended only from London to Edinburgh. Agreement was reached after eight months and a review of the stock was undertaken, leading to the provision of 17 new vehicles, comprising five composites with two 1st class and two 2nd class compartments; five composites with one 1st, one 2nd and two 3rds; one composite with one 1st, one 2nd and one 3rd; and six 3rds. A similar number of old vehicles was dispersed among the three original partners. To accommodate the use of ECJS coaches over the Scottish North Eastern and Perth & Inverness lines the stock was separated into four divisions: Aberdeen and King's Cross; Inverness and King's Cross, Glasgow and King's Cross, and Edinburgh and King's Cross. The value of each division to be divided among the companies concerned on a mileage basis. The stock allocated to the various services was: Aberdeen traffic ten composites; Inverness traffic nine composites, Glasgow traffic six composites and six 3rds, Edinburgh traffic six 1sts, 4 2nds, twelve 3rds and ten brake vans.

Again it was stressed that the Joint carriages were to be restricted exclusively for through traffic by the East Coast Route and on no account were they to be used for local traffic by any of the companies. The Clearing House numbertakers were to be instructed to watch the working of East Coast stock and to report any improper use.

By March 1865 there were 63 East Coast vehicles in use and it was decided that instead of the individual companies having a certain number of carriages apportioned to them the stock should be dealt with as a whole, each company paying its mileage proportion of the entire cost.

Towards the end of 1867 the Minutes of the East Coast Joint Committee became available and one of the earliest entries relates to the replacement of the original carriages dating from 1861–4. In the Minutes of the meeting held on 19th December a brief summary of the position was given, pointing out that the Joint Stock was the property of the GN, NE, NB, the Caledonian (as the representative of the Scottish North Eastern and the Scottish Central) and the Highland. However, it was reported that the Highland wished to withdraw. Thus arrangements had to be made for the cost of the new stock, together with the Highland's share, to be divided among the remaining four companies. At the same time it was reported that 13 East Coast vehicles had been damaged in two accidents (at Ratho and Grant's House) and that they were being sent to Doncaster for repairs. Authority was also given for some of the old coaches to be withdrawn and replaced by carriages of improved construction from designs furnished by Mr Stirling. By January 1868 four specimen carriages were under construction at Doncaster—a 1st, 2nd, 3rd and composite—'to replace the existing stock by as perfect a coach as can be had without extravagance'. These four vehicles cost: 1st (4-compartment) £385; 2nd (4-compartment) £248, 3rd (5-compartment) £205 and composite (4-compartments, including two 1st) £314. All were on four wheels. On 19th May 1868 the tender of R. Crossley & Co. for 100 rugs at 8s 0d was accepted.

A stock list of 1870 provides an illustration of the vehicles and their numbering: 1st 1–9; 2nd 10–13; composites with two 1st and two 2nd 14–28; composites with two 1st, one 2nd and one 3rd 29–38; 3rds 39–44; vans 45–54; 3rd 55–63. A total of 63 vehicles.

A Doncaster drawing dated 24th August 1866 shows a 5-compartment 4-wheel 3rd class carriage 23 ft 6 in long and 7 ft 9 in wide over body, with a wheelbase of 15 ft $3\frac{1}{2}$ in. The height of the side under the cornice was 6 ft 0 in, and from rail to top of roof 10 ft 10 in, with another 12 in to the top of the oil lamps. The wheels appear to be 4 ft 0 in although no dimension is given on the drawing. One partition rose to the full height but the others were mere low backrests, carried barely 18 in above the unpadded seats; only two lamps were provided. Quarter-lights were glazed (an improvement on the 3rds of 1855, which had lights only in the doors) and 9 in wide. The compartments were only 4 ft $6\frac{1}{4}$ in wide and the doors 2 ft 0 in. No brakes appear on the drawing.

More improvements were soon found necessary. On 19th May 1870 it was stated that 'the West Coast third class carriages are now fitted with hat and umbrella rails or netting' and it was decided that the East Coast 3rds should be similarly fitted; and on 21st November 1871 'East Coast 2nd class passengers are not provided with foot-warmers north of York, as is done by the West Coast'. A month later it was reported that 'foot-warmers have been ordered and will be supplied as soon as possible'.

By October 1871 additional stock was required as 'the 8.20 pm down express has, during the autumn, generally been formed of Great Northern carriages and there should be provided for it: eight 4-bodied 1st and 2nd class composite carriages with luggage body; two 3rd class carriages; and four large 6-wheel brake vans'. This was approved on 4th March 1872 but on 23rd March, following the decision to attach 3rd class carriages to all trains from 1st April, the new vehicles were altered to: eight composites, each with two 1st and two 3rd and one luggage body; two 3rd brakes with three passenger compartments, and four brake vans. All to be on six wheels, and not to carry luggage on the roof. On the same day it was proposed to build 15 additional 5-compartment 3rds and five 3rd brakes with three compartments. The allocation on 21st May 1872 was:

	London–Edinburgh	London–Glasgow	London–Aberdeen
1st class	9	6	—
2nd class	4	—	—
3rd class	9	—	—
Composite	—	9	16
Brakes	10	—	—
New compos 3rd-1st-luggage-1st-3rd	4	—	—
New compos 3rd-1st-luggage-2nd-3rd	—	—	4
3rd brakes	—	2	—
New brakes	—	—	4
	36	17	24

A total of 77 vehicles.

At that time 66 carriages were in use daily in the ordinary formations, but as it had been decided to run an additional train between London and Edinburgh or Glasgow it was agreed to recommend the construction of twelve additional vehicles with as little delay as possible. All were to be 6-wheel, with the contemporary flat segmental roof contour used by the Great Northern. The appropriate Doncaster drawing dated December 1872 shows a 6-wheel composite coach; 3rd-1st-luggage-2nd-3rd, with a wheelbase of 20 ft 8 in. The height to the top of the roof was 10 ft 11 in, and to the top of the oil lamps 12 ft 1 in, with the height of the side under the cornice now 6 ft 2 in. The Mansell type wheels were 3 ft 6 in diameter. Both 2nd and 3rd class compartments were 5 ft 6 in wide having upholstered seats and backs, while the 1st class were 7 ft 0 in wide, with more elaborate padding and elbow rests for three-a-side seating. The central luggage compartment was 7 ft 2 in with double doors. The quarter-lights of the 2nd and 3rd class were now 12 in wide and those of the 1st 14 in.

In October 1873 it was reported that the ten brake vans dating from 1861 and 1863 were nearly worn out and Mr Stirling estimated he could build 6-wheel replacements at £293 9s 7d each. These were in traffic by May 1874 and a month later the old vans were divided among the NBR (1), NER (4) and GNR (5). During 1873 two sleeping cars were introduced on East Coast services, one owned by the North British and one by the Great Northern. In the following year it was suggested that these two vehicles should be taken into East Coast stock but this was not accomplished until 1877.

On 14th October 1875 more vehicles were requested and when this came up for discussion in March 1876 the stock at that time was: 13 1st Nos 1–9 and 86–89; 4 2nd 10–13, 37 composite 14–38 and 64–75, 15 3rd 39–44 and 55–63; 6 3rd brake 76–81 and 14 brake vans 45–54 and 82–85. It was left to Mr Stirling and Mr Fletcher to settle the details of the new coaches, and it was decided not to provide any more sleeping carriages for the present. However, on 24th May 1876 the Committee decided to provide sleeping accommodation on the 8.30 pm and 9 pm expresses from King's Cross and the 7.30 pm and 10.30 pm from Edinburgh.

In July 1876 Mr Stirling submitted his design of sleeping carriage, 36 ft in length and carried on six wheels. This had the newly adopted higher roof contour, 12 in radius at the sides, with a flat-segmental section of about 17 ft radius, referred to as the 'round-top' to distinguish it from the 'old flat top' used hitherto. It had two compartments, each containing four couches, with two lavatories in the centre. One door per compartment (between two longitudinal couches) was provided on either side, while the central gangway between the couches was only 1 ft 9 in wide. One oil lamp was provided per pair of couches, i.e. two per compartment.

In October 1876 Mr Cockshott called the attention of

the East Coast Committee to the fact that the West Coast companies were 'now running saloon coaches specially constructed for the service between London and Edinburgh by the day express trains' and a special meeting was ordered to be held at York to consider East Coast policy. By this time East Coast 6-wheel composite carriages were 33 ft long, with a 22 ft 2 in wheel base; 2nd and 3rd class compartments were 5 ft $5\frac{7}{8}$ in and the 1st compartments 6 ft $11\frac{7}{8}$ in, the luggage compartment remaining at 7 ft 2 in. Quarter-lights were now 16 in for 1st class and 14 in for 2nd and 3rd class.

In April 1877 there was much discussion about the comfort of 3rd class passengers and it was reported that the Glasgow & South Western had actually padded the backs of the seats in the 3rd class compartments of their vehicles used between Glasgow and London. Consequently it was decided not to remove the stuffing from some East Coast vehicles about to be downgraded from 2nd to 3rd. Two months later the London & North Western also decided to stuff the backs in their 3rd class carriages, but the North Eastern would not agree to such luxury being provided in East Coast stock! By June 1878 the London & North Western had provided their latest 3rd class stock with sprung seats and the North Eastern and North British then agreed to improvements in the East Coast 3rd class 'to the extent adopted by the London & North Western and Midland Railways'.

In the meantime three sleeping carriages, Nos 104, 105 and 106, started running on 1st July 1877, one on the 8.30 pm to Perth and another on the 9.30 pm to Glasgow.

When further replacement vehicles were requested in 1877 Doncaster was fully occupied on Great Northern work and the construction of 47 coaches was put out to tender. The tenders were opened on 15th March 1878 and eventually 38 vehicles were ordered: ten 32 ft 5 in 1st with four 7 ft 0 in compartments, and twelve 33 ft 1st and 2nd composites from Ashbury, and 16 33 ft $1\frac{5}{8}$ in 3rd with six 5 ft 6 in compartments from Midland Carriage & Wagon Co. All were delivered in 1879, together with 13 1st, 2nd and 3rd composites built at Doncaster as no outside tender had been accepted. The additional stock totalled 51 vehicles but only the number of coaches authorised initially (47) were disposed of, 20 going to the GN, 16 to the NE, eight to the NB and three to the Caledonian. This left only one 4-wheel vehicle in East Coast stock and at Mr Cockshott's suggestion it was withdrawn and replaced, not by a 6-wheel 2nd as authorised but by a 6-wheel 4-compartment brake third, with the same number. In addition four 2nd class vehicles built for the Great Northern were transferred to East Coast stock and four new carriages built for the GN; those transferred to the East Coast having remained in the works for a time awaiting a decision as to whether they should be lettered GN or ECJS!

On 3rd May 1878 it was decided that three additional sleeping cars should be built for the autumn Scotch traffic, but first came two Pullman sleeping cars, which commenced working between London and Perth on 19th August 1878. They were planned to run to Perth for a trial period of three months, but after two months they were transferred to the Glasgow service. Then, on 20th February 1879 it was reported to the Great Northern Board that the North Eastern was prepared to join in an Agreement with the Pullman Company to provide three or four sleeping carriages of a shorter and lighter construction.

By November 1881 the East Coast stock amounted to 117 vehicles, with sleeping cars 118, 119 and 120 under construction, but soon afterwards it was recommended that 110 new vehicles should be built in the Great Northern shops for East Coast service, to be ready for use by Easter 1883. A similar number of old vehicles would then be divided amongst the GN, NE and NB. In January 1882 48 vehicles were authorised to be built at Doncaster, with all the displaced vehicles going to the Great Northern, although eventually (Oct. 1884) only 47 were transferred, becoming GN Nos 1722 and 2090–2135.

One of the new designs represented a notable departure when produced by Mr Stirling, in March 1882, having four 1st class compartments, a side corridor and two lavatories. Three months later the GN Board approved such a vehicle, to run on six wheels 'with a closet at each end and a ladies' compartment', it was to be fitted 'with side gallery but without end platforms'. The North Eastern gave a qualified approval and suggested that one or two corridor carriages be provided by way of experience. In April 1883 Mr Tennant, the NER General Manager, inspected the new corridor coach and pointed out that doors should be fitted between each compartment and the corridor, and that blinds were required. He concluded by saying "Of course it will be understood that you will not build any more carriages of the same type". However, Mr Oakley of the Great Northern expressed the opinion that Mr Tennant's caution was because if the corridor coach proved a success it would make the rest of the stock unpopular and involve considerable expense in providing a fleet of corridor coaches. Nevertheless two further corridor carriages were ordered.

The pioneer vehicle was No. 87 and the two subsequent coaches, built in 1884 were Nos 122 and 123, although over the years an illustration of No. 176 has been published, with the incorrect statement that this was the first East Coast corridor coach. This appears to be another fallacy fostered by the Drawing Office at Doncaster Works! (See 'The First British Railway Dining Car' by K. Hoole, *Railway World* September 1979). No. 176 was actually built in 1891 and it was a 3rd corridor with lavatory; the initial corridor coaches were, as might be expected, for the benefit of 1st class passengers only.

Another incorrect statement which has appeared in print is to the effect that the original vehicle eventually became half of an articulated twin; this was only a proposal, mooted in 1911 and not implemented.

On 27th February 1883 the firm of John King Ltd submitted a small-tube system of hot water apparatus for heating coaches, stating that this type of equipment was already being supplied to the LNWR. The matter was referred to Mr Stirling, who pointed out that there was no novelty about it as the apparatus was exactly the same as the Pullman heater, with a small furnace requiring an attendant. Five weeks later Mr Oakley expressed the view that after the experience of the past winter some means of carriage heating was desirable, particularly in family saloons and sleeping cars. Although he received permission for Mr Stirling to try out some form of heater in the East Coast sleeping cars no further action appears to have been taken at that time.

During 1883 and 1884 the 48 vehicles authorised in January 1882 were delivered, all running on six wheels; the passenger carrying stock varying in length between

THE EAST·COAST JOINT STOCK, ON OCTOBER 13th, 1891.

REFERRED TO IN MINUTE 5220. *of Nov. 92*

No.	Class.	Compartments.	Makers.	Year when Built.	No.	Class.	Compartments.	Makers.	Year when Built.
1	First	Four 1st & W.C. at end	Midland Carr. & Wagon Co.	1879	58	Third	Six 3rds	Midland Carr. & Wagon Co.	1879
2	"	"	"	"	59	"	"	"	"
3	"	"	"	"	60	"	"	"	"
4	"			"	61	"	"	"	"
5	"			"	62	"	"	"	"
6	"			"	63	"	"	"	"
7	"			"	64	Composite	3rd, 3rd, 1st, 1st, 2nd, Lug.	G.N.R.	1883
8	"			"	65	"	"	"	"
9	"			"	66	"	"	"	1884
10	"			"	67	"	"	"	"
11	Composite	Lug., 2nd, 1st, 1st, 2nd, Lug.	Ashbury Co.	"	68	"	"	"	"
12	"	"	"	"	69	"	3rd, 2nd, 1st, 1st, Lav., Lug.	"	"
13	"	"	"	"	70	"	"	"	
14	"	"	"	"	71	"	2nd, 2nd, 1st, 1st, Lav., Lug.	"	1883
15	"	"	"	"	72	"	"	"	
16	"	3rd, 3rd, 1st, 1st, 2nd, Lug.	G.N.R.	1883	73	"	"	"	1884
17	"	Lug., 2nd, 1st, 1st, 2nd, Lug.	Ashbury Co.	1879	74	"	3rd, 2nd, 1st, 1st Lav., Lug.	"	"
18	"	"			75	"	2nd, 2nd, 1st, 1st, Lav., Lug.	"	"
19	"	Lug., 1st, Lav., Lav., 1st, 2nd, 3rd	G.N.R.	1890	76	3rd Cl. Brake	Four 3rds and Brake	"	1883
20	"	Lug., 2nd, 1st, 1st, 2nd, Lug.	Ashbury Co.	1879	77	"	"	"	"
21	"	"	"	"	78	"	"	"	"
22	"	"	"	"	79	"	"	"	"
23	"	3rd, 3rd, 1st, 1st, 2nd, Lug.	G.N.R.	1883	80	"	"	"	"
24	"	Lug., 1st, Lav., Lav., 1st, 2nd, 3rd	"	1890	81	"	"	"	1879
25	"	Lug., 2nd, 1st, 1st, 2nd, Lug.	Ashbury Co.	1879	82	Lug. Bk. Van		"	1883
26	"	"	"	"	83	"		"	"
27	"	Lug., 1st, Lav., Lav., 1st, 2nd, 3rd	G.N.R.	1890	84	"		"	1890
28	"	"	"	"	85	"		"	1883
29	"	"	"	"	86	First	1st, 1st, Lug., 1st, 1st	"	1880
30	"	"	"	"	87	Corridor (1st)	Lav., 1st, 1st, 1st, 1st, Lav., Corr.	"	1883
31	"	"	"	"	88	First	1st, 1st, Lav., Lav., 1st, 1st	"	1884
32	"	"	"	"	89	"	"	"	
33	"	"	"	"	90	Sleepg. Compo (old G.N.)	2nd, Sleepg., Lav., Lav., Sleepg., Lug.	"	1878
34	"	"	"	"	91	First	1st, 1st, Lav., Lav., 1st, 1st	"	1884
35	"	"	"	"	92	"	"	"	
36	"	"	"	"	93	Second	Five 2nds and Lug.	"	1883
37	"	"	"	"	94	"	"	"	"
38	Third	Six 3rds	Midland Carr. & Wagon Co.	1879	95	"	"	"	"
39	"	"	"	"	96	Composite	2nd, 2nd, 1st, 1st, Lav., Lug.	"	"
40	"	"	"	"	97	"	"	"	"
41	"	"	"	"	98	"	3rd, 2nd, 1st, 1st, Lav., Lug.	"	1884
42	"	"	"	"	99	Second	Five 2nds and Lug.	"	1883
43	"	"	"	"	100	Lug. Bk. Van		"	"
44	"	(Corridor) Lav., 3rd, 3rd, 3rd., 3rd, 3rd, Lav. Corr.	G.N.R.	1889	101	"		"	"
45	Lug. Bk. Van		"	1883	102	"		"	"
46	"		"	"	103	"		"	"
47	"		"	"	104	Sleeping (1st Class)	Lav., Sleepg., Sleepg., Lav., Lav., Sleepg., Sleepg., Lav.	"	1890
48	"		"	"	105	"	"	"	"
49	"		"	1890	106	"	"	"	"
50	"		"	1883	107	"	"	"	"
51	"		"	"	108	"	"	"	"
52	"		"	"	109	"	"	"	"
53	"		"	"	110	Lug. Bk. Van		"	"
54	"		"	"	111	"		"	1880
55	Third	Six 3rds	Midland Carr. & Wagon Co.	1879	112	"		"	1890
56	"	"	"	"	113	Second	Five 2nds	"	1879
57	"	"	"	"	114	"	"	"	1880

[Handwritten note bracketing Nos. 1–10:] Withdrawn & to be replaced by Composite Carriages.

No.	Description of Vehicle. (All 6 Wheels.)		Makers.	Year when Built.	No.	Description of Vehicle. (All 6 Wheels.)		Makers.	Year when Built.
	Class.	Compartments.				Class.	Compartments.		
115	Second	Five 2nds	G.N.R.	1879	151	Sleeping	Lug.,1st,Lav.,Sleepg., Sleepg., Lav., 2nd	G.N.R.	1889
116	"		"	"	152	"	"	"	"
117	Sleeping (1st Class)	Sleepg., Sleepg., Lav., Lav., Sleepg, Sleepg.	"	1881	153	"	"	"	"
					154	"	"	"	"
118	"	"	"	1882	155	Third (Corr.)	Lav., 3rd, 3rd, 3rd, 3rd, 3rd, Lav., Corr.	"	"
119	"	"	"	"					
120	"	"	"	"	156	"	"	"	"
121	First	1st, 1st, Lav., Lav., 1st, 1st	"	1884	157	"	"	"	"
122	Corridor	Lav., 1st, 1st, 1st, 1st, Lav.	"	"	158	"	"	"	"
					159	"	"	"	"
123	"	"	"	"	160	"	"	"	1890
124	Sleeping (1st Class)	Lav., Sleepg., Sleepg., Lav., Lav., Sleepg., Sleepg., Lav.	"	1885	161	"	"	"	"
					162	"	"	"	"
125	"	"	"	"	163	"	"	"	"
126	Composite	3rd,1st,Lav.,Lav.,1st, 2nd, Lug.	"	1888	164	"	"	"	"
					165	Composite	Lug., 1st, Lav., Lav., 1st, 2nd, 3rd	"	"
127	"	"	"	"	166	"	"	"	"
128	"	"	"	"	167	"	"	"	"
129	"	"	"	"	168	"	"	"	"
130	"	"	"	"	169	"	"	"	"
131	"	"	"	"	170	"	"	"	"
132	"	"	"	"	171	Third (Corr.)	Lav., 3rd, 3rd, 3rd, 3rd, 3rd, Lav., Corr.	"	1891
133	"	"	"	"					
134	"	"	"	"	172	"	"	"	"
135	"	"	"	"	173	"	"	"	"
136	"	"	"	"	174	"	"	"	"
137	"	"	"	"	175	"	"	"	"
138	Third	Five 3rds	"	"	176	"	"	"	"
139	"	"	"	"	177	"	"	"	"
140	"	"	"	"	178	"	"	"	"
141	"	"	"	"	179	"	"	"	"
142	Third Cl. Bks	Four 3rds and Brake	"	"	180	"	"	"	"
143	"	"	"	"	181	Under construction (Sleeping Composites)		"	1892
144	Lug. Bk. Van	"	"	"	182				
145	"	"	"	"	183	Sleeping	Lav., Sleepg., Sleepg., Lav., Lav., Sleepg., Sleepg., Lav.	"	1891
146	Sleeping	Lug., 1st, Lav., Sleepg., Sleepg., Lav., 2nd	"	1889	184				
147	"	"	"	"	185	"	"	"	"
148	"	"	"	"	186	"	"	"	"
149	"	"	"	"					
150	"	"	"	"					

List of the East Coast Joint Stock on 13th October 1891.

33 ft 8$\frac{3}{8}$ in and 37 ft, with the brake vans only 29 ft long.

On 24th November 1886 Mr Cockshott wrote to Mr Oakley, 'There are but two first class carriages. These are in daily use on the 10 am down and 10 am up expresses. The carriages are much liked and compartments are ordered daily in advance. They are specially appreciated by users of these particular trains, and are in constant use. They now require to be overhauled and should be for a time in the shops, but we have no similar vehicles to replace them, and I would beg to recommend that two additional carriages be constructed and added to East Coast stock.' This is odd when there were actually three corridor coaches, although as only one additional vehicle was suggested later perhaps someone realised that there was one spare vehicle available. However, this one extra corridor vehicle was not approved by the North Eastern, neither were the additional lavatory-fitted carriages for which Mr Oakley was pressing, after seeing that much of the West Coast stock had lavatories. The East Coast could provide such stock only to a limited extent and

there were frequent complaints, especially about the Aberdeen and Highland district through coaches. The North Eastern's reply was, that 'the question might safely be allowed to stand over for a period of, say, twelve months'.

The next move was in November 1887 when the East Coast Committee complained that 'By reason of there being insufficient stock, and of the exceptionally long distances it has to travel, there is difficulty in maintaining the appearance of the carriages which it is desirable they should have' and it was recommended that 24 6-wheel vehicles of various types should be added, all fitted with the vacuum and Westinghouse brakes:

12 lavatory 1st/2nd/3rd composites (Nos 126–37)
4 sleeping cars
2 4-compartment brake 3rds (Nos 142/3)
4 5-compartment 3rds (Nos 138–41)
2 'side light' brake vans (Nos 144/5)

At this time the stock amounted to 125 vehicles built

⟶❄ DINING TRAINS. ❄⟵

First and Third Class DINING SALOONS are run in the 11.20 a.m. and 2.20 p.m. Express Trains from LONDON (King's Cross) to EDINBURGH, and the 12.20 p.m. and 2.20 p.m. Express Trains from EDINBURGH to LONDON (King's Cross).

The DINING SALOONS are connected with Corridor Carriages by covered gangways.

Luncheon, Dinner, and other refreshments will be served *en route*, the respective charges being as follows:—

LUNCHEONS.

Served in the
Down Train between
KING'S CROSS and DONCASTER,
and
Up Train between
EDINBURGH and DARLINGTON.

First Class ... ... 2s. 6d.
Third Class ... ... 2s. 0d.

Also a la Carte, at Buffet charges
as per daily bill of fare.

DINNERS.
TABLE D'HOTE.

Served in the
Down Train on leaving
YORK,
and
Up Train on leaving
YORK.

First Class ... ... 3s. 6d.
Third Class ... 3s. 6d. & 2s. 6d.

TEA and COFFEE.

Served between
KING'S CROSS and EDINBURGH
at any time on the journey.

Tea or Coffee, with Roll and
Butter ... ... 6d.

Other Refreshments at Buffet
charges as per daily bill of fare.

LUNCHEON BASKETS.—Hot or Cold Luncheon Baskets can be obtained at Darlington, Harrogate, Hull, Leeds Newcastle, Scarborough, and York at a charge of 3/- each; or without wine, ale, stout, or aerated water, 2/6 each.

FREE TELEGRAMS ordering Luncheons will be sent to any of these Stations on notice being given to the conductor or guard of the train, or to the station master or other official at any of the principal stations *en route*.

Passengers due in **Perth** between 10 p.m. and midnight may have a hot meal in the Station Hotel there on arrival by having a telegram sent from Edinburgh or any station south thereof. The telegram will be sent free on application.

Notice from NER Timetable for July 1899 when only two trains in each direction had dining cars.

between 1877 and 1885. All the vehicles above, except the sleeping cars, were delivered in 1888 and raised the fleet numbering to 145. Nine 6-wheel sleeping composites with two double-berth cabins and on 3rd class compartment (Nos 146–154) followed in 1889; ten corridor 3rd (Nos 155–164) with five 6 ft 1 in compartments in 1889/90 and six 1st/3rd composites (Nos 165–70) in 1890. The corridor 3rds (Nos 155–64) were the first East Coast coaches with lavatory accommodation for 3rd class passengers.

Also in 1889/90 a number of vehicles similar to the above were built to replace older vehicles and took their numbers, followed in 1891 by ten 6-wheel 3rds, Nos 171–180; of these 171/2/3/9 were later provided with end connections for which the toilet had to be reduced in size. In 1892 six further sleeping cars were built and numbered 181–6: 181 and 182 were sleeping composites similar to 146–154, and 183–6 were full sleepers similar to 124 and 125. Of the displaced vehicles the GNR took ten, the NER took eight and the NBR six when they were distributed in 1891.

In 1892 all ten of the Midland Carriage & Wagon built lavatory 1sts of 1879 (Nos 1–10) were divided amongst the partners (GN four, NE three, NB three) in preparation for the appearance of new 6-wheel composites 37 ft 6 in long, with 24 ft 8 in wheelbase, delivered in 1893. These had a luggage compartment and two 1st class compartments at one end and two 3rd class compartments at the other, with two central lavatories reached by two short corridors on opposite sides of the coach, giving all compartments access to the toilet

facilities. Two further vehicles to this design (Nos 26 and 129) were built in 1893, together with van No. 51, corridor 3rd (later composite) No. 60, and corridor 3rd No. 163, all five as replacements for vehicles destroyed in the Thirsk accident in the previous year.

In 1893 bogie vehicles made their appearance although, of course, the bogie Pullmans had been in use for some years. The new vehicles were for the first East Coast dining car trains, and to form four complete set trains 24 6-wheel coaches were built:

198–201	Kitchen cars by Birmingham Carriage & Wagon Co.
202–205	Corridor 1sts by Gloucester Carriage & Wagon Co.
206–213	Corridor 3rds by Oldbury Carriage & Wagon Co.
214–221	Luggage brake vans by Craven Bros Ltd.

Four bogie 1st class dining saloons (Nos 190–193) were built by the Lancaster Railway Carriage & Wagon Co. and four bogie 3rd class dining saloons, (Nos 194–197) by the Oldbury Carriage & Wagon Co.

The last 6-wheel sleeping cars were built in 1893 (Nos 117–120) and these continued to run until the end of 1909, latterly with the letter 'A' suffix to their numbers. In 1894 6-wheel corridor 3rd No. 63 and brake vans Nos 224–7 were built, followed in 1895 by 6-wheel 3rd No. 139 as a replacement for a similar vehicle destroyed in the Northallerton accident of 4th October 1894. The last 6-wheelers to be built were brake vans Nos 257–261, built in 1896 and all but No. 260 lasted until 1922.

3 Dining Cars

For many years the East Coast companies showed a surprising lack of initiative as far as dining cars on London-Edinburgh trains were concerned. Such facilities were not actually provided until 1893—and then only on one train in each direction—although dining facilities on the Great Northern had developed since the introduction of a Pullman dining car in 1879. Even when they did appear the 1st and 3rd class dining cars were comparatively small vehicles seating only 24 passengers each and used with a 6-wheel kitchen car marshalled between them, whereas vehicles of 60 ft, with kitchen and pantry, were in use on Great Northern internal services from 1885.

For the inauguration of dining cars on the East Coast four 1st class and four 3rd class vehicles were built to form part of four complete new trains, but the spaciousness and comfort of the 3rd class cars attracted passengers from the 1st class and the four 3rd class cars were replaced in 1894 by four cars seating 42 passengers. All the 1893 and 1894 cars were classed as 'Dining Saloons', although they were merely open vehicles with no kitchen or pantry, whereas other open vehicles which could be

used for the same purpose were not graced with the title. Consequently it has been difficult to decide which vehicles should be included in this section and only those officially classed as dining saloons, dining cars or kitchen cars, and open vehicles with a pantry, are included.

There was also some delay in introducing bogie coaches on East Coast services. Stirling of the Great Northern was sometimes in favour of bogies, but at others he was dead set against them, whilst the North Eastern seem to have resisted bogie coaches until the 1890s. Thus, except for the 8-wheel dining saloons, the first East Coast dining car trains of 1893 were made up of 6-wheel stock—and yet Stirling had introduced two fine 60 ft dining cars between London and Leeds in 1885. These two coaches, GN Nos 2182 and 2183, were built by Craven Bros of Sheffield for £1,800 each and could—or should—have set the pattern for East Coast stock, but the opportunity was not taken, and ten years development was lost.

Plans for the proposed dining car trains made up of 1st, 2nd and 3rd class corridor coaches were generally approved on 31st March 1892, but later in the year it was decided that the trains should consist of a brake van, 1st corridor, 1st dining car, kitchen car, 3rd dining car, two 3rd corridors, and a brake van; all were on six wheels except the dining cars, which were 8-wheel bogie vehicles, and all except the vans were connected by gangways. A smoking section (four tables) was to be separated by a glazed door in each saloon, and the 1st and 3rd class compartment stock was to have a lavatory at each end. The heating was to be by steam or hot water, confined at first to the dining cars, and lighting was to be by gas on Pope's system. No charge was to be made for use of the dining saloons. By the time the trains were introduced 2nd class had disappeared.

Four trains were to be built and because of pressure of work at Doncaster the designs and specifications for tendering were to be prepared by the North Eastern Railway. In November 1892 the first tenders were accepted: from Lancaster Carriage & Wagon Co. for four 1st dining saloons at £2,195 each (Nos 190–3), and from Oldbury Railway Carriage & Wagon Co, for four 3rd class dining saloons (Nos 194–7) at £1,313 each—all to be carried on bogies.

In December 1892 it was decided that the gangways of the new vehicles should be 'in the centre instead of at one side of the carriage end', but all were turned out with side gangways. Tenders for the remaining cars, all on six wheels, were accepted in February and March 1893, namely:

Birmingham Railway Carriage & Wagon Co.
4 kitchen cars at £1,050 each exclusive of Pope's gas fittings (Nos 198–201).

Gloucester Railway Carriage & Wagon Co.
4 1st class corridor carriages at £850 each (Nos 202–5).

Oldbury Railway Carriage & Wagon Co.
8 3rd class corridor carriages at £794 each (Nos 206–13).

Craven Bros Ltd
8 luggage vans at £370 each (Nos 214–21).

It was hoped to start the new service in May 1893 but the vehicles were not ready until mid-July, and on Thursday, 20th, it was announced that the new dining

Great Northern, North Eastern, & North British Railways.

THE EAST COAST EXPRESS ROUTE

BETWEEN

ENGLAND & SCOTLAND.

Commencing on Monday, 24th July, first and third class CORRIDOR DINING CARS will be run in the under-mentioned through express trains. These Cars will be connected by covered gangways throughout each train :—

			P.M.					P.M.
LONDON (King's Cross)	dep.		2 30	EDINBURGH	..	.. dep.		2 30
NOTTINGHAM	..	,,	4 0	BERWICK	..	..	,,	3 50
GRANTHAM	..	,,	4 37	NEWCASTLE	..	..	,,	5 15
YORK	..	,,	6 25	DARLINGTON	..	..	,,	6 1
THIRSK	..	,,	6 55	THIRSK	..	..	,,	6 33
DARLINGTON	..	,,	7 27	YORK	..	..	,,	7 10
NEWCASTLE	..	,,	8 19	DONCASTER	..	..	,,	7 52
BERWICK	..	,,	9 41	NEWARK	..	..	,,	8 38
EDINBURGH	..	arr.	11 0	GRANTHAM	..	..	,,	9 1
				PETERBOROUGH	..	..	,,	9 38
				LONDON (King's Cross)	arr.		11 10

Luncheon, Dinner, and other refreshments will be served en route, the respective charges being as follows :—

LUNCHEONS.	**DINNERS.**	**TEA AND COFFEE.**
Served in the Down Train between KING'S CROSS and DONCASTER, and Up Train between EDINBURGH and DARLINGTON.	TABLE D'HOTE. ———— Served in the Down Train on leaving YORK, and Up Train on leaving YORK.	Served between KING'S CROSS and EDINBURGH at any time on the Journey. ———— Tea or Coffee, with Roll and Butter, 6d.
First Class .. 2s. 6d. Third Class .. 2s. 0d.	First Class .. 3s. 6d. Third Class, 3s. 6d. and 2s. 6d.	Other Refreshments at Buffet charges as per daily bill of fare.
Also à la carte, at Buffet charges as per daily bill of fare.		

On and after 24th July passengers will not be conveyed by the train leaving London (King's Cross) at 2.30 p.m., except for Darlington, Durham, Newcastle, and places beyond Newcastle.

An additional express train (to which it is intended from the 1st August to attach a first class Dining Car) will leave London (King's Cross) at 2.35 p.m., and arrive at York at 6.23 p.m., Thirsk 6.58 p.m., Stockton 7.38 p.m., Middlesbro' 7.50 p.m., West Hartlepool 8.28 p.m., Sunderland 8.30 p.m., South Shields 8.55 p.m., and Newcastle 8.55 p.m.

HENRY OAKLEY, General Manager, G.N. Railway.
GEORGE S. GIBB, General Manager, N.E. Railway.
J. CONACHER, General Manager, N.B. Railway.

Printed by McCorquodale & Co. Limited, Leeds.

Timetable and Menu issued for the first East Coast Dining Car trains introduced on 24th July 1893.

E. C. J. S. KITCHEN CAR (6 WHEELS)

Nos 198. 199. 200. 201.

Built by the Birmingham Carriage & Wagon Cº 1893
Maintained by G.N.Cºy

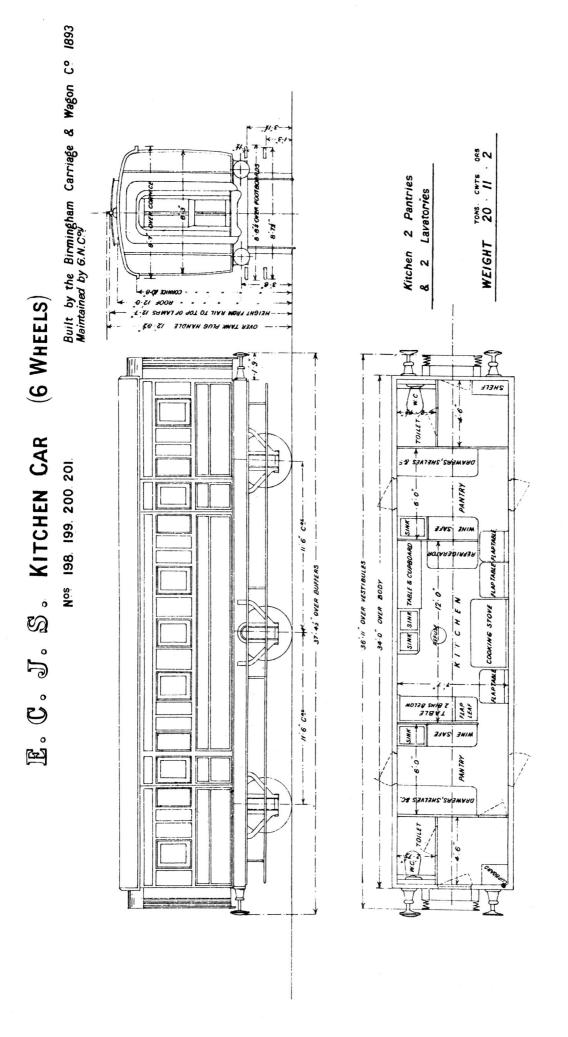

Kitchen 2 Pantries
& 2 Lavatories

WEIGHT TONS. CWTS ORS 20 . 11 . 2

Dgm. 80. The four 6-wheel Kitchen Cars Nos 198–201 were built for the first East Coast dining car trains. They originally had side gangways.

18

car trains would commence running on Monday 24th July. On Friday, 21st July, a press demonstration run was made from London to Edinburgh, with about fifty reporters aboard, although *The Times* could not send a representative. The train left King's Cross at 2.35 pm, following the normal 2.30 pm 'down' 'Scotch express', which the special preceded from Newcastle. From Newcastle to Edinburgh the special was worked by one of the North Eastern's top drivers from Gateshead shed, Enoch Shipley, with the new Worsdell-von Borries compound 4-4-0 No. 1619, arriving in Waverley station five minutes early. On the following Saturday morning the party was taken to see the Forth Bridge, opened three years earlier, and then left Waverley for King's Cross at 2.25 pm.

Regular running commenced two days later, on Monday 24th July, but although the first 'down' train arrived at Edinburgh on time the 'up' train was two hours late into King's Cross. This was due to a coach axle heating south of Newcastle and, after two attempts had been made to cool it, slow running was necessary to York, where the offending coach was detached. Unfortunately the new rubber connections between the coaches were unfamiliar to the staff and it took 41 minutes to remove the coach, so that the train was 112 minutes late away from York. Immediately steps were taken to simplify the coupling arrangement on the existing coaches and on those that had not yet been put into service.

The new trains were not sufficiently capacious to carry all the passengers and from 1st August the 'down' train carried only passengers for Darlington, Newcastle and beyond, with an additional train at 2.35 pm to serve York, Stockton, West Hartlepool, and Sunderland. The 2.35 pm 'down' and the 'up' working at 7 am from Newcastle utilised one of the 6-wheel kitchen cars and one of the 8-wheel 1st class diners: no 3rd class dining car was provided but it was stated that one would be run if demand warranted.

At the same time the opinion was expressed that 'the 3rd class cars provided for the Scotch train are too good and we propose to take them out of the Scotch service and use them in the Newcastle train, simply rubbing out the word *THIRD*. To replace them we recommend that four new 3rd class dining saloons be built as quickly as possible, on the bogie principle, but capable of seating three passengers on each side instead of two'. Formal approval to convert the 3rd class diners to 1st class and to construct four additional 3rd class dining cars was given on the Friday of the same week in which the new service commenced operations—namely on 28th July 1893.

The two Scotch trains were made up of:

Brake van	216	215
3rd corridor	209	206
3rd corridor	207	208
1st corridor	202	204
3rd dining car	194	195
Kitchen car	198	199
1st dining car	191	190
Brake van	214	221

Kitchen car No. 200 and 1st diner No. 192 were used on one of the Newcastle trains and kitchen car No. 201 and 1st diner No. 193 on the other.

The timings of the trains were:

LONDON	dep.	2.30	EDINBURGH	dep.	2.30
Grantham	arr.	4.32	Longniddry	pass	2.47
	dep.	4.37	Dunbar	pass	3.6
Doncaster	pass	5.36	Grantshouse	pass	3.24
Selby	pass	5.51	Berwick	arr.	3.45
YORK	arr.	6.15		dep.	3.50
	dep.	6.25	Belford	pass	4.9
Alne	pass	6.40	Alnmouth	pass	4.30
Thirsk	arr.	6.53	Morpeth	pass	4.50
	dep.	6.55	NEWCASTLE	arr.	5.10
Northallerton	pass	7.7		dep.	5.15
Darlington	arr.	7.23	Durham	pass	5.33
	dep.	7.27	Darlington	arr.	5.59
Durham	pass	7.54		dep.	6.1
NEWCASTLE	arr.	8.14	Northallerton	pass	6.17
	dep.	8.19	Thirsk	arr.	6.30
Morpeth	pass	8.40		dep.	6.33
Alnmouth	pass	9.0	Alne	pass	6.46
Belford	pass	9.20	YORK	arr.	7.0
Berwick	arr.	9.39		dep.	7.10
	dep.	9.44	Selby	pass	7.27
Grantshouse	pass	10.4	Doncaster	arr.	7.49
Dunbar	pass	10.20		dep.	7.52
Longniddry	pass	10.41	Newark	arr.	8.36
EDINBURGH	arr.	11.0		dep.	8.38
			Grantham	arr.	8.57
				dep.	9.1
			Peterborough	arr.	9.34
				dep.	9.38
			LONDON	arr.	11.10

Luncheon was served in the 'down' train between King's Cross and Doncaster, and in the 'up' train between Edinburgh and Darlington. Dinner was served in both 'up' and 'down' trains on leaving York.

The 2.35 pm to Newcastle ceased running on 11th September 1893, leaving the East Coast with four spare dining cars—two 1st and two 3rd, and this became eight spare—two 1st and six 3rd when the four 42 seat diners were ready in mid-1894. Although it was intended that the North Eastern designed 3rd class cars should be reclassified as 1st class this was not, in fact, implemented, and neither was the scheme to transfer the same four cars to a 'North Eastern and Great Northern Joint Account'.

It was not until November 1896 that it was decided that they be sold to the North Eastern for £1,100 each. The NER Locomotive & Stores Committee approved the transfer on 3rd December 1896.

At a meeting of the East Coast partners on 10th April 1895 the main topic of discussion once again appears to have been the provision of new carriages. The general opinion was that those with bogies were the most suitable, that they should be built with clear-stories (sic), and that sliding doors into the corridor should be fitted instead of swing doors.

This preliminary discussion was to lead to a great change in the appearance and design of East Coast vehicles; whereas the first dining car train of 1893 had consisted mainly of 6-wheel stock, with only the two dining cars on eight wheels (and only 46 ft long) the new trains, when introduced in 1896/7 were made up of magnificent 12-wheel coaches up to 65 ft 6 in long—except for the dining cars, of which more later. At a meeting on 18th June 1895 Mr Gibb of the NER expressed a preference for saloons with centre gangways for 1st and 3rd class, whereas Mr Stirling of the GNR proposed that the 3rds be open and the 1st class have compartments and corridors.

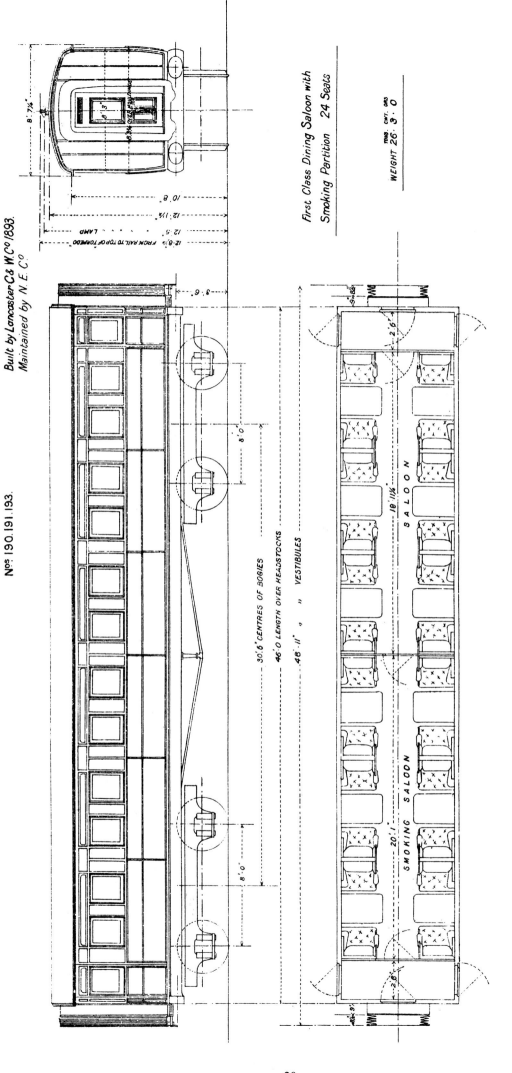

E. C. J. S. First Class Dining Saloon

Nos 190. 191. 193.

Built by Lancaster C. & W. Co. 1893.
Maintained by N. E. Co.

First Class Dining Saloon with
Smoking Partition   24 Seats

WEIGHT 26 · 3 · 0

8' 7¾"

10' 8"
12' 11½"
12' 5"   LAMP
12' 8½"   FROM RAIL TO TOP OF TORPEDO

8' 6"

8' 0"

30' 6" CENTRES OF BOGIES
46' 0 LENGTH OVER HEADSTOCKS
48' 11" " " VESTIBULES

8' 0"

SALOON
18' 11½"

SMOKING SALOON
20' 1"

2' 6"

Dgm. 59. The first East Coast Dining Cars were on eight wheels and were built to run with the Kitchen Cars. This is the 1st class version. They were numbered 190–3, but 192 differed in having the smoking saloon 26 ft 8 in long and the non-smoking saloon 13 ft 4¼ in long.

Dgm. 59. 1st class Dining Saloon No. 193 by Lancaster Carriage & Wagon Co. 1893.

Interior of No. 193.

On 28th June 1895 it was decided that the new coaches would be 'about 60 ft long (but not over 65 ft), clipper built, with clerestories, doors at the ends but not in the sides, sliding doors between compartments and corridor, and centre vestibules. Width of compartments to be 7 ft 2 in 1st class and 6 ft 3 in 3rd class'. Seven-coach trains were envisaged, and it was suggested that a conductor should travel with the train, with a compartment from which he could serve tea, coffee and light refreshments.

On 5th July 1895 Mr Stirling's designs were produced and various modifications suggested, and a fortnight later amended designs were put before the Committee by Mr Howlden, who stressed the fact that the new trains would weigh 224 tons against the present 176 tons! On 12th August 1895 it was reported that the North Eastern and the North British had approved the designs, but that the Great Northern decision was still awaited. Eight days later Mr Stirling said he could build the *three* trains at Doncaster. On 4th October 1895 approval was formally given for three trains, each of six carriages and two luggage vans; five of the six cars to be of ordinary corridor design but one to be an experimental open 3rd.

Some of the new stock was used on a trial run on 29th

June 1896 and on 6th August 1896 it was reported that the account of Norman D. MacDonald of Edinburgh, 'in preparing blazons for the sides of the new East Coast cars' amounted to £24 4s 0d.

The complete order was as follows:

6 12-wheel composites with luggage compartment	239/42/3/4/7/8
6 12-wheel composites with luggage compartment	240/1/5/6/9,250
3 12-wheel 3rd	251/3/5
3 12-wheel 3rd open with pantry	252/4/6
5 6-wheel brake vans	257–61
6 12-wheel 3rd brake	262–7

According to the 1903 Diagram Book Nos 239/42/3/4/7/8 had the luggage compartment on the left when facing the corridor side of the vehicle, and Nos 240/1/5/6/9,250 had the luggage compartment on the right. Also, Nos 262/3/4 had the brake van section to the left when facing the corridor side and Nos 265/6/7 had the brake van on the right, but these diagrams do not always agree with photographic evidence. Nos 243/6/7 had the luggage compartment altered to an attendant's compartment, although they had reverted to their original use in the 1909 Book. Nos 239–45 were altered to composite brakes in 1906.

⚜ LUNCHEON AND DINING TRAINS. ⚜

First and Third Class LUNCHEON and DINING CARS are run on the trains leaving **LONDON** (King's Cross) at **10.0 a.m.** for **GLASGOW, PERTH,** and **ABERDEEN,** and at **10.10 a.m., 11.25 a.m.,** and **2.20 p.m.** for **EDINBURGH**; also on the trains leaving **EDINBURGH** at **10.0 a.m., 10.10 a.m., 12.20 p.m.,** and **2.20 p.m.** for **LONDON** (King's Cross). A **Breakfast Car** is also run from **ABERDEEN** to **EDINBURGH** on the **6.20 a.m.** train.

Only passengers for **beyond Edinburgh** will be conveyed by the **10.0 a.m.** train from **King's Cross.**

Table d'Hote Breakfasts, Luncheons, and **Dinners** will be served *en route* at the times given below, or meals *a la carte*, Tea, or Coffee at any time during the journey (except during *Table d'Hôte*), at the following prices:—**Breakfast, 2/6; Luncheon,** First Class, **2/6;** Third Class, **2/- Dinner,** First Class, **3/6;** Third Class, **2/6.**

BREAKFAST. . .	. . DINNER. . .
7.0 a.m.—9.0 a.m.	On leaving York for King's Cross at 6.50 p.m
LUNCH.	" " " " Edinburgh at 6.15 p.m.
12.0 noon—3.30 p.m.	" " Edinburgh for Aberdeen at 6.40 p.m.
TEA OR COFFEE	And at 6.30 p.m on the 11.25 a.m. train from King's Cross
With Bread and Butter at any hour *(except during Table d'Hôte).* price **6d.**	and the 12.20 p.m. train from Edinburgh.

Breakfast, Luncheon, Tea, and **Dining Cars** are also run on the following trains:—

8.30 a.m. Scarborough to Leeds.	7.5 a.m. Newcastle to Bournemouth.
5.5 p.m. Leeds to Scarborough.	10.47 a.m. Bournemouth to Newcastle.
7.40 a.m. York to Newcastle.	9.15 a.m. Hull to London (King's Cross).
11.10 a.m. Newcastle to Edinburgh.	10.55 a.m. London (King's Cross) to Hull.
4.55 p.m. Newcastle to London (King's Cross).	

Hot Meals will be served in the Station Hotel at **Perth** to passengers arriving at that Station between 10.0 p.m. and 12.0 midnight, if notice be given to the Station Master at Edinburgh or any Station south thereof.

Luncheon Baskets (Hot or Cold) can be obtained at **York, Darlington, Newcastle, Leeds, Harrogate, Scarborough,** or **Hull,** at a charge of 3/-, or without Wine, Ale, Stout, or Aerated Water, 2/6 each.

Telegrams ordering Luncheon Baskets, Meals, &c., will be sent **Free of Charge** on notice being given to the Conductor or Guard of the Train, or to the Station Master, or other Official, at any of the principal Stations *en route*.

Notice from NER Timetable dated July 1902, by which time there were four dining car trains in each direction, including the 10 am trains. Note that the 10 am from London conveyed only passengers for beyond Edinburgh.

Even when the new trains were completed in 1897, for the 11.20 am 'down' and the 12.15 pm 'up', no new catering vehicles were available except for the three open 3rds with pantry (Nos 252/4/6). However, in 1897 the NER made available to the ECJS two 1st class dining saloons with kitchen. These had started life as two of the four 'too good' 3rd class dining saloons of 1893, sold to the NER in November 1896 for £1,100 each, where two were converted to 3rd class saloons and two were rebuilt at York as 1st class diners. The renumbering involved appears to have been:

Original East Coast	NER	Number on Return to ECJS
194	2649	–
195	2648	–
196	2647	194
197	2646	195

During the course of their rebuilding the two diners were fitted with clerestory roofs. In their original condition they were fitted with gangway connections to one side of the centre line of the coach, but when returned they had centre gangways. However, the kitchen and pantry were the full width of the car and thus effectively divided the train into two halves.

In the very first volume of the *Railway Magazine* W. J. Scott described the new train, which first ran on Monday 12th July 1897:

'Thanks to its 'Gould' vestibules it had at first sight almost the look of being one endless seventy-wheeled vehicle—an impression which the uniform lines of gilding further bore out. On looking closer, one could discern the rounded 'bows' of one coach from the 'stern' of the next, rounded in like manner—a most attractive shaping outside, and within giving a kind of 'observation car' gratis; a 'look-out' seat with splendid views of all that passes, mile-posts or mountains, from the big curved windows at each end. In harmony with the rest, but not in unison, is the dining car, as cleverly refitted (for it is not a new vehicle) and decorated by Mr Bain. It harmonises well with the other vehicles, but, unlike them, is only on eight wheels and bears the arms and initials of the North Eastern Company, instead of the mystic letters 'E.C.J.S.'

These two dining cars were sold back to the ECJS later in the year at what the NER had paid for them (£1,100 each) plus the cost of the alterations (£1,135 10s 0d each).

The new stock delivered in 1896 included the three Doncaster built 12-wheel open 3rds with pantry; at a later date two of these were paired with the NER modified cars to provide 3rd class dining accommodation. Until 1897 the seating of the open 3rds was quoted as, '54 when not dining; 42 when dining', the difference being accounted for by the use of the long seats on one side of the central passage for three or two passengers respectively. The discrepancy of two seats is accounted for by the fact that the long seats at each end (adjacent to the door into the vestibule at one end, and into the kitchen at the other) where shorter than normal and seated only two when not dining instead of the usual three.

E. C. J. S. First Class Dining Saloon and Kitchen

Nos 194 and 195

Built in 1893 by the Oldbury Carriage and Wagon Company & Altered at York in 1897.

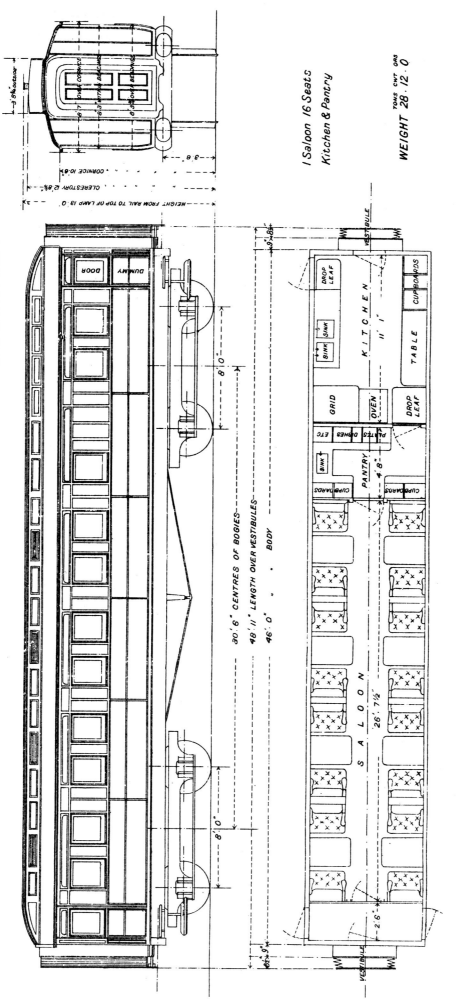

1 Saloon 16 Seats
Kitchen & Pantry

WEIGHT 28.12.0

Dgm. 75. The 1893 3rd class Dining Cars also seated 24 passengers and were soon replaced as they were 'too good'. The NER, which had designed the cars in the first place, took them over and rebuilt two with a full width kitchen and pantry, reclassified them as 1st class, fitted a clerestory roof to the new ECJS standard and returned them to the Joint Stock as Nos 194 and 195.

GREAT NORTHERN, NORTH EASTERN & NORTH BRITISH RAILWAYS.

OCTOBER, 1902, AND UNTIL FURTHER NOTICE.

East Coast 'Express' Route

BETWEEN

England and Scotland.

FIRST AND THIRD CLASS CORRIDOR DINING CARS,

connected throughout by covered gangways, are run in the under-mentioned through express trains:—

		a.m.	a.m.	a.m.		p.m.	p.m.	p.m.
				October.		after 13th October.		C
				11th run not Will		D		
LONDON (King's Cross)	dep.	10	0	11 25		6 20	12 20	2 20
Nottingham (Vic. Sta.)	"	11	15	12 30		8 10	11 35	8 32
Nottingham (London Road)	"					10	12 20	2 20
High Level	"	11	20	12 35		11 15	1 35	8 32
Grantham	"	12	7			12 42	2 59	4 55
Newark	"			2 31		1 31	3 49	5 45
Doncaster	"	1	55				4 44	
York	"			3 34	arr.	6 20		6 50
Harrogate	"			4 26				7 29
Darlington	"	3	35	5 18		4		8 15
Newcastle	"	4	26	6 42		5	7 33	9 18
Berwick	"	6	15	7 55		5	7 38	9 31
EDINBURGH (Waverley)	arr.	6	15	8 10		6	3 45	10 45
DUNDEE (Tay Bridge)	"	8	10					
ABERDEEN	"	10	5					

Notice from Great Northern Timetable dated October 1902.

Notice from NER Timetable dated July 1906, by which time the service included 'Breakfast, Luncheon and Dining Car' trains.

BREAKFAST, LUNCHEON, AND DINING CARS
FIRST AND THIRD CLASS.

TABLE D'HÔTE BREAKFASTS, LUNCHEONS and DINNERS
WILL BE SERVED EN ROUTE AS SHEWN HEREUNDER:—

BREAKFAST
Served between 7.0 a.m. and 9.0 a.m. in the
6.20 a.m. up express from Aberdeen ... 2/6

LUNCHEON
WILL BE SERVED IN THE

10.0 a.m. from King's Cross, on leaving GRANTHAM
11.25 a.m. " King's X at 12.20 p.m. and on leaving NEWARK
2.20 p.m. on leaving King's Cross

10.0 a.m. from Edinburgh at 12.15 noon and on leaving NEWCASTLE

12.20 p.m. from Edinburgh, on leaving EDINBURGH.
2.20 p.m.

FIRST CLASS, 2/6 | THIRD CLASS, 2/-
Also à la carte at buffet charges, as per daily bill of fare.

DINNER
WILL BE SERVED IN THE

10.0 a.m. from King's Cross, on leaving EDINBURGH
11.25 a.m. " " " BERWICK
2.20 p.m. " " York

12.20 p.m. from Edinburgh, on leaving NEWARK
2.20 p.m. " " York

FIRST CLASS, 3/6 | THIRD CLASS, 2/6

TEA OR COFFEE
Served at any hour (except during the time Luncheon or Dinner is being served).
Tea or Coffee with Bread and Butter 6d

Table d'Hôte Breakfasts, Luncheons, and Dinners, or meals à la carte, will be served en route:—
Breakfast or Luncheon, First Class, 2/6; Third Class, 2/6; Dinner, First Class, 3/6; Third Class, 2/6.
Luncheon Baskets containing Hot or Cold Luncheon can be obtained at York, Darlington, Newcastle, Leeds, Harrogate, Scarborough, or Hull, at a charge of 3/-, or without Wine, Ale, Stout, or Aerated Water, 2/6 each.

Telegrams ordering Luncheon Baskets, Meals, &c., will be sent Free of Charge on notice being given to the Conductor or Guard of the Train, or to the Station Master, or other Official, at any of the

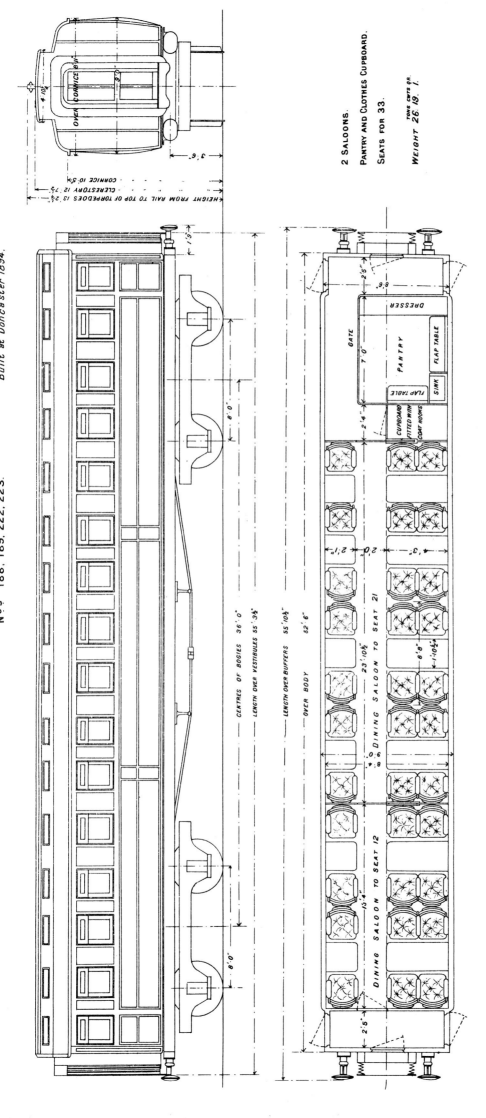

E. C. J. S. DINING SALOON, THIRD CLASS.

Nos 188, 189, 222, 223.

Built at Doncaster 1894.

2 SALOONS.
PANTRY AND CLOTHES CUPBOARD.
SEATS FOR 33.
WEIGHT 26. 19. 1. TONS CWTS QR.

OVER CORNICE 8'11"

CORNICE 10'5"
CLERESTORY 12'7½"
HEIGHT FROM RAIL TO TOP OF TORPEDOES 13'2¾"

4'10½"
3'6"

9'0"

CENTRES OF BOGIES 36'0"
LENGTH OVER VESTIBULES 55'3½"
LENGTH OVER BUFFERS 55'10½"
OVER BODY 52'6"

8'0"
1'3"
8'0"

DINING SALOON TO SEAT 21
23'10½"
8'8"
1'10½"
2'1"
2'0"
1'3"

2'5"
GATE
8'6"
7'0"
DRESSER
PANTRY
FLAP TABLE
SINK
FLAP TABLE
2'4"
CUPBOARD FITTED WITH COAT HOOKS

9'0"
8'4"
DINING SALOON TO SEAT 12
13'4"

2'5"

Dgm. 25. The four 24-seat 3rd class cars were replaced in 1894 and the four new vehicles had a clerestory roof, although it did not slope down at the ends. The seating was originally for 42 passengers in three saloons, but this was reduced to 33 in two saloons when nine seats were removed to allow a pantry to be fitted.

Dgm. 25. 3rd class Dining Saloon No. 222 built at Doncaster in 1894. (*BR*)

When the time came to withdraw the 1896/7 stock from East Coast service in 1925–7 they were disposed of as follows:

Nos	GN	GC	Condemned
239–45	1	–	6
246–50	3	2	–
251–6	3	–	3
262–7	2	3	1

Three similar open 3rds built at York in 1900, Nos 304, 305 and 306, were distributed in 1929: 304 to the NE Area as No. 22239; 305 to the Southern Scottish Area as No. 3652; and 306 to the GN Section as No. 42181.

Next, in August 1898, came the proposal to provide new stock for the 10 am from King's Cross and the 10 am from Edinburgh, both of which made a 20 minute meal halt at York. Mr Ivatt said that the earliest date by which he could build the vehicles would be 1st July 1900, and on 5th January 1899 his plans were considered and it was decided to spread the work between Cowlairs, Doncaster and York, with orders for 42 vehicles:

Cowlairs	9 Brake 3rds	280–8
	3 Brake vans	289/90/1
York	12 Composites	292–303
	3 Open 3rds	304/5/6
	3 Brake 1st	307/8/9

Doncaster	3 1st Dining Cars	310/1/2
	With kitchen and pantry.	
	3 3rd Dining Cars	313/4/5
	With attendant's compartment.	
	3 Composite Dining Cars	316/7/8
	With centre kitchen and pantry.	
	3 Corridor 3rd	319/20/1

At last Doncaster was to build dining/kitchen cars for the East Coast services and Nos 310/1/2 were 62 ft 0½ in long divided thus—kitchen 13 ft 1¾ in; pantry 4 ft 10 in; and two saloons 18 ft 3 in and 14 ft 4 in seating ten and eight passengers respectively, with one seat each side of the gangway. In 1913, as a process of modernisation got under way, authority was given for the fitting of large windows, and two extra seats were provided by removing a lavatory, cupboard and wine safe, all formerly fitted at the end opposite to the kitchen. All three were reclassified 'Restaurant Car' in 1924. Nos 310 and 311 went to the GN Section in 1929 as Nos 43246 and 43247, and 312 was condemned in 1935.

The three 3rd class dining saloons, Nos 313/4/5 were 64 ft 5¾ in long, divided into three saloons seating 12 and 18 (both non-smoking) and 12 (smoking), with an attendant's compartment across the full width of the car at one end. A gents' lavatory was entered from the attendant's compartment, with a ladies' lavatory at the opposite end of the car. Seating was generous for 3rd

Cont. p 31

Dgm. 28. Open 3rd No. 252 built at Doncaster in 1896.

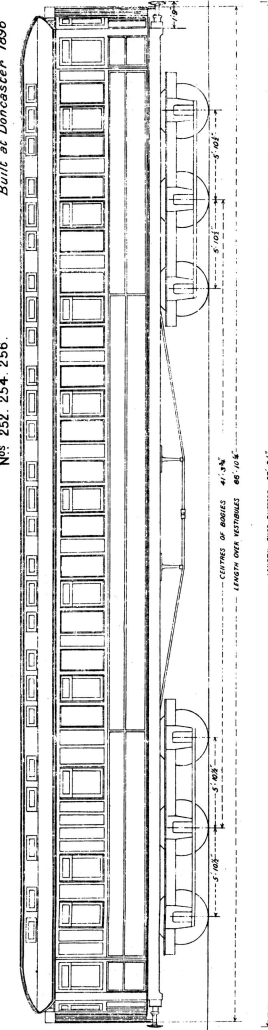
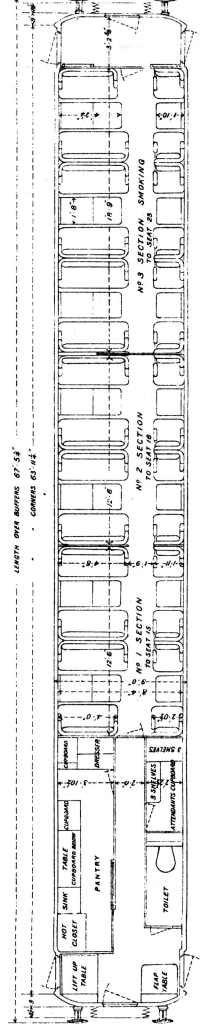
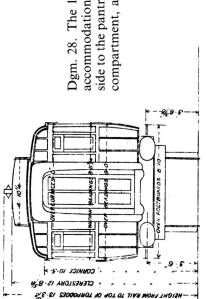

E. C. J. S. OPEN THIRD

Built at Doncaster 1896

Nᵒˢ 252. 254. 256.

Dgm. 28. The 12-wheel Open Thirds 252/4/6, built at Doncaster in 1896, and a pantry at one end and the passenger accommodation divided into three saloons. The idea of full-width pantries had been abandoned, and on the opposite side to the pantry were two toilets, one for Ladies and one for Gents. However, the Ladies was altered to an attendant's compartment, as in the above diagram.

3 Saloons

Pantry & 2 Lavatories

SEATS FOR 54 (but when dining)

WEIGHT − 36 . 8 . 3 ᵀᴼⁿˢ· ᶜʷᵀˢ· ᵠᴿˢ·

27

E. C. J. S. DINING SALOON (FIRST CLASS)

2 Saloons, Kitchen, Pantry, & 2 Lavatories

Nᵒˢ 310. 311. 312.

Built at Doncaster 1900

SEATS FOR 18.

WEIGHT	TONS	CWTS	QRS.
	37	14	0

Dgm. 76. By 1900 the catering vehicles had developed into a 12-wheel Dining Saloon, with a body 62 ft 0½ in long. A kitchen and pantry were fitted and the two saloons seated only 18 passengers in spacious 1 + 1 seating. Nos 310/1/2. In 1913 it was decided that large windows should be fitted to the saloons of these three coaches, and at the same time to remove a lavatory, a cupboard, and a wine safe, to increase the seating from 18 to 20. The estimated cost of the alterations was £230 16s 1d per coach. The kitchen section retained the small windows.

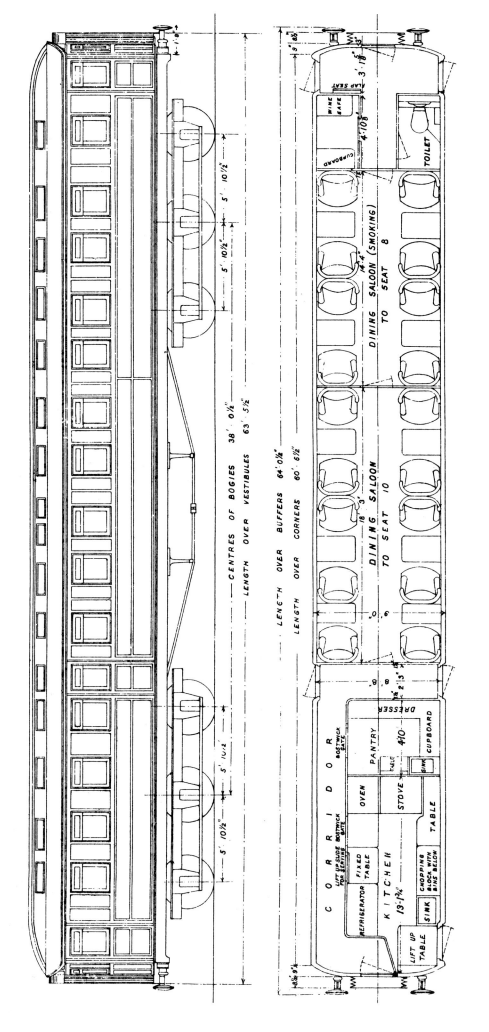

Dgm. 76. 1st class Dining Saloon No. 310 built at Doncaster in 1900, as built with small windows. (*BR*)

No. 310 as rebuilt with large windows.

Dgm. 30. 3rd class Dining Saloon No. 314 built at Doncaster in 1900. (*BR*)

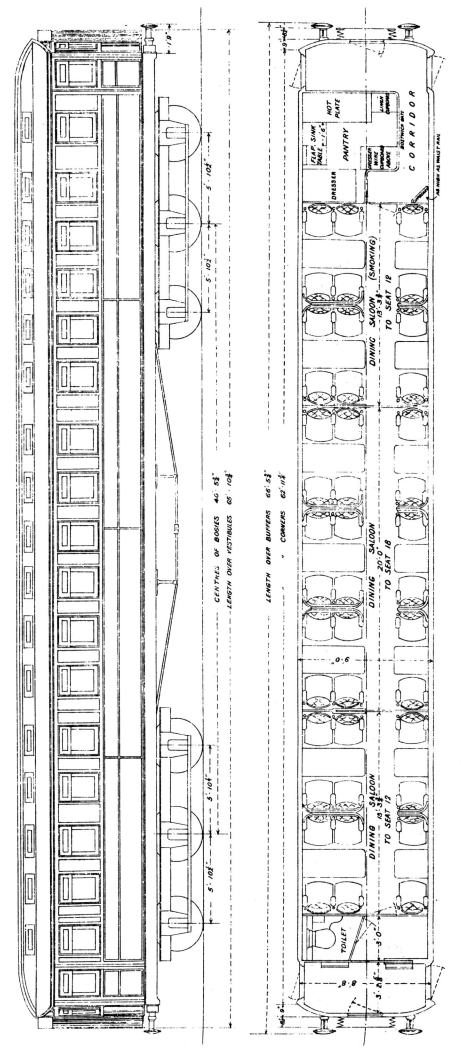

E. C. J. S. Third Class Dining Saloon

Nos. 313. 314. 315.

Built at Doncaster 1900

Dgm. 30. The contemporary 3rd class vehicles, 313/4/5, were longer, with a 64 ft 5¾ in body accommodating 42 passengers, with a full width attendant's compartment at one end. This was modified by removing a lavatory and converting the attendant's compartment into a pantry, at the same time providing a side corridor to give through access.

3 Saloons. Attendant's Compt.

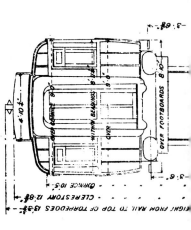

TONS. CWTS. QRS.

class passengers, with accommodation for 42 passengers whether in use for dining or not. The attendant's compartment was later made into a pantry to one side of the car, allowing for through circulation of passengers. The Gents was removed and the 'Ladies' made available to both sexes. All three cars were removed from East Coast services in November 1929, Nos 313 and 314 going to the GN Section as 43248 and 43249, and 315 to the GC Section as 52026.

Three 12-wheel composite dining saloons with centre kitchen and pantry also appeared in 1900 (Nos 316, 317 and 318), this time 63 ft 8½ in in length; on one side of the catering accommodation was a 3rd saloon 13 ft 3½ in long seating twelve and on the other, a 7 ft 2 in 1st saloon seating four, with another, twice the length, seating eight. All three were distributed in March 1925, Nos 316 and 317 to the GC Section as 2003C and 2004C (later 52003 and 52004), and No. 318 to the NE Area as 446Y—later 2446.

The *Locomotive Magazine*'s report on the new stock read:

'These splendid trains, the latest addition to the long list of corridor trains running on the three trunk lines between London and the Scottish cities, may not only claim to be the most up-to-date from the passengers' point of view, but embodying as they do such contrivances as automatic couplers, self-adjusting vestibules and the quick-acting Westinghouse brake, etc, may also claim to hold the first place from a mechanical point of view.'

The four 1st dining saloons, Nos 332, 333, 334 and 335 built at Doncaster in 1902, were similar to 310–2 of 1900 except that the kitchen was extended by 3 ft 11 in, reducing the seating by two to 16, divided equally between two saloons 14 ft 4 in long. The length of the coach was the same at 62 ft 0½ in, but for the first time the weight was over 40 tons—by 12 cwt. Another similarity was the fact that in 1913 authority was given for large windows to be fitted in place of the small variety originally provided. At the same time the seating was increased by two, the cost of both operations being £230 16s 1d per vehicle.

Between 1899 and 1902 York Works turned out seven 8-wheel 55 ft open 3rds with pantry—Nos 274 (1899), 273 and 275 (1900), 95 (1901) and 64, 65 and 66 (1902). When built these coaches had six bays, each seating

eight, although only the four centre bays were of the usual 3 + 1 arrangement. The bay at each end had no single seat at the outer end, and the seat on the opposite side of the gangway was longer than usual, seating four. The single seat at the pantry end was later replaced by a serving table. In 1923/4 all seven were lettered RESTAURANT CAR. They were all withdrawn between 1932 and 1938. The final 12-wheel clerestory dining cars were four built at Doncaster in 1905, Nos 196, 197, 352 and 353. They had a central kitchen and pantry, with a 3rd class saloon seating twelve on one side and two 1st class saloons on the other seating four and eight. Nos 196 and 353 were sold to the North British Railway in 1913 for £2,567 12s 9d, becoming NBR 162 and 163, and eventually LNER 32429 and 32430. After Grouping Nos 197 and 354 also went to Scotland, 197 in November 1928 becoming 32452, followed by 354 in January 1929 becoming 32453.

The last catering vehicles for the ECJS fleet were three kitchen cars built at York in 1914 for use on the new 10 am trains. These were the only ECJS kitchen cars with the Gresley elliptical roof and they were 53 ft 6 in long, of all-steel construction and designed to run with a 1st class dining saloon on one side (Nos 190 and 191), and a 3rd class dining saloon on the other (Nos 192 and 193). They were divided into 1st pantry (9 ft), entrance vestibule (2 ft 6 in), kitchen (22 ft) entrance vestibule (2 ft 6 in), 3rd pantry (6 ft 6 in), attendants' compartment (5 ft 11½ in) and lavatory (4 ft). The walls of the kitchen were covered with enamelled iron plates, and the floor consisted of $\frac{1}{8}$ in steel deck plates covered with $\frac{3}{4}$ in 'Decolite' patent cement. The sides of the cars were formed of Lysaght's No. 16 gauge charcoal finish, cold rolled, hydraulically-flattened panel plates, but the doorway pillars and the door frames were of teak. The roof was of No. 16 S.W.G. steel plates covered with cotton duck. Access to the two pantries and the kitchen from the corridor was through Bostwick folding gates.

The three vehicles were numbered 211, 212 and 213, and became 1211, 1212 and 1213 in 1926. When they became redundant on the East Coast services they were disposed of, two to the Great Northern Section and one to the Great Central, but there are two official versions of their renumbering; one records 1211 became 52039, and 1212 and 1213 became 42182 and 42183. The other version is that 1211 and 1212 became 42182 and 42183, with 1213 becoming 52039.

Dgm. 79. 1st class Dining Saloon No. 317 built at Doncaster in 1900. (*BR*)

E. C. J. S. Composite Dining Saloon

Nᵒˢ 316. 317. 318.

Built at Doncaster 1900.

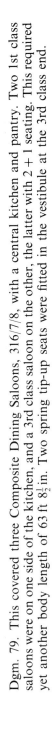

Dgm. 79. This covered three Composite Dining Saloons, 316/7/8, with a central kitchen and pantry. Two 1st class saloons were on one side of the kitchen, and a 3rd class saloon on the other, the latter with 2 + 1 seating. This required yet another body length of 63 ft 8½ in. Two spring tip-up seats were fitted in the vestibule at the 3rd class end.

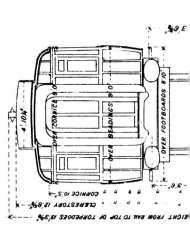

E.C. & J.S. COMPOSITE DINING CAR

Nos 196. 197. 352. 353.

Built at Doncaster 1905

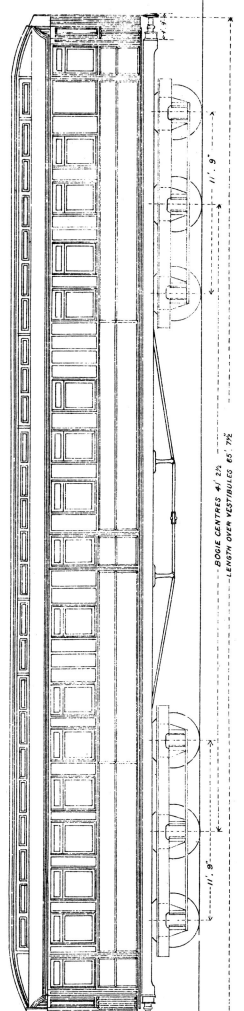

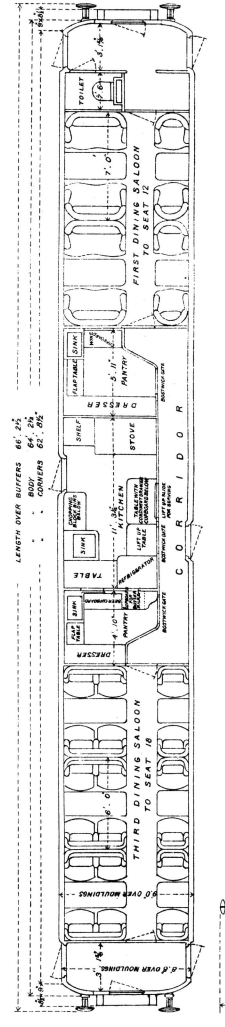

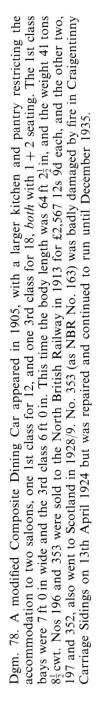

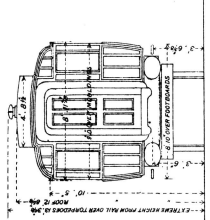

Dgm. 78. A modified Composite Dining Car appeared in 1905, with a larger kitchen and pantry restricting the accommodation to two saloons, one 1st class for 12, and one 3rd class for 18, *both* with 1 + 2 seating. The 1st class bays were 7 ft 0 in wide and the 3rd class 6 ft 0in. This time the body length was 64 ft 2½ in, and the weight 41 tons 8½ cwt. Nos 196 and 353 were sold to the North British Railway in 1913 for £2,567 12s 9d each, and the other two, 197 and 352, also went to Scotland in 1928/9. No. 353 (as NBR No. 163) was badly damaged by fire in Craigentinny Carriage Sidings on 13th April 1924 but was repaired and continued to run until December 1935.

1 First Saloon, 1 Third Saloon.
1 Kitchen, 2 Pantries, 1 Toilet.

WEIGHT	TONS.	CWTS.	QRS.
	41	8	2

SEATS FOR 12 FIRSTS & 18 THIRDS

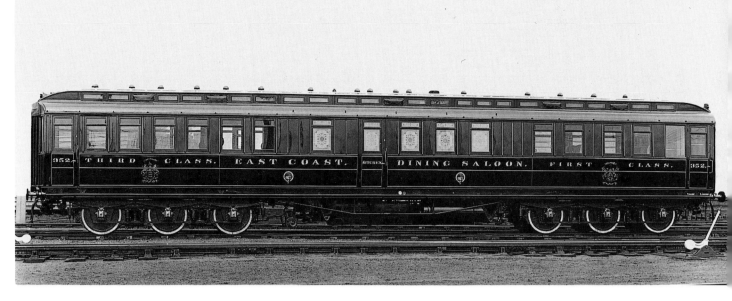

Dgm. 78. 1st class Dining Saloon No. 352 built at Doncaster in 1905.

6-Wheel Kitchen Cars Nos 198–201

KITCHEN EQUIPMENT

To be fitted in the most complete manner, with all the necessary cooking utensils, to be made of copper, tinned inside, and to include the following to be marked E.C.J.S.:

1 1-gallon kettle	1 grater
2 ½-gallon kettles	1 meat chopper
1 8″ saucepan and steamer	1 saw
1 10″ saucepan and steamer	1 set skewers
1 each 6″, 8″, 10″, 12″ stewpans	1 spice box
1 17″ fishkettle	1 2-gallon milk can
1 10″ chop pan	1 spring balance to weigh
1 10″ steak pan	60 lbs
1 10″ omelette pan	3 cook's knives
1 sauce ladle	1 pair meat carvers
a soup ladle	1 pair game carvers
2 vegetable strainers	1 fork and steel
2 gravy strainers and gravy spoon	1 champagne opener
2 fry sieves	1 ice pick
1 egg whisk	2 ginger beer openers
1 sugar and 1 flour dredger	2 corkscrews

Sundry tins for tea, coffee, sugar, flour etc.

To be fitted with shelves, tables and cupboards as drawings, also one James Slater's Patent Gas-heated 'Express Kitchener, copper hot water tank heated by two bunsen burners' and a refrigerator.

PANTRY

List of articles for each pantry. Cutlery and electro-plate, A1 quality, to be marked E.C.J.S.:

6 8″ meat dishes	6 milk jugs
3 10″ meat dishes	3 tea and 3 coffee pots
9 double vegetable dishes	4 toast racks
9 8″ entree dishes	3 pickle frames
6 10″ entree dishes	2 bread baskets
3 large sauceboats	2 doz fishknives
6 small sauceboats	2 doz fishforks
12 cruet frames, 3 bottles	3 doz dessert forks
1 salad bowl and helper	6 doz large knives
6 soup basins	6 doz large forks

2 doz soup spoons	4 doz small knives
2 doz dessert spoons	2 doz small forks
1 doz table spoons	1 Kent's circular knife
2 doz large tea spoons	cleaner
2 doz small tea spoons	1 filter
	6 sugar basins

CROCKERY, marked E.C.J.S.

6 doz dinner plates	3 doz dessert plates
6 doz soup plates	2 doz tea cups and saucers
6 doz pudding plates	1 doz coffee cups and
3 doz cheese plates	saucers

CRYSTAL, marked E.C.J.S.

2 doz soda glasses	2 ice pails
2 doz ale glasses	6 butter dishes
3 doz wine glasses	12 water bottles
2 doz liqueur glasses	

NAPERY, marked E.C.J.S.

3 doz damask table cloths	2 doz glass cloths
6 doz damask table knapkins	1 doz cooks' cloths
1 doz waiters' cloths	½ doz huckaback towels

The fittings to be made of teak, the sideboard to be fitted with four drawers lined with green baize, and loose trays also lined with baize, underneath to be fitted with plate rack. Wine lockers to be fitted with loose trays, each tray to be made to hold four bottles. The side and roof of kitchen and pantry to be lined with sycamore and french polished; the floors to be covered with sheet lead. Two cold water tanks to hold 66 gallons each to be fastened to the roof with angle irons, covered by wood casing. Each pantry to be fitted with telltale and two indicators for Dining Saloon, and one for corridor carriages, also battery and connections. System to be approved of in writing.

The four kitchen cars were originally fitted with a gas heated boiler at each end for providing hot-water heating for the adjoining dining saloons.

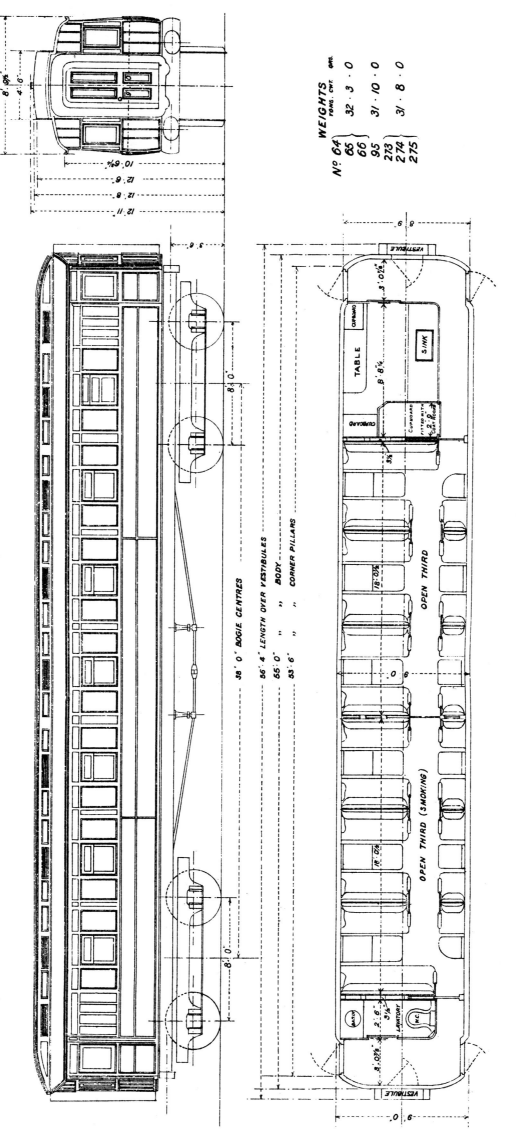

E. C. J. S. Open Third with Pantry

Nos. 64. 65. 66. 95. 273. 274. 275.

Nº 64 Built by N.E.R.Cº. 1902

"	65	" " " 1901
"	66	" " " 1900
"	95	" " " 1901
"	273	" " " 1900
"	274	" " " 1899
"	275	" " " 1900

WEIGHTS

	TONS. CWT. QRS.
Nº 64 } 65 } 66 }	32 . 3 . 0
95 }	31 . 10 . 0
273 } 274 } 275 }	31 . 8 . 0

8' 9¾"
4' 6"
10' 6¾"
12' 6"
12' 8"
12' 11"

38' 0" BOGIE CENTRES
56' 4" LENGTH OVER VESTIBULES
55' 0" " BODY
53' 6" " CORNER PILLARS
8' 0"

VESTIBULE
CUPBOARD
TABLE
SINK
CUPBOARD
CUPBOARD
FITTED WITH
COAT HOOKS
OPEN THIRD
OPEN THIRD (SMOKING)
LAVATORY
W.C.
VESTIBULE
3' 0¾"
8' 8¾"
2' 9"
9½"
18' 0¼"
6' 0"
18' 0¼"
2' 6"
3½"
3' 0¼"
6' 0"

Open Third with Smoking Partition
36 Seats or 34 Seats when Dining
Pantry 1 Lavatory

ELECTRIC LIGHTING

Dgm. 31. The NER built seven 8-wheel Open Thirds with pantry at York between 1899 and 1902, with a 55 ft body and seats for 36 passengers, but because of the layout two passengers could not be accommodated at a table and thus for dining purposes the seating was reduced to 34. However, one seat and table at the pantry end proved an obstacle and they were removed, although a serving table was fitted in their place.

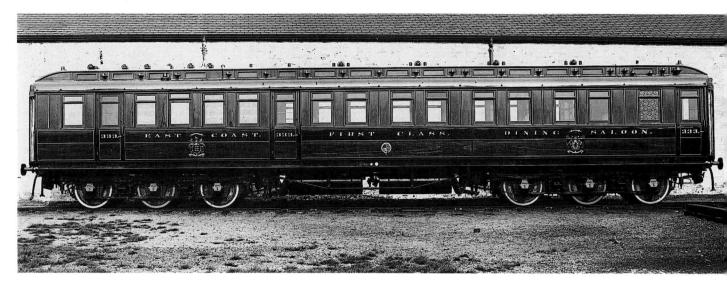

Dgm. 77. 1st class Dining Saloon No. 333 built at Doncaster in 1902.

Above: Dgm. 77. No. 332 fitted with large windows; and below: Dgm. 77. No. 332 interior.

L. C. & D. S. DINING SALOON (FIRST CLASS)

Nºs. 332. 333. 334. 335.   *Built at Doncaster 1902*

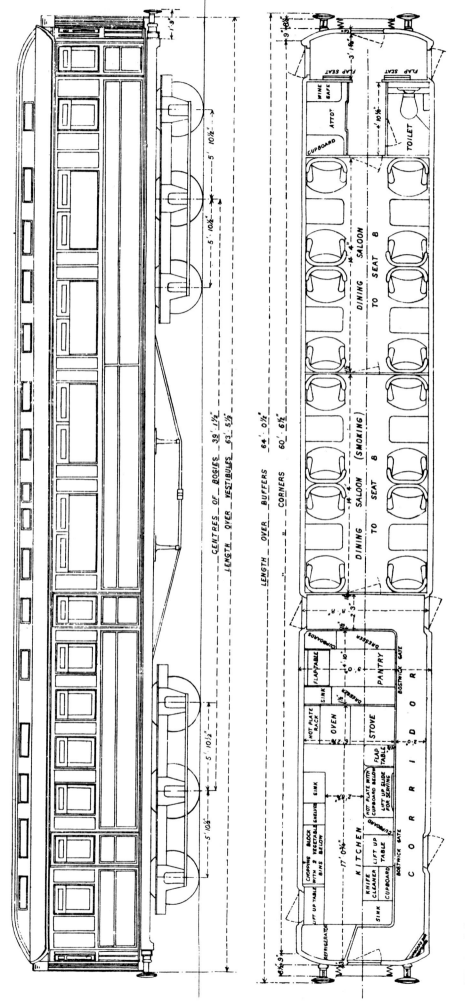

WEIGHT **TONS.** 40 **CWTS.** 0 **QRS.** 12

2 Saloons, 16 Seats,
Kitchen & Pantry
& I Lavatory

Dgm. 77. Other 12-wheel Dining Cars which had their small windows replaced were 332-5, built at Doncaster in 1902. These had an end kitchen, with two saloons, each seating only eight diners on 1 + 1 seating. Authority to fit large windows was given in July 1911, and three years later a lavatory, cupboard and wine-safe were removed to increase the seating by two. The body was 62 ft 0½ in long and the weight was originally quoted as 40 tons 12 cwt, which became 40 tons 12 qtrs on the revised Diagram!

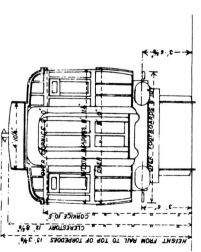

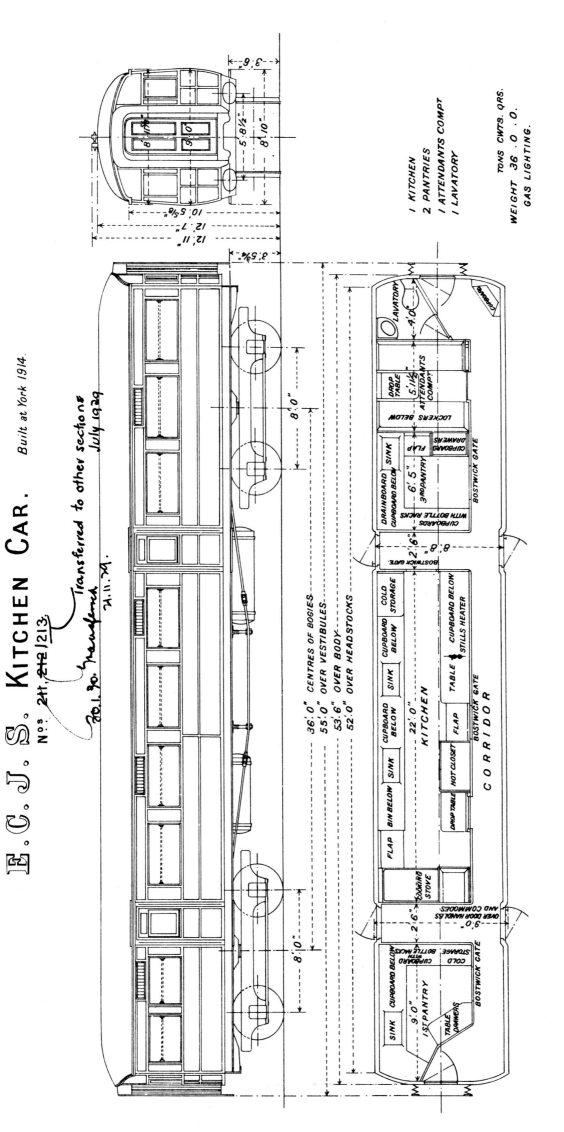

E. C. J. S. KITCHEN CAR.

Built at York 1914.

Nos. 211, 212/213.

Transferred to other sections July 1929

Dgm. 80A. For the 1914 "Flying Scotsman" trains three Kitchen Cars, 211–3 were built at York, with 53 ft 6 in bodies carried on eight wheels. The kitchen was 22 ft long compared with the 12 ft on the original (1893) cars, with a 1st class pantry on one side and a 3rd class pantry on the other; there was also an attendants' compartment. The kitchen and the two pantries were entered from the side corridor via Bostwick Gates—a metal folding gate extensively used on East Coast vehicles.

These coaches were built of steel, with a steel floor covered with a patent cement, and the sides of the kitchen were covered with enamelled plates. The tare weight amounted to 36 tons.

Dgm. 80A. Kitchen Car No. 211 built at York in 1914.

4 Sleeping Cars

The subject of sleeping carriages caused more discussion than any other matter concerning East Coast services. The advent of the sleeping car in America was first mentioned in the late 1860s but no true East Coast Joint Stock sleeping car appeared until 1877, although in 1873 North British and Great Northern sleepers were brought into use on East Coast services. In January 1874 it was proposed that both should be taken over by the East Coast, and it was stated that the GN vehicle (No. 1379) cost £549 and carried more than double the number of passengers carried by the NB coach (No. 145). It was thought that both cars could be transferred to East Coast stock if the North British would accept the same price (£549) for theirs.

In 1872, and again in 1874, Mr Stirling submitted plans for a proposed 8-wheel bogie sleeping carriage, and in May 1874 asked if his latest design should be fitted up on the Pullman principle, or as a composite car. Its estimated cost was £700. It was resolved that the approval of the North Eastern be obtained and that two such carriages should be tried over the East Coast route. However, nothing transpired, although in December 1875 Mr Stirling was instructed to design and build two sleeping carriages 'on the plan which he may consider best suited for the purpose', but in March 1876 it was decided to do nothing further. Nevertheless, in May 1876 the East Coast Committee finally made up its mind and decided to provide sleeping accommodation on the 8.30 pm and 9 pm from King's Cross and the 7.30 pm and 10.30 pm from Edinburgh. As only two sleeping carriages were available for the four services, ordinary 1st class compartment stock was used to provide sleeping facilities, one side of a compartment being allowed to a passenger on payment of the sleeping car berth supplement.

Three weeks later, on 16th June 1876, instructions were given for plans to be prepared for a sleeping carriage, and in the following month the design was presented for discussion; it was described as holding 'eight good couches of ample length and width on the ground floor of the car, with lavatory. Mr Stirling does not contemplate any upper tier. It will not serve well for any day pasengers as the couches will be too broad for anybody to sit on in comfort. In the event of its becoming unnecessary hereafter to use it, it could readily be turned into a double saloon carriage and used in general traffic.' The body was 7 ft 9 in wide and 36 ft long, carried on six wheels; there was a saloon at each end holding four couches, with a communicating door between those on either side. The centre of the car was occupied by two lavatories. Three days later, on 7th July 1876, three sleeping carriages were authorised and they were ready to go into use from 1st July 1877, one on the 8.30 pm King's Cross-Perth and another on the 9.30 pm King's Cross-Glasgow. In the meantime (23rd Jan. 1877) the GN and NB vehicles were purchased at £500 and £549 respectively: the three new East Coast cars (Nos 104/5/6) costing £646 each. The former GN car, ECJS No. 90, was damaged in the Morpeth derailment of 25th March 1877 and the repairs were estimated to cost the NER £50.

Three further sleeping cars were authorised in may 1878, to be ready for the autumn traffic, but these were not proceeded with at once because of the introduction in August of two Pullman sleepers. However, in January 1881 four further East Coast sleepers were ordered to be built at Doncaster. At that time facilities were still provided on only four trains, two 'down' and two 'up', but on occasions it was necessary to add one or two cars to some of the trains, particularly in the 'down' direction, and the supply of sleeping cars did not always allow this to be done without returning cars empty from Scotland. The new vehicles, delivered in 1881, were numbered 107/8/9/17, with 118/9/20 in hand for delivery in 1882.

This made a fleet of twelve East Coast sleepers, of which ten (Nos 104-9 and 117-20) were considered 'good, though probably not equal to the new sleeping cars recently added to the West Coast Joint Stock'.

The old North British sleeper, East Coast No. 91, was replaced in 1884, but not by a sleeping car, and two new sleepers authorised in January 1885 were delivered later in that year (Nos 124/5).

During the winter months there were sleeping cars to spare and in November 1885 permission was given to hire three or four East Coast sleepers to the Great Northern at 10s 0d per day, for use on the night trains to and from Manchester and Yorkshire.

In October 1888 Mr Stirling submitted proposals for new sleeping cars, one on six wheels and the other on eight, although the latter had a rigid wheelbase and was not on bogies, expressing at the same time his preference for the former as the '8-wheel with a 32 ft wheelbase might be objected to by some of the companies'. Henry Oakley of the Great Northern suggested that an attendant should be able to circulate through the carriage so that he could attend to the wants of the passengers, and that the 6-wheel design should not be entertained; heating equipment should also be provided.

As a result Stirling came back the following month with an improved design fulfilling the conditions that it could be warmed during the winter and could carry an attendant, but nevertheless, when the new cars were ordered (and delivered) in 1889 they were on six wheels, with no heating and no attendant. They were numbered 146–54, with two double-berths, a 1st class compartment; a 2nd class (later 3rd) compartment; and a luggage compartment. Each double-berth had its own lavatory. The total length of each vehicle was 36 ft 5 in.

These were followed in 1890 by six replacement cars, Nos 104–9, but 106 was destroyed in the Thirsk accident two years later. The displaced vehicles dating from 1877 and 1881 were divided amongst the GN (104/6/9), NE (107/8) and NB (105). Next came two further composite cars, Nos 181 and 182, and four full sleepers, 183-6, in 1892. On 4th January 1893 it was pointed out that four sleepers were due for renewal and on 3rd March approval was given for cars 37 ft 6 in long, having seven berths, with an attendant, and fitted with central connections between vehicles; these appearing later in the year as Nos 117–20. The old cars dating from 1881/2 were later 'reconstructed internally' and renumbered 228–31, but they passed to the NER in 1903 and put in another ten years work, but not as sleeping cars! They were NER Nos 3172–5.

Sleepers Nos 117–20 dating from 1893 were replaced after seven years but continued to run with a letter "A" suffix until, in January 1909 it was stated that they were

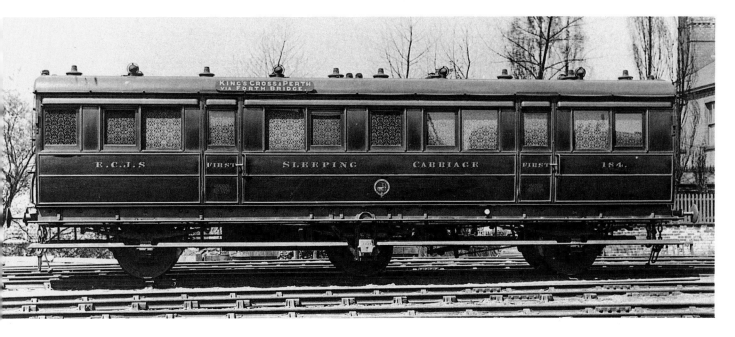

6-wheel Sleeping Car No. 184 built at Doncaster in 1892.

E. C. J. S. COMPOSITE SLEEPING CARRIAGE (6 WHEELS)

Nos 146. 148. 150. 151. 152. 153. 154. 181. 182.

Built at Doncaster 1889
" " " 1892

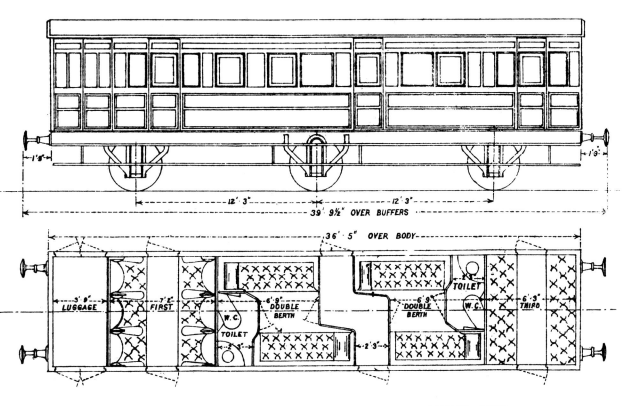

WEIGHT 15 · 12 · 2 TONS. CWT. QRS.

2 DOUBLE BERTHS
6 FIRST & 10 THIRD CLASS BERTHS

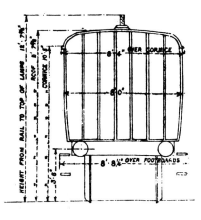

Dgm. 71. The 6-wheel sleepers on the East Coast services underwent numerous design changes, and it was not until the introduction of the transverse sleeper in 1895 that some form of standardisation was achieved. One 6-wheel design dating from 1889 had two double berths, two toilets, one 1st class compartment, one 3rd class (originally 2nd) compartment, and a luggage compartment—all in a body 36 ft 5 in long outside. The berths were two on each side of a staggered transverse passage, and each pair of berths had its own toilet, not accessible from any of the compartments.

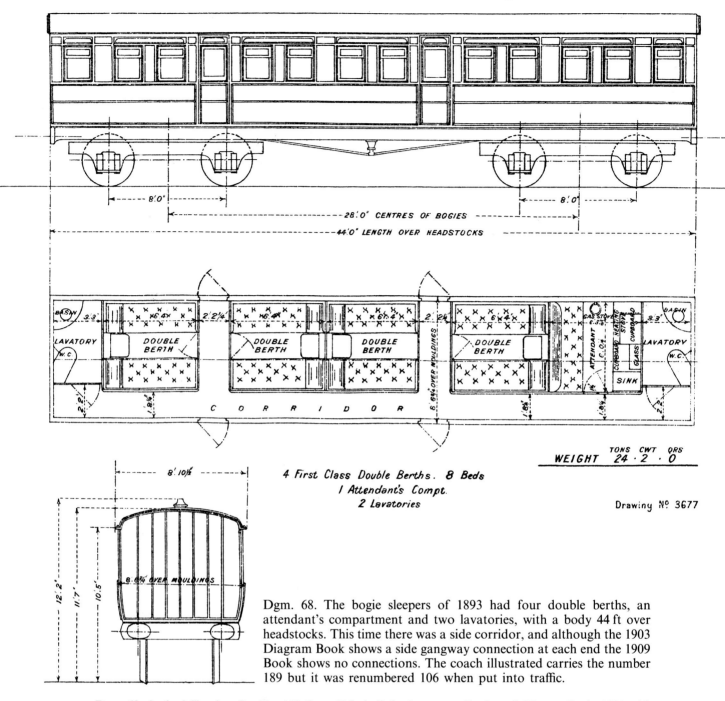

E. C. J. S. Sleeping Carriage

Nᵒˢ 90ᴬ 106ᴬ 187ᴬ   Built by Lancaster C.& W. Cᵒ 1893. Maintained by N.E. Cᵒʸ

4 First Class Double Berths. 8 Beds
1 Attendant's Compt.
2 Lavatories

WEIGHT 24 · 2 · 0 (TONS CWT QRS)

Drawing Nᵒ 3677

Dgm. 68. The bogie sleepers of 1893 had four double berths, an attendant's compartment and two lavatories, with a body 44 ft over headstocks. This time there was a side corridor, and although the 1903 Diagram Book shows a side gangway connection at each end the 1909 Book shows no connections. The coach illustrated carries the number 189 but it was renumbered 106 when put into traffic.

Dgm. 68. 8-wheel Sleeping Car No. 189 (later 106), built by Lancaster Carriage & Wagon Co. in 1893 with longitudinal berths.

deteriorating through standing idle. Six months later they were reported as 'seldom used, and when used give rise to complaints'. In January 1910 it was noted that No. 117A had gone to the GN, 118A to the NE, and 119A and 120A to the NB. These were the last East Coast 6-wheel sleepers to be built and, as with most of the full sleepers, they had a short life, whereas some of the composite sleepers lasted much longer because of a greater demand; for instance, although 146/8/50/1 only continued in use until 1910, Nos 152/3/4 ran until 1914 and 181/2 until 1922.

The short life of the full sleepers was no doubt due to the introduction of bogie sleeping cars in 1894 and transverse sleepers in 1895—both NER designs breaking away from the 20 years of GN supremacy favouring 6-wheelers and longitudinal berths. The reason for the much longer life of the composite sleepers is more difficult to explain, although it is probably due to the fact that one of these could be hired by a family travelling to Scotland, complete with servants. The master and mistress, with their children, could occupy the sleeping berths, with the servants in the compartment.

Also in January 1893 the North Eastern proposed a 46 ft long bogie sleeping car with side corridor, toilet at each end, central compartment for attendant, and four cabins with two couches in each. Mr Stirling, however, did not like bogies and he sent a strongly critical letter to his General Manager, attacking Mr Worsdell, 'who has not the slightest experience of bogies as far as I am aware should so strongly advocate them against this Company's view, who have had considerable experience of the bogie and have altogether discarded them'. Stirling also took exception to the North Eastern designed bogie dining cars, then out to tender. In return the North Eastern was asked to give a trial to 8-wheel (non-bogie) sleeping carriages for ECJS use but declined. Nevertheless, on 16th March 1893, only thirteen days after the GN pattern 6-wheel cars had been approved, the tender of the Lancaster Railway Carriage & Wagon Co. was accepted for one bogie car at £1,535, with two more at the same price to follow.

It was planned for these three bogie sleeping cars to be numbered 187, 188 and 189 but 188 became 90, and 189 became 106. Of the vehicles replaced, old No. 90, the pioneer Great Northern-built car for the East Coast, went to the Great Northern and became 2681, and 106 replaced a sleeper of 1890 vintage destroyed in the Thirsk accident in 1892. No. 187, which retained its originally allocated number, was considered as replacing

the Pullman sleeper *India*, also destroyed at Thirsk. Although officially listed as being built in 1893 these three new vehicles were not placed in service until 1894, on the 8 pm King's Cross-Aberdeen and the 6.50 pm Aberdeen-King's Cross; two GN-built 6-wheel cars worked to Perth, also on the 8 pm from King's Cross, returning at 7.55 pm, and the two Pullmans worked down to Glasgow on the 8.30 pm and returned at 9.5 pm.

These Lancaster built cars had four double-berth cabins arranged along one side and, of necessity, had side corridors. A ladies' lavatory was provided at one end and a gents' at the other, with a compartment for the attendant between the gents' and the berths. Access from the non-corridor side of the coach was by two transverse passages, each having on either side a door into one of the cabins. Length over headstocks was 46 ft, with 8 ft bogies at 28 ft centres.

The building of three straight-sided sleepers in 1905 relegated these three cars to the duplicate list as Nos 90A, 106A and 187A, but they continued to run until 1910, when 90A went to the GNR, and 106A and 187A to the NER. The two North Eastern cars were converted to 3rd class saloons and numbered 3758 and 3759; 3758 continued to run until September 1938 and 3759 until June 1937.

In the same year that the first bogie cars went into service (1894) the North Eastern was preparing drawings for a transverse-berth sleeper, having two double-berths, four single, a smoking compartment (which could be converted to a double-berth if required and was later so converted permanently), an attendant's compartment, and two lavatories. A preliminary design which has survived shows a clerestory roof stopping short about 2 ft 6 in from each end. The ends were not shaped in any way and no gangway connection was provided for. On 14th September 1895 Mr Bain, the NER Chief Carriage & Wagon Works Manager, reported that he was arranging to build the sleeping car in teak, 'so as to correspond with the ordinary type of East Coast carriage' and the go-ahead was formally given on 4th October 1895, although work had obviously been started during the previous month.

When the first transverse-berth car appeared in 1895 its interior layout was as in the preliminary design, with the ends still flat, probably with the clerestory sloping down at each end, a feature which was to become so familiar on East Coast stock; a gangway connection was provided. One feature not perpetuated in later cars was that the sleeping-berth doors were hinged and opened

Dgm. 65. No. 234, the first East Coast sleeper with transverse berths, built at York in 1895. (*BR*)

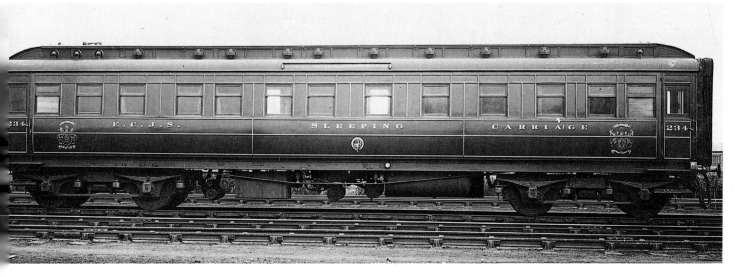

E. C. J. S. First Class Sleeping Carriage

Nos 234   Built by N.E.R. 1895

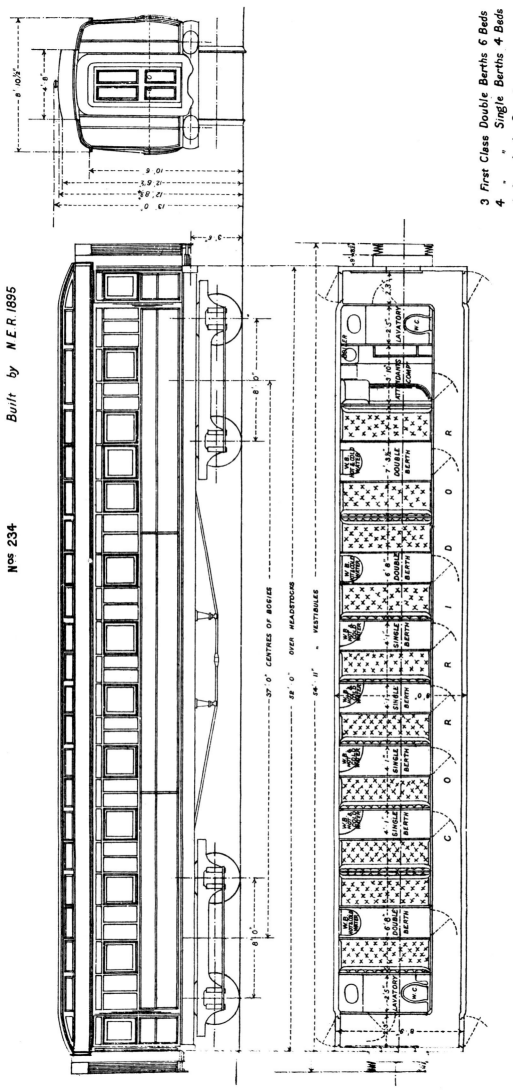

3 First Class Double Berths 6 Beds
4 " Single Berths 4 Beds
1 Attendants Compt.
2 Lavatories

WEIGHT	TONS	CWTS.	QRS.
	26	17	0

ELECTRIC LIGHTING

Dgm. 65. No. 234, the first transverse sleeper appeared from the NER York Carriage Works in 1895, with three double-berths and four single, two lavatories and an attendant's compartment. It was carried on 4-wheel bogies and had a body 52 ft over headstocks.

⇥ SLEEPING CARRIAGES. ⇤

SLEEPING CARRIAGES, provided with sheets, rugs, &c., and fitted with separate lavatories for ladies and gentlemen, are attached to the undermentioned trains.

STATIONS.	Weekdays.						Sundays.		
	A B	**J**			**B**	**C**			
King's Cross ..dep	7 45 p.m.	8 15 p.m.	8 45 p.m.	10 30 p.m.	11 30 p.m.	11 30 p.m.	8 15 p.m.	8 45 p.m.	11 ⁰0 p.m.
York .... "	11 27 "	11 57 "	1 15 a.m.	3 35 a.m.	3 12 a.m.	3 12 a.m.	11 57 "	1 15 a.m.	3 12 a.m.
Edinburgh .... arr	3 30 a.m.	4 0a.m. ‡	6 0 " ‡	e8 58 "	7 15 " ‡	7 15 " ‡	4 0 a.m.‡	6 0 " ‡	7 15 " ‡
Glasgow ...... "	—	—	d7 23 " ‡	—	8 50 " ‡	10 43 "	—	7 23 " ‡	8 50 " ‡
Perth .... "	4 40 "	5 14 " ‡	—	—	8 55 "	8 40 " ‡	5 14 " ‡	—	⁸ 55 " ‡
Aberdeen ...... "	—	7 20 " ‡	—	—	10 50 " ‡	11 10 " ‡	7 2¹ " ‡	—	10 50 " ‡
Inverness...... "	8 35 "	9 10 " ‡	—	—	—	—	9 10 " ‡	—	—

A—Will run from 24th July to 11th August.   B Saturdays excepted.   C—Saturdays only.   d—On Sunday mornings is due at Glasgow at 7.30 a.m.
e—No arrival at Edinburgh on Sunday mornings.

STATIONS.	Weekdays.						Sundays.		
		A							
Inverness......dep	—	—	—	5 45 p.m.‡	—	—	3 30 p.m.‡	—	—
Aberdeen ...... "	—	—	—	7 45 " ‡	—	—	—	—	—
Perth .... "	—	7 55 p.m.	—	9 40 " ‡	—	—	—	—	—
Glasgow ...... "	6 0 p.m.‡	—	9 35 p.m.‡	—	—	—	5 0 " ‡	9 ³5 p.m.‡	—
Edinburgh .... "	7 35 " ‡	9 4⁰ "	10 50 " ‡	11 15 " ‡	—	—	7 35 " ‡	11 0 " ‡	—
York......... arr	1 15 a.m.	2 25 a.m.	3 15 a.m.	3 30 a.m.	—	—	1 15 a.m.	3 45 a.m.	—
King's Cross .. "	5 50 "	6 40 "	7 10 "	7 35 "	—	—	5 50 "	8 5 "	—

A—Will commence on 3rd July.

‡ Corridor Sleeping Carriage with Transverse Berths, or Pullman Sleeping Carriage, accompanied by an attendant who provides tea, coffee, &c.

The charges are:—Between G.N. stations, including York, 3s.; between G.N. stations and stations north of York, 5s., in addition to first class railway fares.

Between N.E. stations, including York, and Glasgow, Perth, and Aberdeen, 3s.; and between N.E. stations, including York, and stations on the Highland Railway, 5s., in addition to first class railway fares.

FOR LADIES TRAVELLING ALONE a separate compartment is reserved. On the Pullman Sleeping Carriages this compartment contains four berths, and can be reserved on payment of 15s., in addition to three first class fares.

⇥ BERTHS CAN BE SECURED IN ADVANCE ⇤

By giving notice to the Great Northern Company's Superintendent at KING'S CROSS; the North Eastern Company's Superintendent at YORK; the North British Company's Superintendent at EDINBURGH, and at the East Coast Companies' Offices, 16, South St. Andrew Street, EDINBURGH; 37, West George Street, GLASGOW; General Station, Perth; 28, Market Street, ABERDEEN; and 6, Academy Street, Inverness; or by giving notice to the Stationmasters at any station at which the express trains call, between London, Edinburgh, Glasgow, Perth, Aberdeen, and Inverness.

Passengers travelling in the Sleeping Carriages by the up trains due to arrive at King's Cross at 5.50 a.m., 6.4⁰ a.m., and 7.10 a.m. may, if they wish, remain in them until 8.0 a.m.

SUPPLY OF RUGS AND PILLOWS TO PASSENGERS BY NIGHT EXPRESS TRAINS.—Rugs and Pillows are supplied for first and third class passengers of the through East Coast Trains to and from Stations south of, and including Edinburgh, Glasgow, Perth, and Aberdeen, at a charge of 6d. per Rug, and 6d. per Pillow.

Notice from NER Timetable for July 1899, by which time the NER-designed transverse berth sleeping cars were in use, and the Pullman sleepers *Iona* and *Columba* were still in service.

into the corridor; later cars had sliding doors. Only one vehicle, No. 234, was built to the initial design; it was 52 ft long, with 8ft bogies at 37 ft centres and it remained in service until October 1925.

This car set the pattern for East Coast Joint Stock and LNER sleeping cars. From 1895 to 1922 the North Eastern carriage works at York built all the East Coast bogie sleeping cars and the Great Northern works at Doncaster did not re-enter the field until 1922 with the articulated sleeper, No. 181 + 181A.

Two minor matters which received attention in 1895 were the provision of a water-bottle and glass in each compartment of sleeping carriages, and confirmation that the attendants in the Pullman cars on the Glasgow service ceased sleeping in the cars at Glasgow from 1st June.

The Pullman sleeper *Iona* was damaged in the St Neots accident in November 1895 and when the transverse car was ready it was decided to use it as a replacement on the 11.30 pm to Glasgow, commencing on 10th December 1895. Within a matter of six weeks the new car was reported to be very popular with passengers, leading to authority being given for four more, to be ready for the summer season. These turned out to be Nos 235/6/7/8, basically the same as the pioneer car but 18 in longer over headstocks. However, by cutting the smoking compartment down to a coupé, and with the extra length, it was possible to accommodate an additional single-berth compartment. This design also perpetuated the flat ends. The smoking coupé could be used as a single-berth if required and it later became a permanent berth. Nos 235, 237 and 238 were withdrawn in April 1923 and 236 in July 1925.

Four new sleepers to two designs appeared in 1897: Nos 268 and 269 were similar to the previous batch, 235–8, still on eight wheels, but with bowed ends. The length over headstocks remained at 53 ft 6 in but the length over body was now 55 ft. End windows were fitted on each side of the vestibule connection. With the flat-ended sleepers it had been the practice to fit sliding doors to the connections at each end, but with bowed ends this became difficult and henceforward hinged doors were provided. The bowed ends allowed more space in the end vestibules, which were now $8\frac{3}{4}$ in wider (in the centre) at 3 ft.

The other two cars built at York in 1897 were Nos 147 and 149, and they brought back composite sleeping cars with 1st class berths and 3rd class compartments. They were actually replacements for the two 6-wheel composite cars with the same numbers lost in the St Neots accident. The accommodation consisted of two double-berths, with two single-berths in between, two 3rd class compartments, two lavatories, and an attendant's compartment, which also accommodated luggage. No. 147 was withdrawn in February 1925 and 149 in January of the same year.

On 4th August 1898 three further transverse sleepers were ordered, together with 20 more on 1st December 1899, the latter order to include replacements for the two remaining Pullmans, and actually 21 were built between 1899 and 1902. Although the same length as the previous cars, 53 ft 6 in, these were all carried on two 6-wheel bogies: 19 were full sleepers, although with a smoking coupé, and were numbered 104/5/9/17–20/4/5/83: 6, 232/3, 276–9. The other two were composites numbered 107 and 108 and had two 3rd class compartments

45

E. C. J. S. Composite Sleeping Carriage

Nos 147, 149.

Built by N.E.R Cº 1897

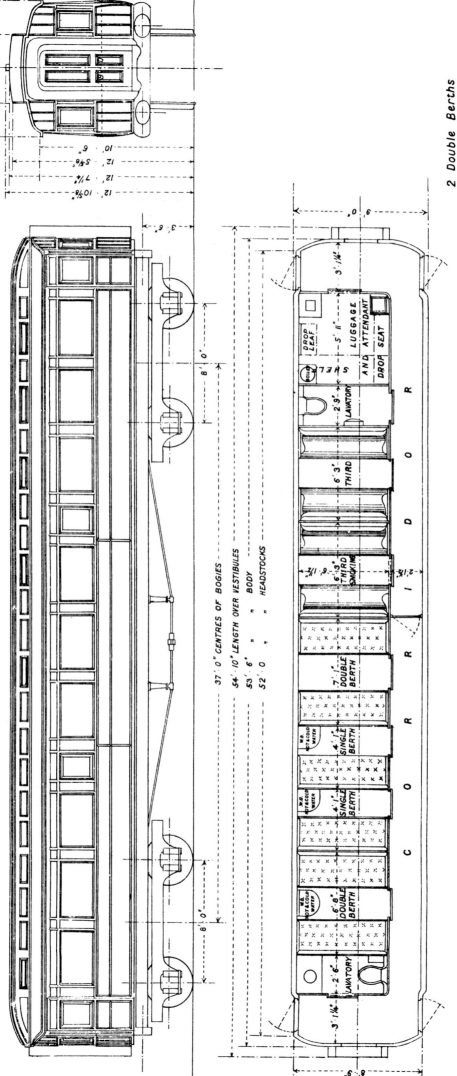

2 Double Berths
2 Single Berths
12 Third Class Seats
2 Lavatories
Luggage & Attendants Compt.

WEIGHT 31 · 8 · 0
TONS. CWTS. QRS.

ELECTRIC LIGHTING

Dgm. 72. Similar Composite Sleeping Cars 147 and 149 had two double-berths and two single-berths, together with two 3rd class compartments, two lavatories and an attendant's compartment, which also provided space for passengers' luggage.

SLEEPING CARRIAGES, provided with sheets, rugs, &c., and fitted with separate lavatories for ladies and gentlemen, are attached to the undermentioned trains. The charge is 5s. per berth, in addition to first class railway fares.

Stations.	Weekdays.							Sundays.				
	A B 7 45 p.m.	**A** 8 15 p.m.	8 45 p.m.	**A** 10 30 p.m.	11 30 p.m.	**C** 11 30 p.m.	11 45 p.m.	**D** 7 45 p.m.	8 15 p.m.	8 45 p.m.	11 30 p.m.	11 45 p.m.
King's Cross .... dep	7 45 p.m.	8 15 p.m.	8 45 p.m.	10 30 p.m.	11 30 p.m.	—	11 45 p.m.	7 45 p.m.	8 15 p.m.	8 45 p.m.	11 30 p.m.	11 45 p.m.
York .... "	11 27 "	11 57 "	1 15 a.m.	3 35 a.m.	3 12 a.m.	3 12 a.m.	3 27 a.m.	11 27 "	11 57 "	1 15 a.m.	3 12 a.m.	3 27 a.m.
Newcastle .... "	1 7 a.m.	1 32 a.m.	3 10 "	6 0 "	4 47 "	4 47 "	5 7 " *‡	1 7 a.m.	1 32 a.m.	3 10 "	4 47 "	5 7 " *‡
Edinburgh .... arr	3 30 "	4 0 "	5 55 "	8f58 " *	7 15 "	7 15 "	7 30 "	3 30 "	4 0 "	5 55 "	7 15 " *‡	7 30 "
Glasgow ...... "	—	5 35 "	7e23 " *‡	—	—	—	8h50 " *	—	5 35 "	7 23 " *‡	—	8 50 " *
Aberdeen ...... "	7 20 " *‡	—	—	11 10 " *‡	11 20 " *‡	—	—	7 20 " *‡	—	—	11 10 " *‡	—
Perth .... "	4g40 "	5 14 "	—	—	8 55 " *‡	8 40 " *‡	—	4 40 "	5 14 "	—	8 55 " *	—
Inverness ...... "	8g35 " *	9 10 " *‡	—	—	—	—	—	8 35 " *	9 10 " *‡	—	—	—
Fort William .. "	—	43 " *‡	—	—	—	—	—	9 43 " *‡	—	—	—	—

A.—Saturdays excepted.   B.—Will run from 7th July to 8th August.   C.—Saturdays only.   D.—Will only run on 10th August.   e.—On Sunday mornings is due at Glasgow at 7.30.   f.—Runs to Berwick only on Sunday mornings.   g.—From 21st July to 8th August.   h.—On Sunday mornings arrives at Glasgow at 10.43.
*.—Through car from King's Cross terminating at this point.

‡ Corridor Sleeping Carriage with Transverse Berths, accompanied by an attendant who provides tea, coffee, &c.

Stations.	Weekdays.				Sundays.	
Fort William .. dep	—	—	4 20 p.m.*‡	—	—	—
Inverness ...... "	—	—	—	5 30 p.m.*‡	4 10 p.m.	—
Perth .... "	—	7 55 p.m.*‡	—	9 40 " *‡	3 30 "	—
Aberdeen ...... "	3 30 p.m.	—	—	7 45 " *‡	—	—
Glasgow ...... "	6 0 " *‡	—	9 35 " *‡	—	5 0 " *	9 35 p.m.*‡
Edinburgh .... "	7 45 "	9 40 " *‡	10 50 " *‡	11 15 " *	7 45 "	11 0 " *‡
Newcastle .... "	a11 15 " *‡	12 37 a.m.	1 34 a.m.	1 49 a.m.	11 15 " *‡	2 0 a.m.
York .... arr	1 15 a.m.	2 22 "	3 15 "	3 29 "	1 12 a.m.	3 45 "
King's Cross .. "	5 50 "	6 40 "	7 10 "	7 35 "	5 50 "	8 5 "

a.—The car which starts from Newcastle does not run on Saturday nights.   *.—Through car between this point and King's Cross.

‡ Corridor Sleeping Carriage with Transverse Berths, accompanied by an attendant who provides tea, coffee, &c.

BERTHS CAN BE SECURED IN ADVANCE

By giving notice to the Great Northern Company's Superintendent at KING'S CROSS; the North Eastern Company's Chief Passenger Agent at YORK; the North British Company's Superintendent at EDINBURGH, and at the East Coast Companies' Offices, 16, South St. Andrew Street, EDINBURGH; 37, West George Street, GLASGOW; General Station, PERTH; 28, Market Street, ABERDEEN; and 6, Academy Street, INVERNESS; or by giving notice to the Station-masters at any station at which the express trains call, between London, Edinburgh, Glasgow, Perth, Aberdeen, and Inverness.

In ordering berths passengers should state whether required for lady or gentleman.

Passengers travelling in the Sleeping Carriages by the up trains arriving at King's Cross at 5.50 a.m., 6.40 a.m., and 7.10 a.m., and by the down train arriving at Newcastle at 5.0 a.m., may remain in them until 8.0 a.m.

SUPPLY OF RUGS AND PILLOWS TO PASSENGERS BY NIGHT EXPRESS TRAINS.—Rugs and Pillows are supplied for first and third class passengers, in the through East Coast Trains, travelling to and from Stations south of, and including Edinburgh, Glasgow, Perth, and Aberdeen, at a charge of 6d. per Rug, and 6d. per Pillow.

Notice from NER Timetable for July 1902. The Pullman sleepers have disappeared and the popular transverse cars were in use on most of the trains running beyond Edinburgh—to Aberdeen, Fort William, Glasgow, Inverness and Perth.

in place of the two double-berths, but still with the smoking coupé. All were fitted with the usual attendant's compartment and two lavatories. No. 120 was destroyed in the Grantham accident of 19th September 1906. The remainder were all condemned in 1925, 1926 and 1927.

Although not the first transverse berth cars on the East Coast the 12-wheel full sleepers were praised for the novelty of their layout, 'which should conduce to the comfort of the sleepers by keeping their heads away from the noise and draughts from the windows, because the berths are placed across the carriage instead of lengthways, with the pillows next the corridor. The beds are specially large and fitted on the outside with an ingenious movable net about 9 in high, which not only prevents the bedding from slipping off, but removes the uncomfortable feeling, inseparable from a narrow bed, that one may fall out'. Lighting was by gas.

Credit for the design was given to Mr D. Bain, the Carriage Superintendent of the NER, under the supervision of Mr Wilson Worsdell, the Locomotive Superintendent. One of the cars was sent to the Paris Exhibition in 1900, shipped with Class S 4-6-0 No. 2006 from Hull.

Four more 12-wheel composites were authorised in 1902 and they appeared in the following year as Nos 228, 229, 230 and 231, generally similar to the previous cars except that instead of having five single-berths they had one double and three single. What had been the smoking coupé in the previous designs was now classed as an additional berth, but it had folding arm-rests so that it could be used as a smoker if required. No 231 was lost in the Grantham derailment. No. 228 was condemned in July 1925, and 229 and 230 were both condemned in April 1927.

In 1905 York Carriage Works turned out three straight-sided composite sleepers with matchboarding below the waist-line. The numbers 90, 106 and 187 were used, relegating the 1893 cars to 90A, 106A and 187A. The new cars reverted to 4-wheel bogies and used, for the first time from the NER works, a high-arched roof. There was an attendant's compartment at one end and a luggage compartment at the other. Only one toilet was provided, placed between the six sleeping berths and the two 3rd class compartments. Sliding doors were fitted between berths in each pair so that a combination of single and double-berths could be provided as required. One berth was fitted with a bed in place of a bunk as an experiment. Each berth was fitted with a washbasin with hot and cold water, and a pull-out dressing-table. Stone's electric lighting was fitted and each berth was provided with an electric fan in the roof.

The bodyside arrangements were dissimilar; on the corridor side at one end there was a set of double doors, one marked *THIRD* and the other *LUGGAGE* (in smaller characters) and these gave access to the corridor leading to the 3rd class compartments as well as the luggage compartment. The only other door on this side was at the opposite end, into the vestibule giving access to the sleeping berths. On the non-corridor side there was a matching door into the vestibule for the sleeping accommodation, a door for each of the 3rd class compartments, and a pair of double doors giving direct access into the luggage compartment and marked *PASSENGERS LUGGAGE*.

The three cars were built in December 1905 and were considered by some—Cecil J. Allen for one—to be ugly. The design was ascribed to a visit to America by a party of NER officers at the end of 1902, but Mr Worsdell subsequently mentioned that he was not at all impressed with American sleeping cars and that he had forwarded plans and drawings of the East Coast cars to America. It seems probable that J. D. Twinberrow played a part in the design as he had returned to the NER in 1905 as

E. C. J. S. Composite Sleeping Carriage

Built by N.E.Cº December 1905

Nºˢ 90. 106. 187.

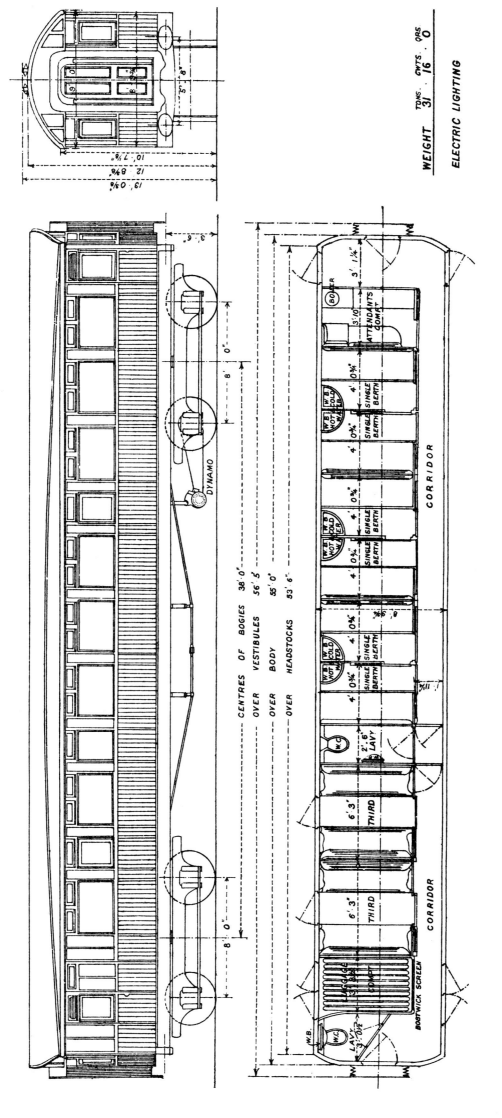

WEIGHT TONS. CWTS. QRS.
          31   16   0

ELECTRIC LIGHTING

6 First Class Single Berths 6 Beds.
2 Third Class Compartments 12 Seats.
1 Attendant's Compartment.
1 Luggage Compartment.
2 Lavatories.

Dgm. 69. The three York-built straight-sided sleepers of 1905 took the numbers of the 1893 Lancaster Carriage & Wagon Company's cars 90, 106 and 187. They had six single-berths (all of which could be converted to double-berths), two 3rd class compartments, luggage compartment, and attendant's compartment with one (later two) lavatories. The clerestory roofed vehicles achieved their maximum height over the clerestory, whereas the straight-sided vehicles with high arched roofs reached the same height in one sweep.

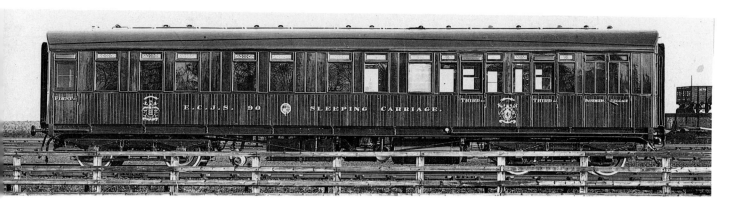

Dgm. 69. Straight-sided sleeper No. 90, built at York in 1905.

Dgm. 69. Straight-sided sleeper No. 90.

Chief Carriage & Wagon Draughtsman. Twinberrow had, of course, long been the protagonist of large-capacity mineral wagons and held a number of patents for their design.

The provision of only one lavatory for 1st and 3rd class passengers was considered unsatisfactory and by reducing the size of the luggage compartment a lavatory for 3rd class passengers was fitted at the end of the coach. In December 1921 No. 187 was converted to a full sleeper by abolishing the additional lavatory and transferring the 1st class lavatory to the luggage compartment, allowing four extra berths.

No. 187 was condemned in November 1931, and 90 and 106 in December 1933. No. 90 was converted to Touring Camping Coach No. 66 (Dgm. NE45) and used in the North Eastern Area; in the summer months it left York on a Saturday and spent two or three nights at various beauty spots in North Yorkshire, returning to York the following Saturday to be prepared for the next week's tenants.

In 1934 No. 106 was converted to the North Eastern Area Mobile Signal School and renumbered 2100 (Dgm. NE43); in BR days it could be seen in the North Eastern Region as Mess and Tool Van (S&T NE HULL) DE 900273.

In 1906 Nos 165–70 appeared from York, having ten single berths, attendant's compartment and lavatory; these were on eight wheels and introduced the Gresley look to East Coast sleeping cars. The body was length-ened to 55 ft and the cars were distinguished by substantial bow-girder (or fish-belly) underframes, but these were removed in 1924/5. All six cars were withdrawn between April 1931 and November 1932.

New construction in 1907 was restricted to two replacement vehicles for sleepers lost in the Grantham accident. No. 120 was a ten-berth car identical in layout, size and weight to 165–70 built the previous year but, for some reason, it was given a separate Diagram. It was condemned in November 1937. No. 231 was built to replace a composite car and thus had six single-berths and two 3rd class compartments. The interior was re-arranged so that the attendant's compartment was between the compartments and the berths, and a 5 ft 2 in luggage compartment was provided. The new vehicle was 18 in longer than the one it replaced and it had the bow-girder type of underframe, but this was replaced in July 1924. It was condemned in December 1932.

The last East Coast bogie sleeping cars, and the last cars to be built before the outbreak of World War I, comprised a batch of four in 1910 numbered 146, 148, 150 and 151, replacing Doncaster-built 6-wheelers of 1889. Again this was a case of composites replacing composites as the four new vehicles had six berths and two 3rd class compartments, although in 1921 they were all converted to full sleepers with ten berths. The attendant's compartment also accommodated luggage, and in their original condition they too had the misleading arrangement of double doors on the non-corridor side labelled *THIRD* and *LUGGAGE*. All four were condemned between January 1935 and February 1936.

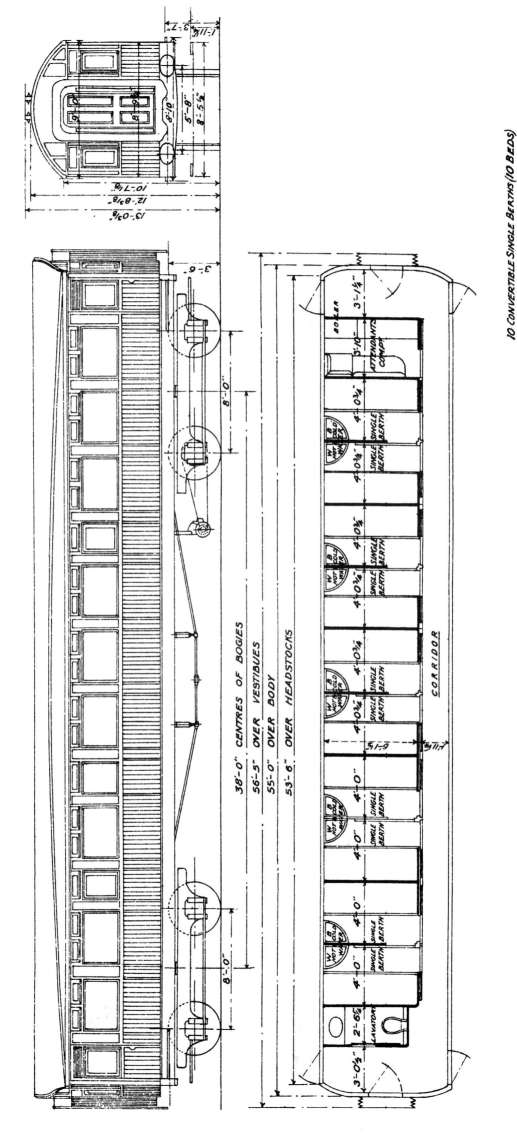

E. C. J. S. Sleeping Carriage

Nº 187. Built by N.E.R.Cº. Dec 1905. Converted to Full Sleeper Nov. 1921.

38'-0" Centres of Bogies

56'-5" Over Vestibues

55'-0" Over Body

53'-6" Over Headstocks

ATTENDANTS COMPT

SINGLE BERTH

SINGLE BERTH

SINGLE BERTH

SINGLE BERTH

CORRIDOR

SINGLE BERTH

SINGLE BERTH

SINGLE BERTH

SINGLE BERTH

SINGLE BERTH

LAVATORY

10 CONVERTIBLE SINGLE BERTHS (10 BEDS)
1 ATTENDANTS COMPARTMENT
1 LAVATORY

	TONS.	CWTS.	QRS.
WEIGHT	31.	3.	9
	33.	10.	0.

ELECTRIC LIGHTING
DUAL BRAKES.

Dgm. 64A. All three cars were to have been converted into full sleepers but only No. 187 was dealt with (in November 1921) giving ten single-berths, or five double-berths.

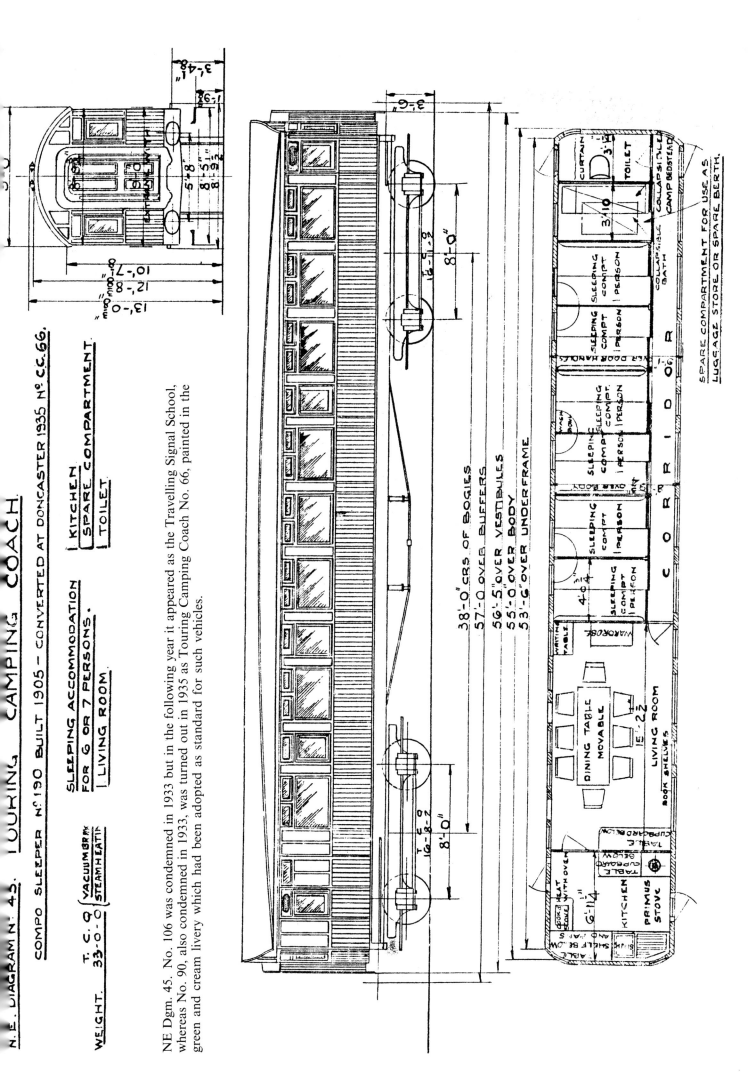

N.E. DIAGRAM Nº 45. TOURING CAMPING COACH.

COMPO SLEEPER Nº 190 BUILT 1905 – CONVERTED AT DONCASTER 1935 Nº C.C.66.

VACUUM BRK	SLEEPING ACCOMMODATION
STEAM HEATIN	FOR 6 OR 7 PERSONS
	LIVING ROOM

T. C. Q
WEIGHT. 33-0-0

KITCHEN
SPARE COMPARTMENT
TOILET

NE Dgm. 45. No. 106 was condemned in 1933 but in the following year it appeared as the Travelling Signal School, whereas No. 90, also condemned in 1933, was turned out in 1935 as Touring Camping Coach No. 66, painted in the green and cream livery which had been adopted as standard for such vehicles.

Dgm. NE 45. Touring Camping Coach No. CC66 at York (ex-Sleeping Car No. 90). (*Real Photographs*)

Dgm. 64. 'Fish-belly' sleeper No. 165, built at York in 1906.

Doncaster Works came into the picture again in 1922 and built the last sleeping car for the East Coast Joint Stock in the shape of an articulated twin with ten single berths in each unit. Each body was 56 ft $2\frac{1}{2}$ in long, making a total length of 113 ft 6 in. All but the two berths at the outer ends could be used as double berths when necessary. A compartment for the attendant was provided at the inner end of one body, whilst at the inner end of the other there was a toilet. For the first time on ECJS sleepers since 1895, the arms of England and Scotland were left off, and each unit carried only the ECJS device.

The interior finish of each berth was mahogany panels to the waist, with white enamelled paintwork above; the roof was plain white. Staples spiral spring mattresses were fitted to the beds and an innovation, fitted for the first time to a railway vehicle, concerned the method of opening and closing the frameless windows. This was performed by turning a small handle and could be done without raising the blinds or drawing the curtains. 'This method of operating the windows has been used on some of the highest-class Limousine bodies for motor-cars' stated one account, probably based on a publicity hand-out! The lighting in each berth could be dimmed by the occupant, and there was a reading lamp by the bed head. A two-speed fan was fitted in the corridor partition.

The original number of this unit was 181 + 181A, but it was renumbered by the LNER to 1181 + 1182. It was slightly damaged in a collision at Retford on 13th February 1923. Two further twins to the same design were built by the LNER in 1923.

E.C.J.S. Sleeping Carriage.

Nos. 165, 166, 167, 168, 169, 170.

Built by N.E.R. Co 1906.

10 First Class Single Berths 10 Beds.

1 Attendants Compartment.

1 Lavatory.

Weight 32 19 0 (T. C. Q.)

Dgm. 64. For a few years new East Coast carriages were provided with a very substantial fish-belly underframe, but these must have had some fault in their design or construction as they were provided with new straight frames in 1924/5. Nos 165–70 had ten single-berth compartments, which could be converted into double-berth cabins when required.

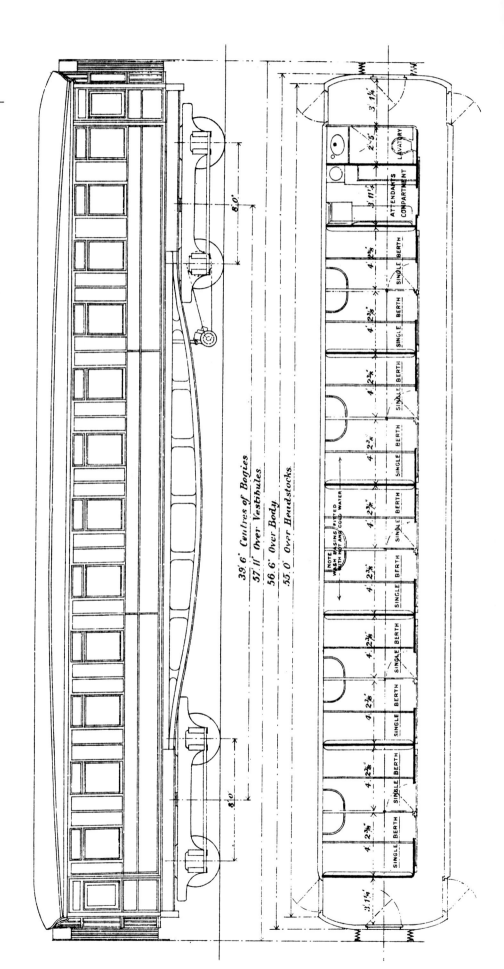

39'6' Centres of Bogies

57'11' Over Vestibules

56'6' Over Body

55'0' Over Headstocks

8'0'

8'0'

[NOTE] WASH BASINS FITTED WITH HOT AND COLD WATER

4'2¾' 4'2¾' 4'2¾' 4'2¾' 4'2¾' 4'2¾' 4'2¾' 4'2¾' 4'2¾' 4'2¾'

SINGLE BERTH (×10)

ATTENDANTS COMPARTMENT

LAVATORY

3'11¼'

2'5'

3'1¼'

3'1¼'

12'11¾'

12'7⅝'

10'6⅜'

3'7'

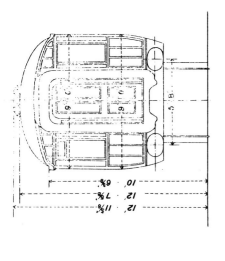

E. C. J. S. Composite Sleeping Carriage

Nº 231. Built December 1907

6 First Class Single Berths .... 6 Beds
1 Attendants Compartment
2 Third Class Compartments ... 12 Seats
2 Lavatories

	TONS.	CWTS.	QRS.
WEIGHT	34	0	0

Fitted with Stones Patent System
of Ventilating and Air Purifying.
Dargue Griffiths Hot & Cold Water
Supply & Water Heating Apparatus

Dgm. 74. Another 8-wheel Sleeping Car with a fish-belly frame was built at York in December 1907 and numbered 231; it replaced a 12-wheel car with the same number (but to Dgm. 73) destroyed in the Grantham accident of 19th September 1906. The underframe was replaced in July 1924, when Stone's electric heating was fitted, and at the same time the 8 ft bogies were replaced by an 8 ft 6 in pattern. Electric fans had been fitted in the sleeping compartments in 1911.

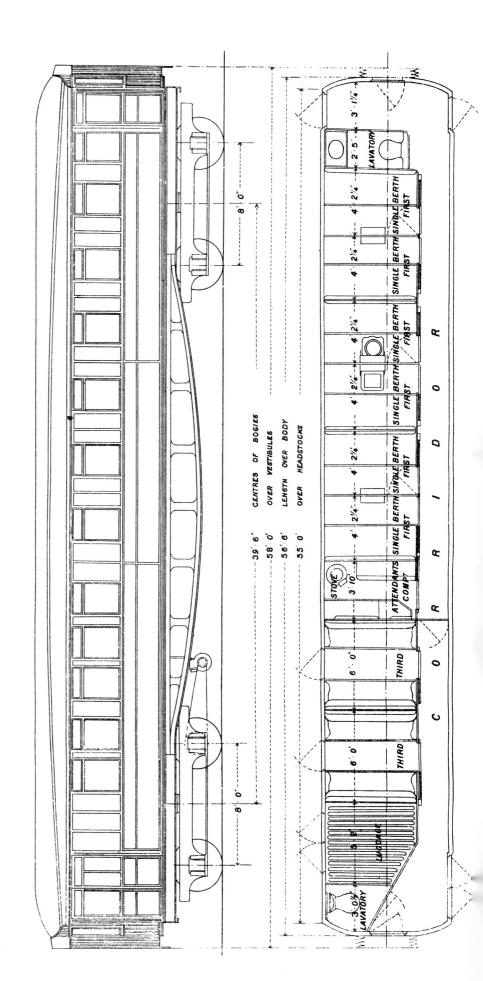

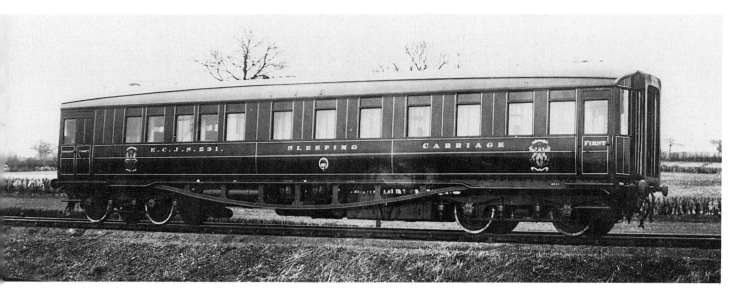

Dgm. 74. Sleeping Car No. 231, built at York in 1907.

Dgm. 62. Close-up view of 6-wheel bogie fitted to Sleeping Car No. 279.

Dgm. 70B. Composite Sleeping Car No. 148, built at York in 1910, with six berths and two 3rd class compartments.

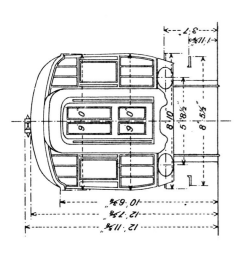

E. C. J. S. Composite Sleeping Carriage

Nos. 146, 148, 150 & 151.

Built at York November 1910.

6 First Class Single Berths   6 Beds
1 Attendants Compartment
2 Third Class Compartments   12 Seats
2 Lavatories
1 Luggage Compartment

WEIGHT   TONS CWT. QRS.   { DUAL BRAKES
         34 .. 0 .. 0   { ELECTRIC LIGHT
                             { STEAM HEATING

Dgm. 70B (later 70A). This covered four 8-wheel Composite Sleeping Cars 146/8/50/1, built at York in 1910 and very similar to Dgm. 64 (No. 231). However, in 1921 the Dgm. 70A cars were altered to full sleepers by taking in the two 3rd class compartments and the luggage space, and moving the attendant's compartment; this led to them being reclassified as Dgm. 63A.

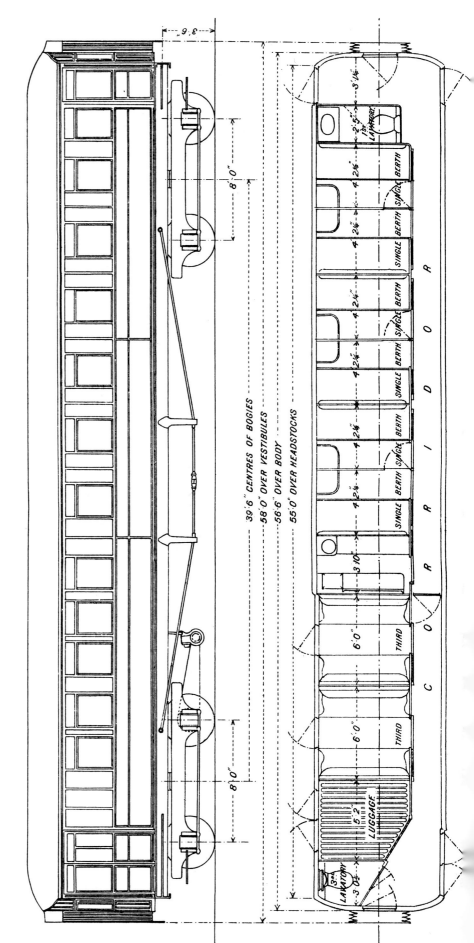

E.C.J.S. FIRST CLASS SLEEPING CARRIAGE

Nos 104. 105. 109. 117. 118. 119. 124. 125. 183. 184. 185. 186. 232. 233. 276. 277. 278. 279.

		WEIGHTS		
		TONS.	CWTS.	QRS.
Nos	104. 105.	36	10	0
"	109. 117.	"	"	"
"	118. 119			
"	124. 125			
"	232. 233.	36	6	0
"	183. 184			
"	185. 186	37	7	0
"	276			
Nos	277.278.279.	36	4	0

Nos 104,105,109,117, Built by N.E.R.Cᵒ 1901
  118,119,124,125, " " 1901
  183,184,185,186, " " 1902
  232, 233,   " " 1901

ELECTRIC LIGHT " 276, 277. " " 1900
    " 278, 279. " " 1899

2 First Class Double Berths 4 Beds
6 First Class Single Berths 6 Beds
1 Attendants Compt 2 Lavatories

Dgm. 62. No less than 19 1st class Sleeping Cars were built to this design, all at York between 1899 and 1901; they were originally arranged with two double-berths, five single-berths, a coupé smoking compartment and an attendant's compartment, but the smoking coupé was changed to a single-berth, which was 6 in wider than the others because of its original use. No. 120 to this design was destroyed in the 1906 Grantham accident.

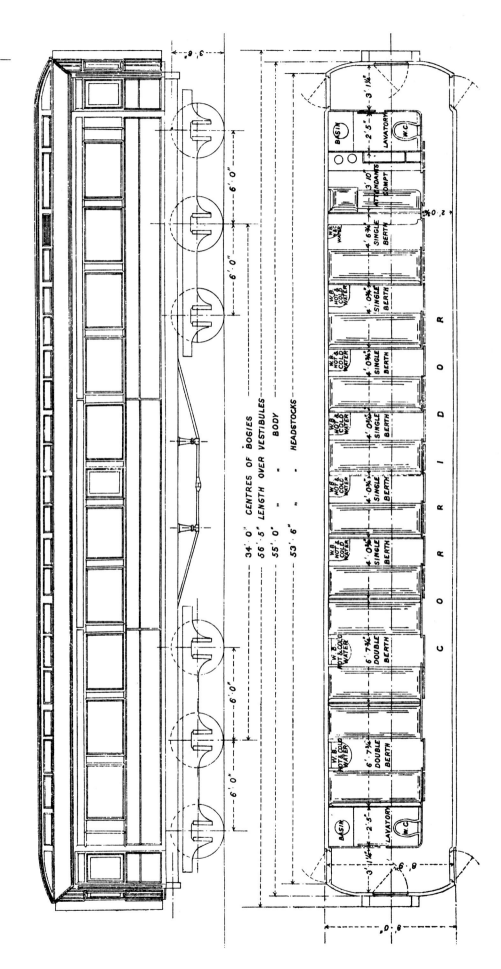

34'.0" CENTRES OF BOGIES
56'.5" LENGTH OVER VESTIBULES
55'.0"   "   BODY
53'.6"   "   HEADSTOCKS

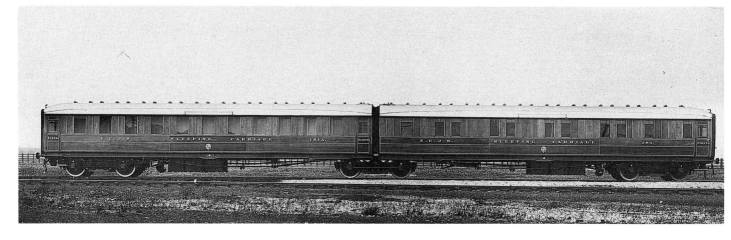

Dgm. 68. Articulated Twin sleeper No. 181A + 181, built at Doncaster in 1922, with 20 berths. (*BR*)

The practice of having normal 1st, 2nd and 3rd class compartments mixed with sleeping berths in one coach dated back to the origin of the sleeping cars on the East Coast in 1873, and it was perpetuated on the bogie cars. Thus many of the York-built sleepers included two 3rd class compartments and the practice did not cease until 1910, last being used on new construction Nos 146, 148, 150 and 151. However, on these four cars, together with 187 of 1905, the compartments were removed and the cars converted to full sleepers in 1921.

With the introduction of transverse berth sleeping cars in 1895 it was usual to provide a smoking compartment for the 1st class passengers. At first this accommodation was a full compartment seating six, but in subsequent cars it was reduced to a coupé seating three. Nos 228–31 built in 1903 had folding arm-rests allowing the coupé to be made up into a single berth, but within a few years the use as smoking compartment/coupé ceased and they were converted to permanent berths.

The rapid turnover of sleeping cars meant that they had to be distributed among the three partners, where they were usually converted into saloons as the companies had no use for sleepers on their internal services. Because of the frequent replacement of cars, vehicles with the same numbers available for disposal only a few years apart. For instance, in 1891 the NER received East Coast Nos 107 and 108, which became 2377 and 2378; and in 1905 another East Coast 107 and 108, which became 3559 and 3560. Both varieties were converted to 3rd class saloons to Dgms. 38 and 136 respectively. One of the Dgm. 136 vehicles lasted in service as a saloon until July 1935—and outlived by eight years the vehicle that had originally replaced it!

In 1915 the Great Northern carried out a surgical operation on three former East Coast 6-wheel sleeping cars (probably Nos 152, 153 and 154) when they were converted to two saloons. One sleeping car was cut in

half and each half was spliced to one of the whole bodies; the resulting body was then mounted on a 51 ft steel frame, placed on two 8 ft bogies—and the result was GN saloons 3290 and 3291.

A similar operation had been performed earlier on two Great Northern 4-wheel composite saloons built in 1887 which, although not ECJS vehicles, were used on the King's Cross–Whitby service and thus traversed almost half of the East Coast Main Line. These two bodies were also mounted on a 51 ft frame, with two 4-wheel bogies. The originals seated nine 1st class passengers in a saloon, and six 3rds in a compartment, with a toilet section between and accessible from saloon and compartment; there was also a 3 ft 9 in luggage compartment with double doors. In the combined version the luggage compartments were placed at the outer ends and one was converted to a toilet; the two saloons of the originals were retained, but the old toilets and compartments were combined to form one large saloon 17 ft 6 in long, with one long seat down each side giving a total seating capacity of 48. The Great Northern numbers when running as 4-wheel vehicles were 2244 and 2245, but the unified vehicle became 2244 (and eventually LNER 42244).

Because of the continuous programme of replacement and renewal of ECJS vehicles, particularly sleeping cars, certain numbers were used time after time, keeping the same series of numbers for the same type of vehicle. This applied especially to the numbers 104–9 and 117–20; No. 120, for instance, was used on a 6-wheel sleeper built in 1882. This was replaced in 1893 by a new 6-wheeler with the same number, but the old car was later rebuilt and renumbered 231. The second 120 was replaced in 1901 by a 12-wheel car with six single-berths and two double, but this was destroyed in the Grantham accident, and a fourth No. 120, this time with ten single-berths, was built in 1907. This in turn was condemned in November 1937.

5 Compartment Stock

Between the 1903 and 1909 Diagram Books more than 50 non-corridor 6-wheelers of seven different types were withdrawn and the 1909 book contains only one diagram of 6-wheel non-corridor vehicles in the form of a 4-compartment brake 3rd, 33 ft 10 in long with compartments only 6 ft wide. The four coaches listed (Nos 76–9) were the survivors from 76–81 and 142/3 built at Doncaster in 1883 and were disposed of to the NBR in 1913.

As mentioned in Chapter 1 a 6-wheel side-corridor coach was introduced in 1883, the pioneer vehicle being No. 87, followed by 122 and 123 in 1884. These were 37 ft over body with four 7 ft 2 in wide 1st class compartments and a toilet at each end, all built at Doncaster. In 1898 all three were converted to composites by downgrading the two outer compartments, and the two toilets were reduced in size to allow vestibule connections to be fitted. No. 122 was destroyed in the Grantham accident of 19th September 1906, but 87 and 123 were both taken over by the NER in 1913, althouh they were condemned in the following year.

Other 6-wheel types which survived long enough to gain entry to the 1909 Diagram Book were:

Dgm. 1 Semi-corridor composites 1–10, 26 and 129, built in 1893, with two 1st class and two 3rd class compartments, each pair having their own short corridor giving access to separate toilets in the centre of the vehicle. Nos 26 and 129 replaced two vehicles destroyed in the Thirsk accident of 2nd November 1892. Nos 6, 7, 8 and 9 went to the NER in May 1910.

Dgm. 3 This vehicle, corridor composite No. 60, was built at Doncaster in 1893—another Thirsk accident replacement coach. It also had the end toilets reduced in size to allow vestibule connections to be added and it was disposed of to the NER in May 1913 or April 1914 (both dates are quoted from official sources) and became NER 3780.

Dgm. 4 Nos 87, 122 and 123 mentioned above.

Dgm. 20 The 1909 Diagram Book lists 16 corridor 3rd vehicles: 44, 155–62, 164, 174–8, and 180. No. 163 was destroyed in the 1892 Thirsk accident. Nos 44, 155–8, 160/1/4, 175/7/8 and 180 went to the NER in 1911/2;159 went to the NBR, and 162, 174 and 176 to the GNR, all in 1922. According to the Diagram these coaches retained the full width toilets at each end as they were not fitted with vestibule connections.

Dgm. 24 These were similar to Dgm. 20 but the toilets had been reduced in size to allow vestibule connections. Their numbers were 171/2/3/9 (1891), 163 (1893) as a Thirsk accident replacement, and 63 (1894). No. 63 went to the NER in November 1922 and 163, 171/2/3/9 to the GNR in 1919 and 1922.

Dgm. 26 The final 6-wheel corridor vehicles were delivered in 1893 for the new trains and there were eight corridor 3rds by Oldbury Carriage & Wagon Co. (Nos 206–13), which became Dgm. 26 in the 1909 book. They originally had side-gangway connections but were altered to centre-gangways from 1898. Some vehicles were paired with a 6-wheel corridor 1st to form articulated units, but No. 208 went to the NER and 209 and 210 to the NBR in October 1922. No. 207 was destroyed in the Grantham accident in 1906.

Dgm. 61 Also for the new 1893 trains four 6-wheel corridor 1sts were obtained from Birmingham Railway

Carriage & Wagon (Nos 202–5) and these also underwent alteration from side to centre-gangways. Some were paired with Dgm. 26 vehicles to form articulated twin composites.

Dgm. 5 In July 1907 Mr Grinling reported to the Great Northern Board: 'With a view of obviating the numerous complaints we have received from time to time with regard to the running of six-wheeled coaches on our express trains, Mr Ivatt about six months ago handed over to the Traffic Department an experimental coach formed by coupling together two East Coast six-wheeled (No. 202 1st class and No. 206 3rd class) and putting them upon three 4-wheeled bogies. This coach has been working almost constantly since January last on the 6.45 pm from King's Cross and the 10.25 am from Edinburgh with most satisfactory results. I think the time has arrived when the system might be safely extended, as these double coaches would be very useful on many of our intermediate main-line expresses.' The cost of conversion was £270 a pair.

It seems probable that the other pairs were: 202 + 206, 203 + 211, 204 + 212 and 205 + 213, and at first they seem to have run as Nos 202, 203, 204 and 205, both sections carrying the same number; but in 1915 it was decided to add the letter 'A' to the 3rd class sections, 'so that each section may earn mileage'. In 1923 204 + 204A became 204J + 205J, and 205 + 205A became 226J + 227J, and both these twins went to the GN Section in December 1924 and September 1925 respectively.

In their combined form the articulated units were unusual in that the two sections in each twin set came from different makers.

In April 1913 H. N. Gresley wrote to V. L. Raven of the NER on the subject of articulated vehicles and included 'I have recently had a large amount of experience with East Coast Twin Compo No. 203 in connection with vestibule trials and I can assure you the working of the two bodies is in perfect harmony; they are very free on curves and will work over any portion of our main line or carriage sidings. The system of arranging two separate bodies and underframes on three bogies allows of longer vehicles to be built without exceeding the Engineer's locking-bar length.'

It seems possible that the trials referred to were in connection with the instructions given on 21st November 1910 for a report on the buckeye centre automatic coupling and the Pullman vestibule, following complaints from the travelling public. A decision was required regarding the future standard for the East Coast—should the buckeye and Pullman vestibule continue to be used and, if not, what system should be adopted in its place?

Bogie compartment stock first appeared in 1896, running on two 6-wheel bogies, and with clerestory roofs; they were all built at Doncaster initially. The composites, Nos 239–250, had three 7 ft 2 in 1st class compartments, and four 6 ft 3 in 3rd class, with two central 2 ft 2 in lavatories. At one end was a 7 ft $2\frac{7}{8}$ in luggage locker, and at the other a compartment for an attendant. Each class had one compartment designated *SMOKING* and one *LADIES*. Nos 239–45 were altered to composite brakes in 1906; these seven vehicles, together with No. 247, had the two central lavatories

E. C. J. S. THIRD CLASS BRAKE (6 WHEELS)

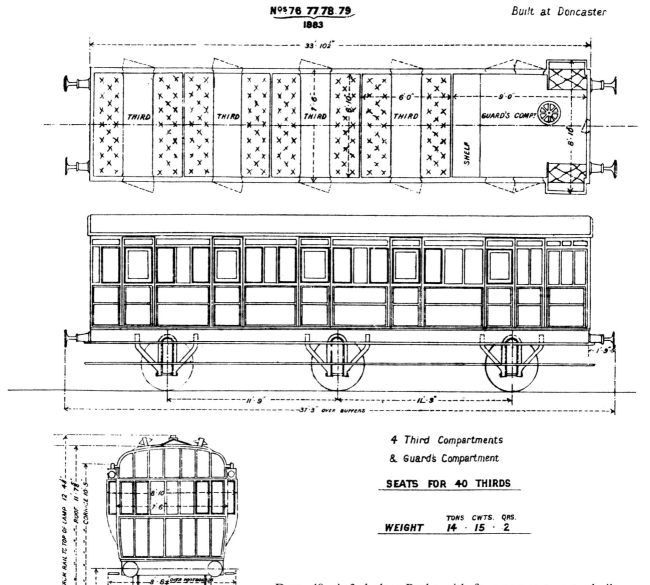

4 Third Compartments
& Guard's Compartment

SEATS FOR 40 THIRDS

WEIGHT	TONS	CWTS.	QRS.
	14	15	2

Dgm. 48. A 3rd class Brake with four compartments, built at Doncaster in 1883. There were originally eight vehicles numbered 76–81 and 142/3.

converted into one 4 ft 5½ in lavatory, but whereas No. 247 had an additional lavatory fitted in the previously unoccupied vestibule next to the luggage locker, Nos 239–45 had the attendant's compartment converted to a lavatory. These were the largest 12-wheel compartment stock at 65 ft 6 in over body.

Three 9-compartment 3rds (Nos 251, 253 and 255) and six 4-compartment brake 3rds (Nos 262–7) followed, and although similar, the latter batch was divided into two Diagrams as there was a right-hand and a left-hand version, with the corridors on opposite sides. However, the Diagrams did not correspond with the vehicles as built. For instance Dgm. 50 (1909 book) illustrates cars 262/3/4 with the corridor on one side, whereas Doncaster photograph negative A39 depicts 264 with the corridor on the opposite side. Presumably Dgm. 51 covering cars 265/6/7 was incorrect in being reversed. The brake ends did not have gangway connections originally.

It is odd that the initial 21 examples of 12-wheel compartment stock, all built at the same works (Doncaster) and at the same time (1896) should have required three different lengths of frames and bodies.

		Length	Between centres of bogies
Dgm. 6	Composites	65 ft 6 in	41 ft 4¼ in
Dgm. 27	3rd	63 ft 5¼ in	39 ft 1½ in
Dgm. 50	Brake 3rd	61 ft 1⅝ in	37 ft 2½ in
Dgm. 51	Brake 3rd	61 ft 1⅝ in	37 ft 2½ in

In 1898 corridor 3rds built at York had six compartments, were 55 ft over body and on two 4-wheel bogies, but in 1900 York built three 61 ft brake 1st (307/8/9), three 65 ft composites (292/3/4), and three 65 ft 6 in composites (298/9, 300).

Compartment stock on twelve wheels built between 1901 and 1905 was largely restricted to brake 3rd coaches from Doncaster (Nos 322–7 and 342–51) and Cowlairs (280–9 and 328–31), a brake composite built at Doncaster in 1905 (No. 23), and four York built straight-sided brake composites (Nos 80, 81, 142 and 143), with two 1st class and three 3rd class compart-

E. C. J. S. Composite Corridor (6 Wheels)

Nos. 87 123 / 1883 1884   Built at Doncaster

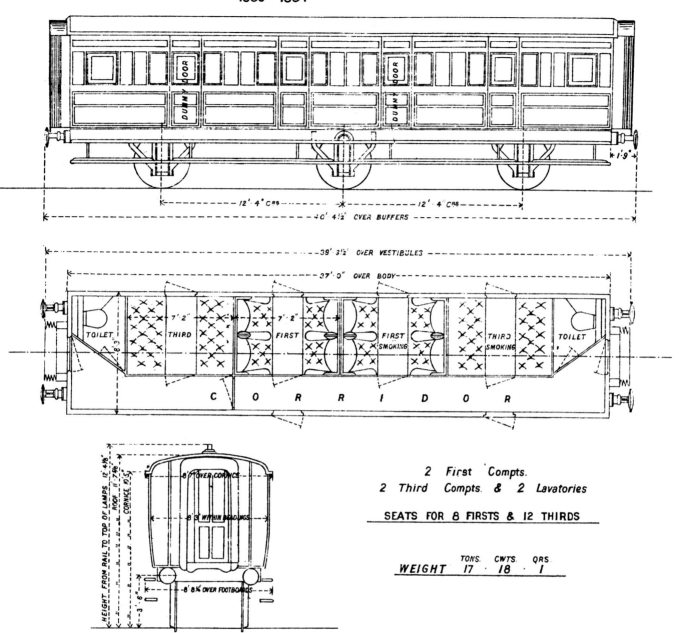

2 First Compts.
2 Third Compts. & 2 Lavatories

SEATS FOR 8 FIRSTS & 12 THIRDS

	TONS.	CWTS.	QRS.
WEIGHT	17	18	1

Dgm. 4. The first East Coast corridor coach was No. 87, built in 1883 as a 37 ft First, but it was converted to a Composite in 1898, retaining the spacious 7 ft 2 in compartments for both classes. The 1909 Diagram shows centre gangway connections and it seems probable that the small lavatories were originally full width and that the connections were a later addition. A second vehicle was built in 1884 (No. 123). Both passed to the NER in 1913 and became 3781 and 3782, but they had a very short life and were condemned in the following year.

ments. The *Railway Magazine* opened a description of these vehicles with, 'Innovations in railway methods are the order of the day, the spirit of change has entered into those responsible for the appearance of the well-known coaches running between King's Cross and various parts of Scotland by the East Coast route. The notable teak panels and curved roofs of these vehicles have now given place to innovations in these details. The compartments, which have a lofty appearance, provide a greater air space than is possible with a clerestory roof.' The *Locomotive Magazine* at the same time stated that the design had been adopted, 'with a view to reducing the cost of construction'.

In 1903 a move was made to 8-wheel 53 ft 6 in corridor 3rd class coaches, each with seven compartments and seating 42 passengers; these were Nos 38–42, 55–9, 61, 62, 113 and 115 from Doncaster, and Nos 93, 94, 99, 114, 116, 138–41 and 336–41 from York.

Combined compartment and open layouts had a temporary vogue; Nos 301, 302 and 303 built at York in 1900 had three 1st class compartments and a 3rd class open saloon (divided into smoking and non-smoking) seating 37 passengers (or 28 when used for dining purposes). Nos 86, 88, 89 and 91 from York in 1903 were semi-open 1st class coaches with three compartments and an irregularly arranged open section seating 36, or 30 when dining. North Eastern built straight-sided vehicles 92 and 121 of 1905 were also semi-open 1st class, with four compartments and a 14-seat open saloon. These continued to run in their original condition until

E.C.J.S. Third Class Corridor (6 Wheels)

Nos 44. 155. 156. 157. 158. 159. 160. 161. 162. 164. 174. 175. 176. 177. 178. 180.
1889   1890   1891

Built at Doncaster

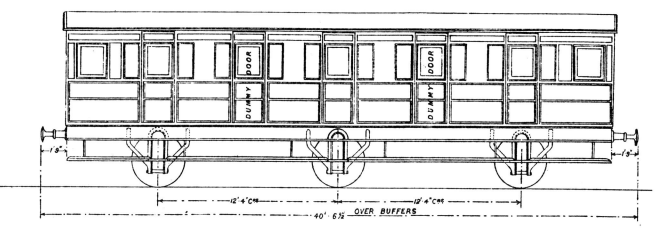

SEATS FOR 30

WEIGHT 15 TONS · 8 CWTS. · 3 QRS.

5 Third Compts.
& 2 Lavatories

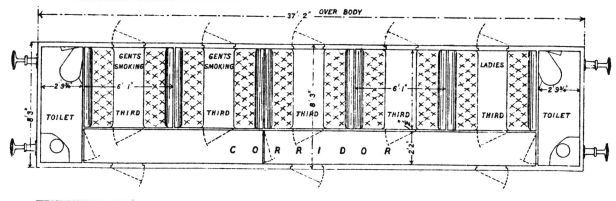

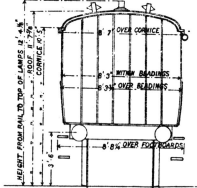

Dgm. 20. This is an 1889 design of side-corridor coach from a series built at Doncaster in 1889–91. These had five compartments, two of which were originally designated *GENTS SMOKING* and one *LADIES*; there was also a full-width toilet at each end. No. 163 was destroyed in the Thirsk collision of 2nd November 1892, involving Signalman Holmes. Four went to the NER in 1911 and another eight followed in 1912, but four were not condemned until 1922, when one went to the North British and three to the Great Northern.

Dgm. 20. 5-compartment 3rd No. 176, built at Doncaster in 1891. (*BR*)

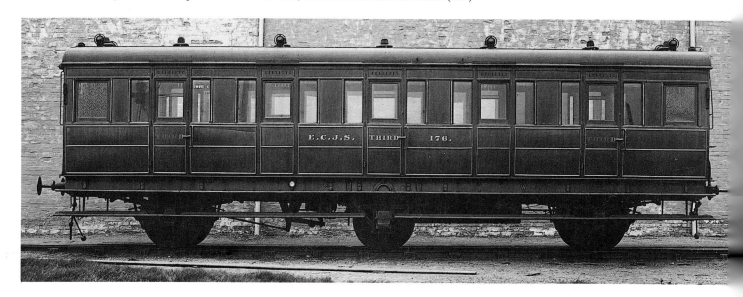

Nos: 1. 2. 3. 4. 5. 6. 7. 8. 9. 10. 26. 129.
1893   1893   1893

Built at Doncaster.

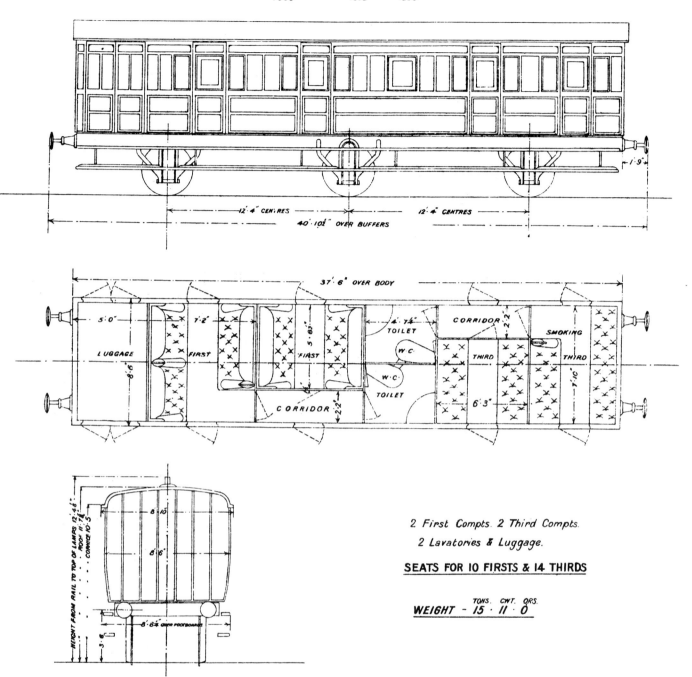

2 First Compts. 2 Third Compts.
2 Lavatories & Luggage.

SEATS FOR 10 FIRSTS & 14 THIRDS

                  TONS. CWT. QRS.
WEIGHT - 15 · 11 · 0

Dgm. 1. This Composite (Semi-corridor) design gave toilet facilities to both the 1st class and 3rd class passengers, with separate accommodation for their luggage. Nos 26 and 129 were built to replace vehicles lost in the Thirsk accident.

1914, when the open section was replaced by three 1st class compartments. No. 92 became GN Section 4149 in August 1931, and 121 became 4150 in February 1931.

The straight-sided brake composites 80, 81 and 142 were renumbered NE Area 2321, 2322 and 2327 respectively in 1936, and 143 was condemned in 1937.

On 21st January 1905 the Great Northern board appointed Nigel Gresley as the company's Carriage & Wagon Superintendent in place of Mr Howlden, who had resigned, and in the following year the East Coast vehicles acquired a new look, with semi-elliptical roofs, large windows, and they were invariably carried on 4-wheel bogies. However, various lengths were still used, such as 53 ft 6 in for 7-compartment vehicles, and 58 ft 6 in for 8-compartment. At first a toilet was provided at one end of the coach, with another sandwiched between the compartments, but a toilet at each end appears to have become standard practice from 1906. A composite brake (No. 347) built in 1911 as a replacement for a clerestory composite brake with the same number destroyed by fire at Wallyford (Inveresk Junction) in 1909, was 61 ft 6 in long, but still carried on 4-wheel bogies, although in this case the wheelbase was increased from 8 ft to 10 ft.

Under Gresley there was a swing away from open stock, and except for the new coaches required for the 10 am trains in 1911, the pre-war period 1906–1914 saw nothing but compartment stock being built at York and Doncaster.

E. C. J. S. First Class Corridor (6 Wheels)

N?? 203. 204.

Built by the Gloucester Carriage and Wagon Company 1893
Maintained by G. N. C?

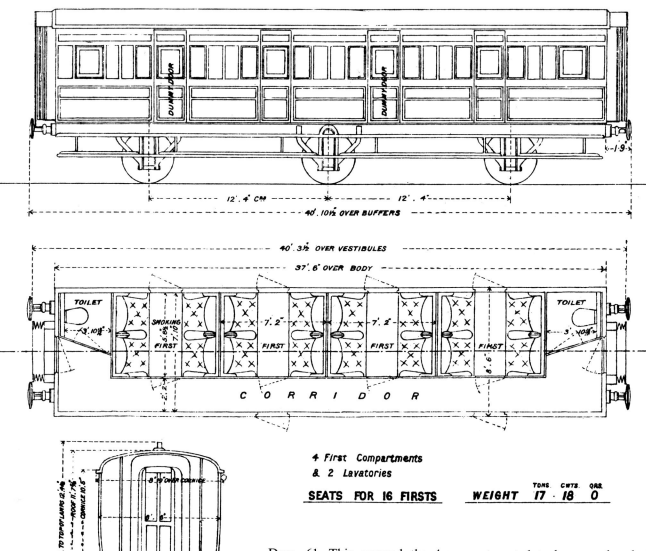

4 First Compartments
& 2 Lavatories

SEATS FOR 16 FIRSTS

	TONS.	CWTS.	QRS.
WEIGHT	17	18	0

Dgm. 61. This covered the 4-compartment 1st class coaches built by the Gloucester Carriage & Wagon Company in 1893 for the first East Coast dining car trains, some of which later formed one half of articulated composites. The Diagram shows a centre gangway connection, but the illustration shows that they were, in fact, built with side gangways. Note the vacuum and Westinghouse brake pipes.

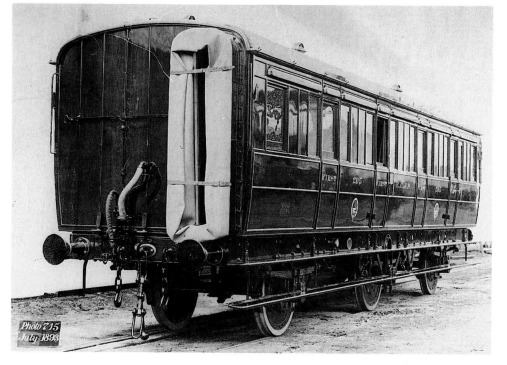

Dgm. 61. 4-compartment 1st No. 205, built by Gloucester Carriage & Wagon Co. in 1893.

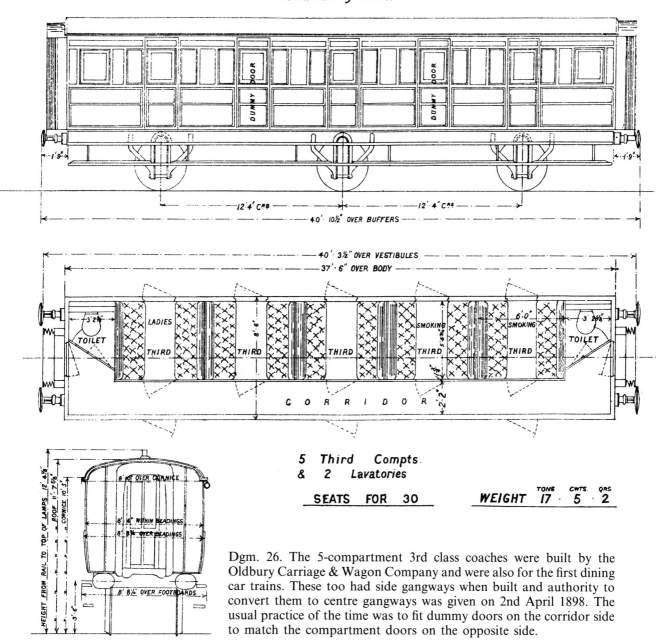

5 Third Compts.
& 2 Lavatories

SEATS FOR 30

WEIGHT 17 · 5 · 2

Dgm. 26. The 5-compartment 3rd class coaches were built by the Oldbury Carriage & Wagon Company and were also for the first dining car trains. These too had side gangways when built and authority to convert them to centre gangways was given on 2nd April 1898. The usual practice of the time was to fit dummy doors on the corridor side to match the compartment doors on the opposite side.

Dgm. 5. Articulated Twin Composite No. 206 + 202, converted at Doncaster in 1907 from two 6-wheel coaches built 1893 for the first East Coast Dining Car train. (*BR*)

E.C.J.S. Twin Bogie Composite Carriage.
202, 205.
Converted to Twin Carriages at Doncaster, 1907.

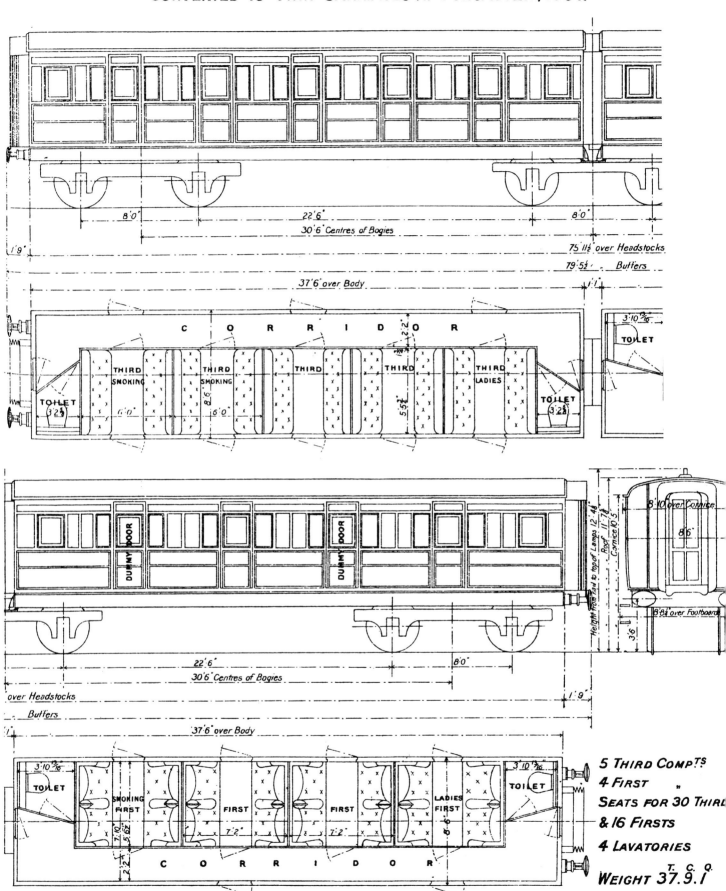

5 Third Comp.ts
4 First "
Seats for 30 Third
& 16 Firsts
4 Lavatories
Weight 37.9.1 T.C.Q.

Dgm. 5. An articulated Twin Composite made up from two of the coaches built for the first dining car trains. The conversion was carried out at Doncaster in 1907 and resulted in bodies by two different makers! Illustrated is 202 + 206, which later became No. 202; however, in 1915 it was decided that each half should have its own number 'so that each section may earn mileage' and No. 202 became 202 + 202A. A further renumbering took place in early LNER days, when 204 + 204A became 204J + 205J and 205 + 205A became 226J + 227J. I have not located the renumbering of 202 + 202A and 203 + 203A, but all four twins passed to the GN Section in 1924/5.

E.C.J.S COMPOSITE BRAKE.

Nos. 239, 240, 241, 242, 243, 244, 245.

Built at Doncaster, 1896.

altered from compo to compo bk. 1906.

2 Toilets & Luggage.

Seats for 8 Firsts & 12 Thirds.

Weight 34. 16. 0.

Dgm. 46. Compartment 12-wheel bogie stock appeared in 1896 in various forms, and these were perhaps the most admired East Coast coaches. The Composite Brakes had two 1st class and two 3rd class compartments—and the 12 3rd class passengers had the benefit of a toilet more than twice the size of that provided for the eight 1st class passengers!

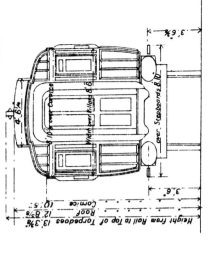

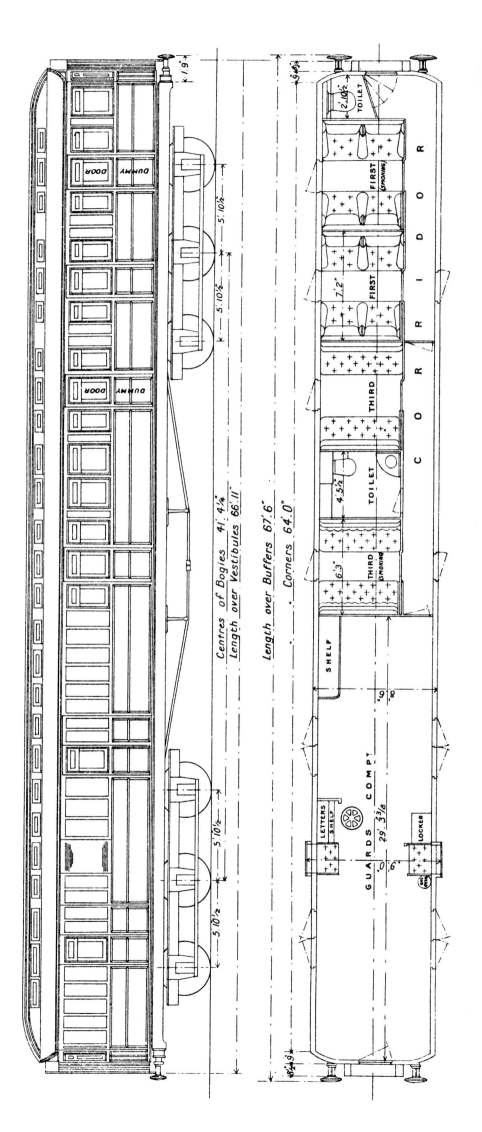

3 First Compts. 4 Third Compts.

Attendants Compt. & 4 Lavatories

SEATS FOR 12 FIRSTS & 24 THIRDS.

E. C. J. S. Composite Corridor

Nos. 246. 247. 248. 249. 250.

Built at Doncaster 1896

WEIGHT – 35 · 18 · 0
TONS. CWTS. QRS.

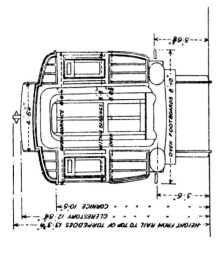

Dgm. 6. These five vehicles had three 1st class and four 3rd class compartments, together with a luggage compartment, two toilets, and an attendant's compartment. The Dgm. mistakenly quotes *four* lavatories. As with the earlier 6-wheel stock, an external door was provided for each compartment, but on the corridor side there were three doors and four dummies.

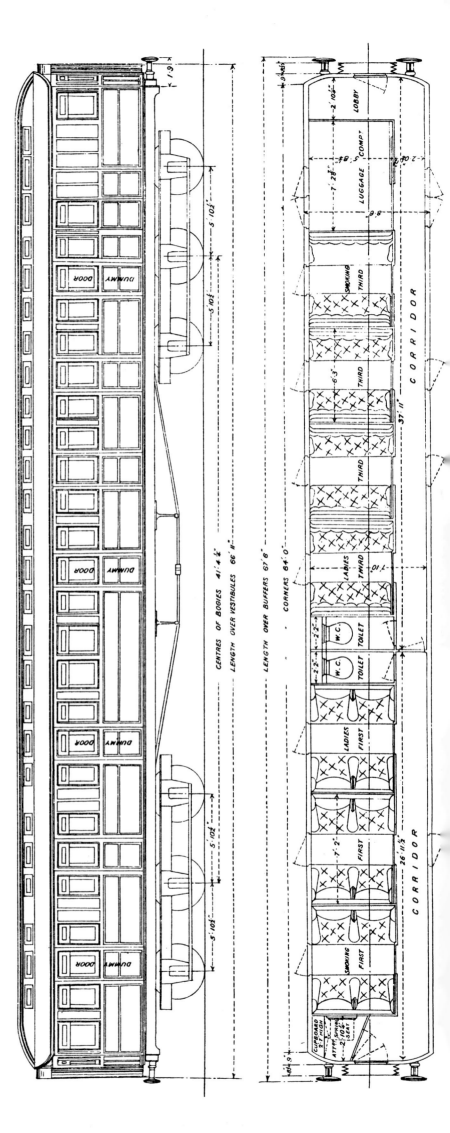

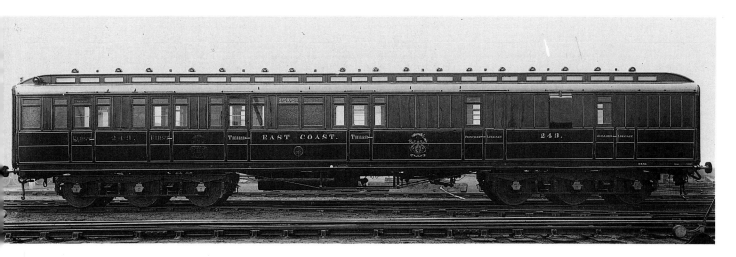

Dgm. 46. 12-wheel Composite Brake No. 243 built at Doncaster in 1896.

Dgm. 27. 12-wheel 9-compartment 3rd No. 251, built at Doncaster in 1896. (*BR*)

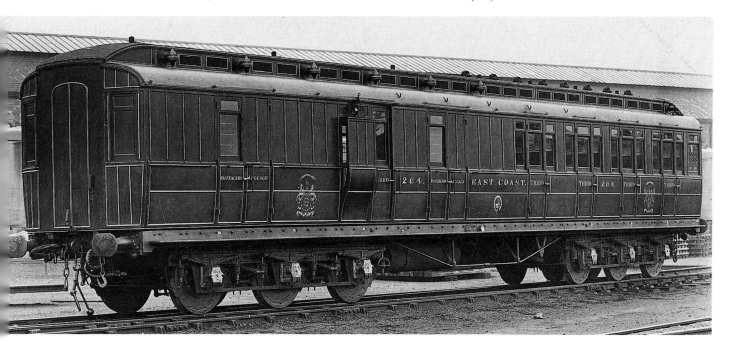

Dgm. 50. 12-wheel 3rd Brake No. 264, built at Doncaster in 1907. Note no end gangway connections. (*BR*)

E. C. J. S. THIRD CLASS.

Nos 251. 253. 255.

Built at Doncaster 1896.

9 Third Compts.
& 2 Lavatories

SEATS FOR 54 THIRDS

	TONS	CWTS.	QRS
WEIGHT	34	19	1

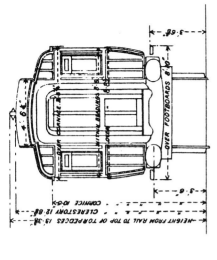

Dgm. 27. This covers a straightforward 9-compartment 3rd, with end lavatories, Nos 251/3/5. All three went to the GN Section in 1927 as 420, 435 and 429 respectively.

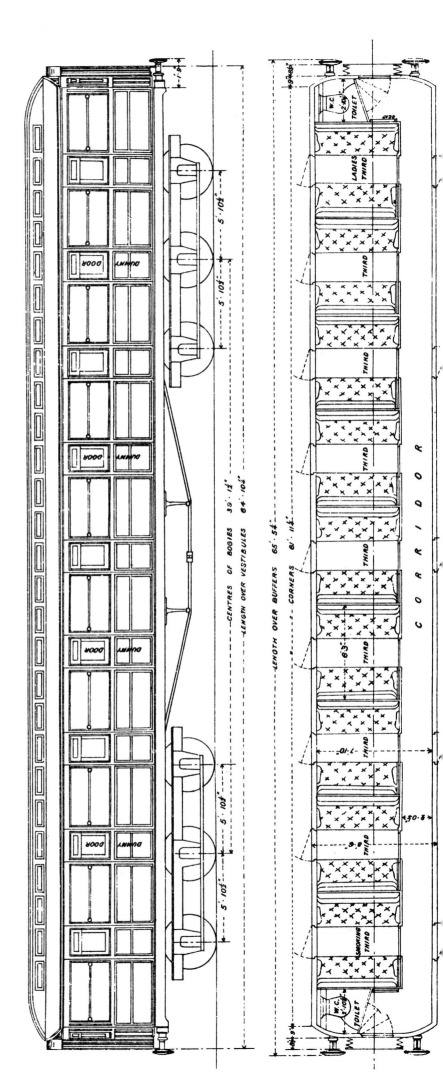

E. C. J. S. THIRD CLASS CARRIAGE BRAKE

Nos 262. 263.
      264.

Built at Doncaster 1896
         ,,   ,,   ,,   1897

4 Third Compts.
1 Lavatory
& Guards Compts.

SEATS FOR 24

TONS	CWTS.	QRS.
WEIGHT 31	18	3

Dgm. 50. Three additional 4-compartment 3rd Brakes were built at Doncaster in 1896/7, Nos 262/3/4 and in this case the vehicles did not correspond with the Dgm. as the corridor and compartments were transposed. Note that the brake end did not have gangway connections. Three similar opposite-handed 3rd Brakes, 265/6/7, were built in 1897 and it is suspected that again the vehicles as built did not correspond with the Dgm.

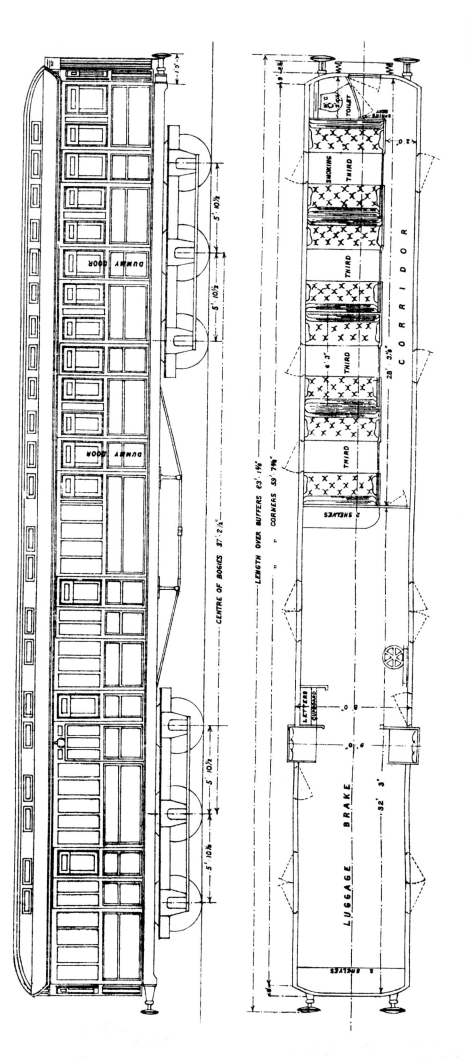

E. C. J. S. CORRIDOR COMPOSITE

Built by N.E.R. C? 1900

Nos 292. 293. 294.

	TONS	CWTS.	QRS
WEIGHT	39	2	0

ELECTRIC LIGHTING

3 Firsts———— 12 Seats
2 Thirds ——————
1 Open Third } 27 Seats or
when dining — 23 Seats

Corridor and Passage
2 Lavatories (First and Third)

Attendants Compt.
Luggage Lobby

Dgm. 10. In 1900 the NER built 12-wheel stock with compartments and open accommodation. Nos 292/3/4 had three 1st class and two 3rd class compartments, with an open (dining) saloon for 3rd class passengers. According to the Dgm. the saloon seating was for 27 — or 23 when dining, but this cannot be reconciled with the Dgm.

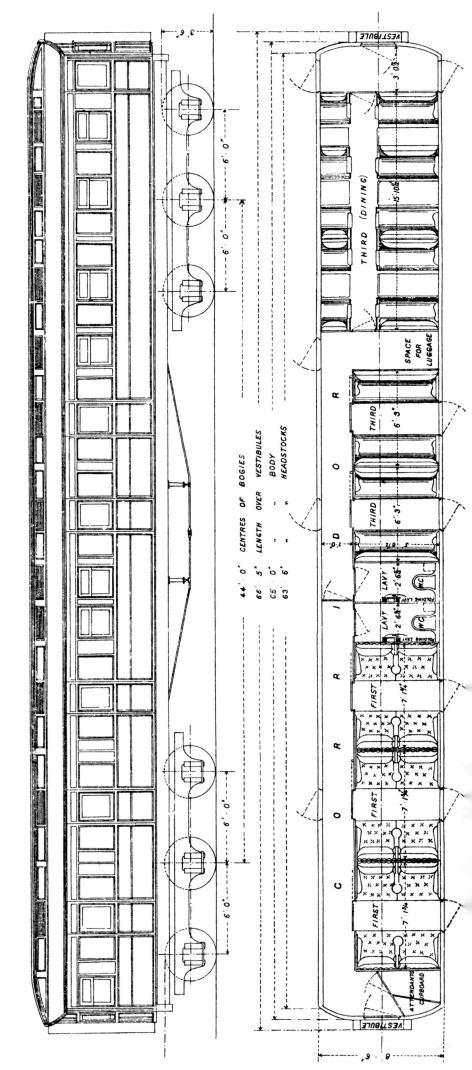

44' 0"	CENTRES OF BOGIES
66' 5"	LENGTH OVER VESTIBULES
65' 0"	" " BODY
63' 6"	" " HEADSTOCKS

E.C.J.S. Corridor Composite First and Open Third

Nos 301. 302. 303.   Built by N.E.R.Co. 1900

3 Firsts ———— 18 Seats or
when dining ———— 12 Seats

1 Open Third with Smoking partition 28 Seats 37 when not dining.

Corridor and Passage

3 Lavatories

WEIGHT   TONS. 38 CWTS. 18 QRS. 0

ELECTRIC LIGHTING

Dgm. 13. Nos 301/2/3 had three 1st class compartments and two open saloons for 3rd class passengers, one (smoking) seating 16 and one seating 21, although this was reduced to 12 and 16 respectively when dining. The seating in the 1st class compartments was divided into 2 + 1 on each seat, separated by an armrest, and the Dgm. states that these compartments could also be used for dining as each compartment was fitted with a folding table.

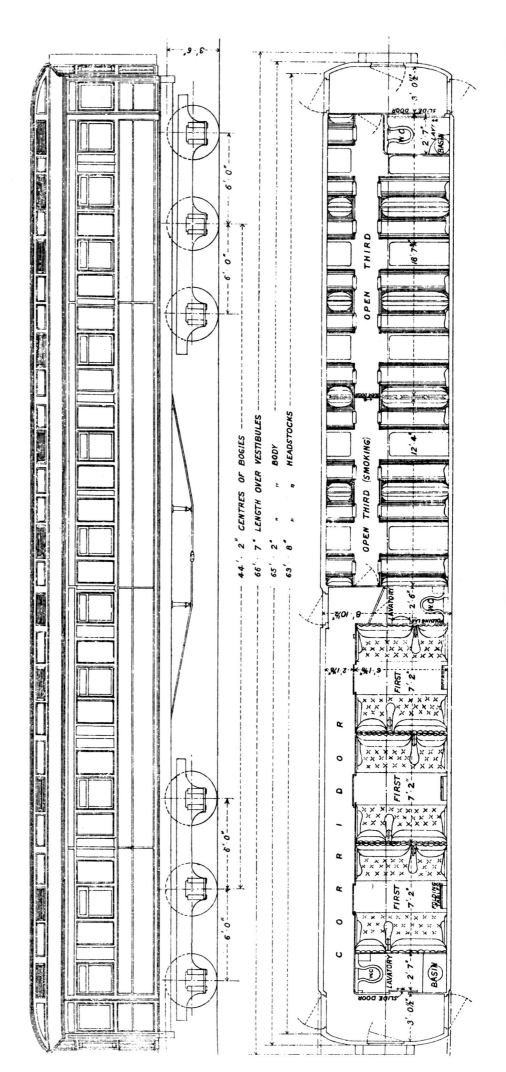

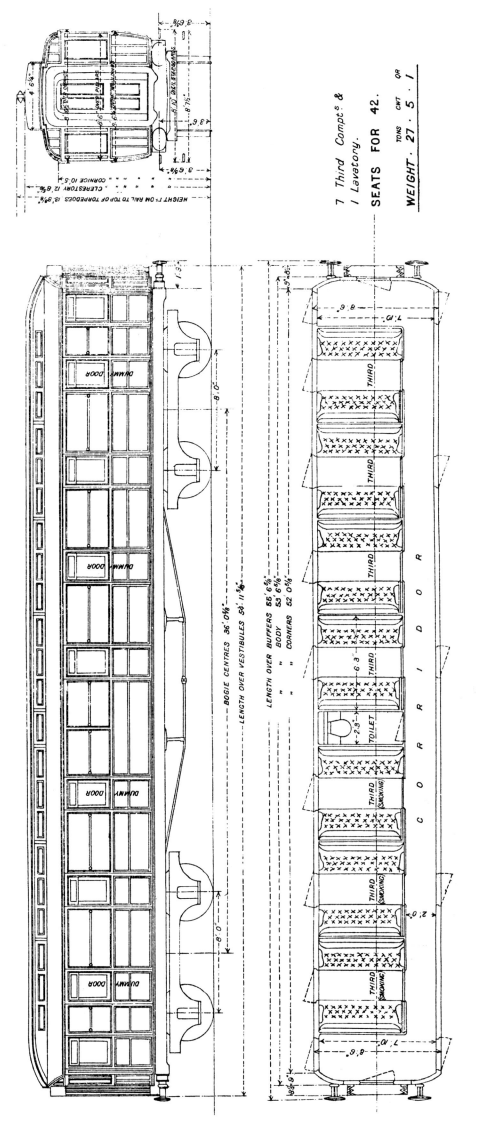

E. C. J. S. Third Class Corridor

Nºˢ 38.39. 40. 41. 42. 43. 55. 56. 57. 58. 59. 61. 62. 113. 115.

Built at Doncaster 1903.

7 Thirdˢ Comptˢ. & 1 Lavatory.

SEATS FOR 42.

WEIGHT. 27 . 5 . 1
TONS   CWT   OR

Dgm. 19. Compartment stock on eight wheels appeared from Doncaster in 1903, with seven compartments and a single toilet. Again dummy doors on the corridor side.

Dgm. 19. 8-wheel 7-compartment 3rd No. 58 built at Doncaster in 1903. Compartment side.

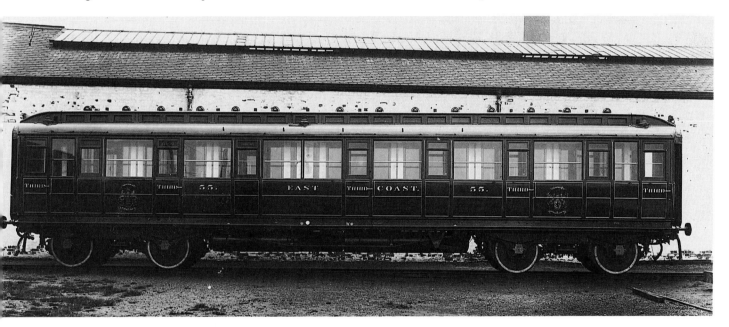

Dgm. 19. 8-wheel 7-compartment 3rd No. 55, corridor side, showing four dummy doors.

Dgm. 23. 8-wheel 7-compartment 3rd No. 94, built at York in 1903.

E. C. J. S. Corridor Third

Nos. 93. 94. 99. 114. 116. 138. 139. 140 141.   Built by N E Cº 1903.

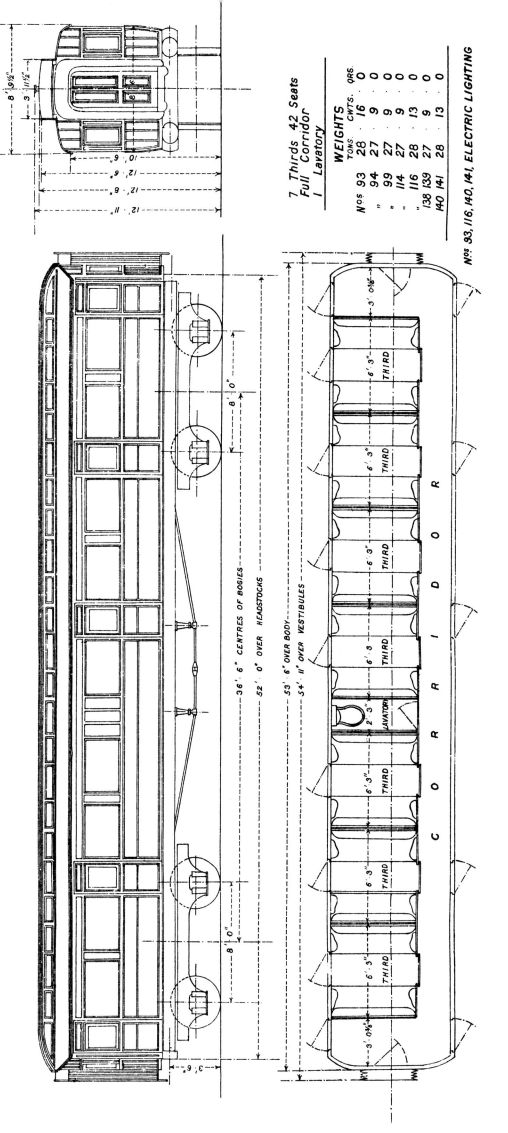

7 Thirds 42 Seats
Full Corridor
1 Lavatory

	WEIGHTS		
	TONS.	CWTS.	QRS.
Nºs 93	28	16	0
„ 94	27	9	0
„ 99	27	9	0
„ 114	27	9	0
„ 116	28	13	0
„138 139	27	9	0
140 141	28	13	0

Nºs 93, 116, 140, 141, ELECTRIC LIGHTING

Dgm. 23. At the same time York also built 7-compartment 3rds, but the NER design did not bother with dummy doors and there were many minor differences; even the quoted dimensions varied by fractions of an inch! The liveries differed considerably, and whereas York used the English and Scottish arms, with the ECJS crest, Doncaster omitted all three, York preferred *E.C.J.S.* but Doncaster used *EAST COAST*, and Doncaster was very fond of using full stops, which York eschewed!

L. & N. E. THIRD CLASS CORRIDOR WITH BRAKE

NOS 280 281 282 328 329
1902

Built at Cowlairs 1901

328 . 329 over 280 281 282

WEIGHT 34 . 1 . 3 TONS CWTS QRS.

4 Compartments to seat
24 Ordinary & 16 Dining

Dgm. 52. Cowlairs built five 4-compartment Brake 3rds in 1901/2, although the official photograph reproduced was taken at Doncaster.

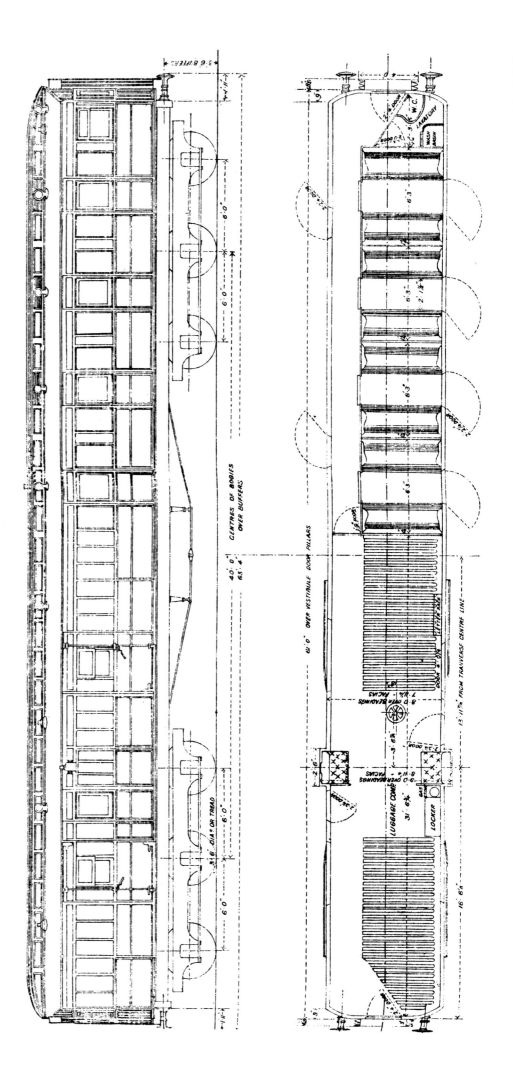

77

E.C.J.S. THIRD CLASS CARRIAGE BRAKE

Built at Doncaster 1902

Nos 322. 324. 326.

4 Third Compt. 1 Lavatory
& Guards Compt.

SEATS FOR 24

TONS.	CWTS.	QRS
WEIGHT 31	18	3

Dgm. 54. Doncaster built some similar Brake 3rds in 1902, but opposite-handed; following Doncaster tradition dummy doors were fitted on the corridor side! There was no gangway connection at the brake van end.

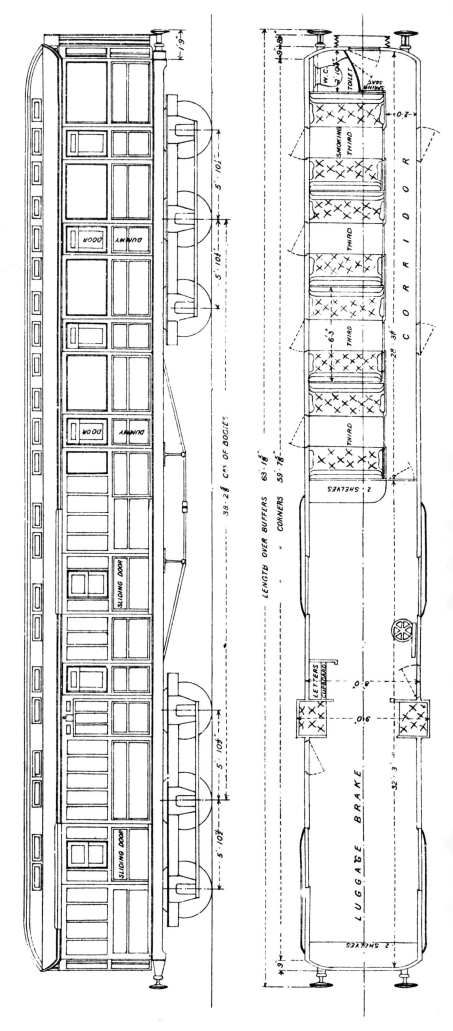

78

Dgm. 51. Cowlairs-built 12-wheel Brake 3rd No. 280, dating from 1900.

Dgm. 54. Doncaster-built 12-wheel Brake 3rd No. 326, dating from 1902.

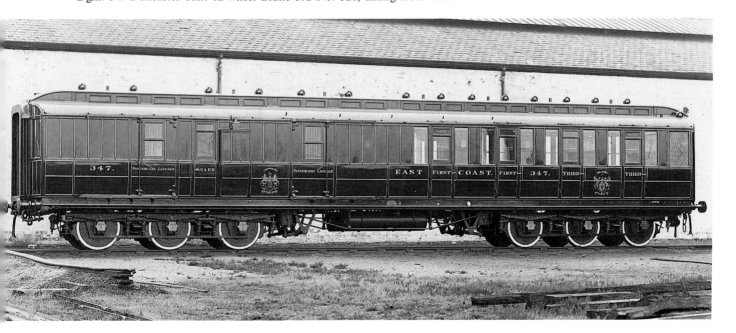

Dgm. 47. 12-wheel Brake Composite No. 347, built at Doncaster in 1903.

E. C. J. S. Composite Corridor with Brake

2 Third Compts. 2 First Compts.
1 Lavatory & Guards Compt.

Nos. 342. 343. 344. 345. 346. 347. 348. 349. 350. 351.

Built at Doncaster 1903
Altered to Compo B.ks 1904

SEATS FOR 12 THIRDS & 8 FIRSTS

WEIGHT	TONS 35	CWTS 6	QRS 2

Dgm. 47. Four Brake 3rds built at Doncaster in 1903 were altered in the following year to Composite Brakes, with two 1st class and two 3rd class compartments. At last the dummy doors had disappeared No. 347 (illustrated) was destroyed by fire at Wallyford, Inveresk Junction, on 6th May 1909.

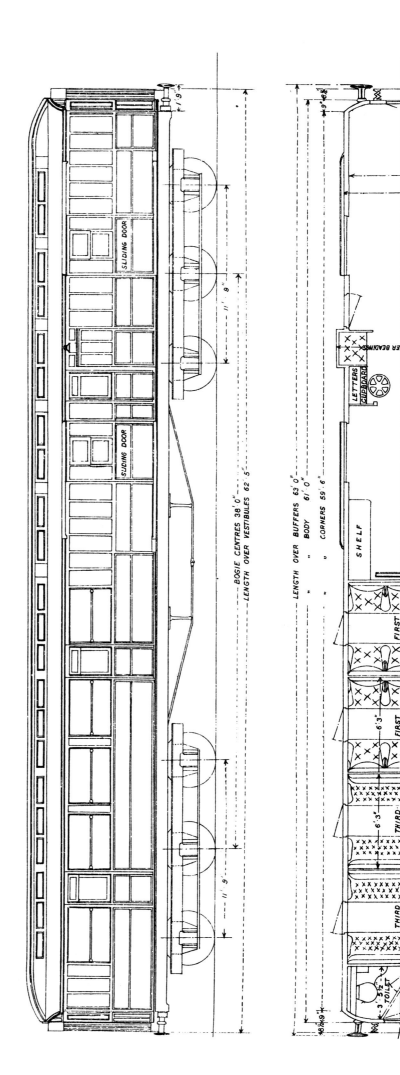

80

E. C. J. S. THIRD CLASS CORRIDOR

6 Thirds 36 Seats
Full Corridor
Luggage Compt
2 Lavatories

Nos 11.12.13

Built by N.E.R.Co June 1898.

WEIGHT TONS. CWT. QRS.
29 . 6 . 0

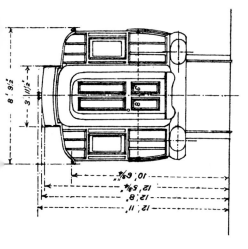

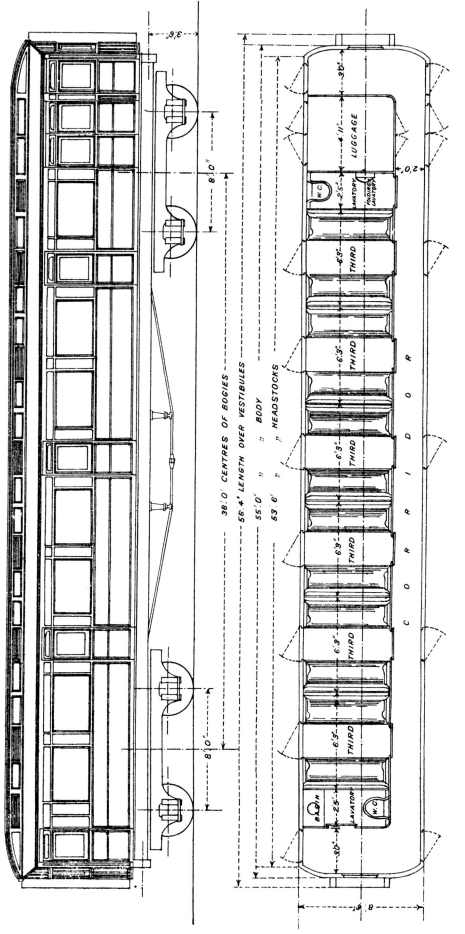

Dgm. 14. Before leaving the clerestory vehicles mention must be made of 3rd class No. 12, one of three coaches built at York in 1898. It went to the GN Section in November 1925, where it became No. 41805, but in 1952 it was repainted in East Coast livery to mark the centenary of King's Cross station.

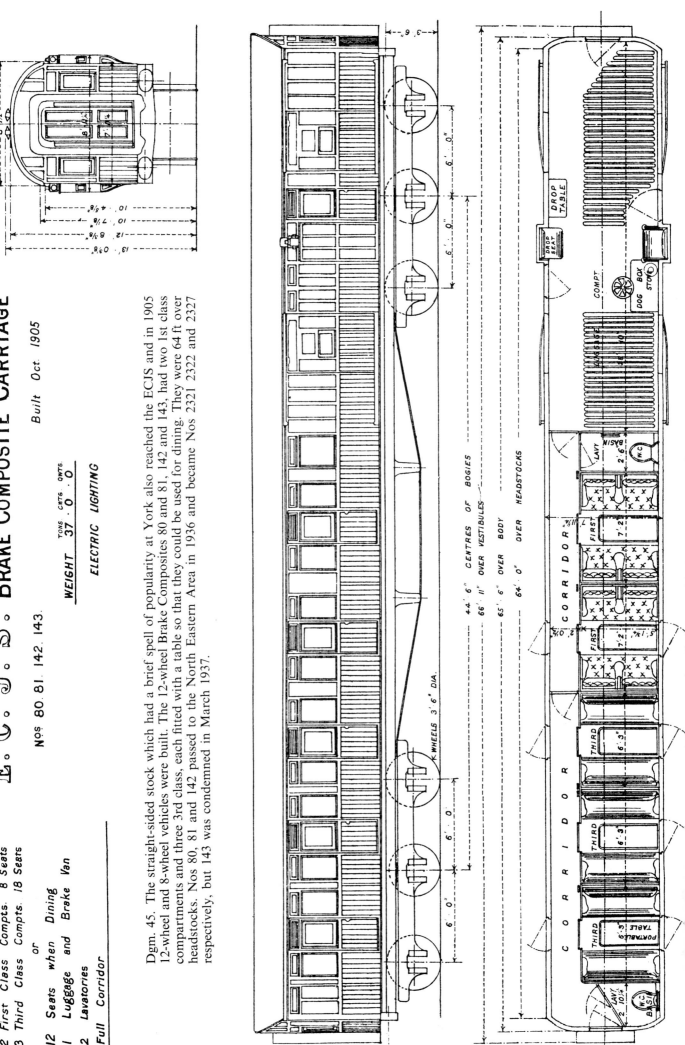

E. C. J. S. Brake Composite Carriage

Built Oct. 1905

Nos 80. 81. 142. 143.

WEIGHT 37 TONS . 0 CWTS . 0 QWTS.

ELECTRIC LIGHTING

2 First Class Compts. 8 Seats
3 Third Class Compts. 18 Seats
  or
12 Seats when Dining
1 Luggage and Brake Van
2 Lavatories
Full Corridor

Dgm. 45. The straight-sided stock which had a brief spell of popularity at York also reached the ECJS and in 1905 12-wheel and 8-wheel vehicles were built. The 12-wheel Brake Composites 80 and 81, 142 and 143, had two 1st class compartments and three 3rd class, each fitted with a table so that they could be used for dining. They were 64 ft over headstocks. Nos 80, 81 and 142 passed to the North Eastern Area in 1936 and became Nos 2321 2322 and 2327 respectively, but 143 was condemned in March 1937.

82

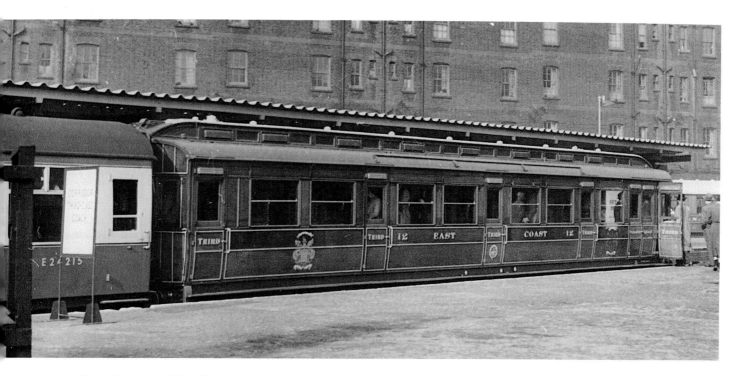

Dgm. 14. 8-wheel 3rd No. 12, restored to East Coast livery in 1952 to mark the Centenary of King's Cross station. (*H.C. Casserley*)

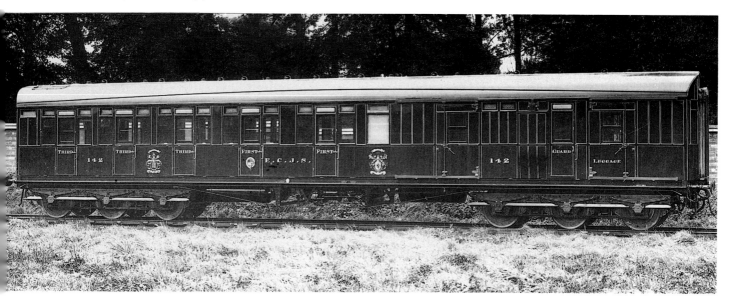

Dgm. 45. Straight-sided Brake Composite No. 142, built at York in 1905. (*BR*)

Dgm. 57. Straight-sided Semi-open 1st No. 121, built at York in 1905. (*BR*)

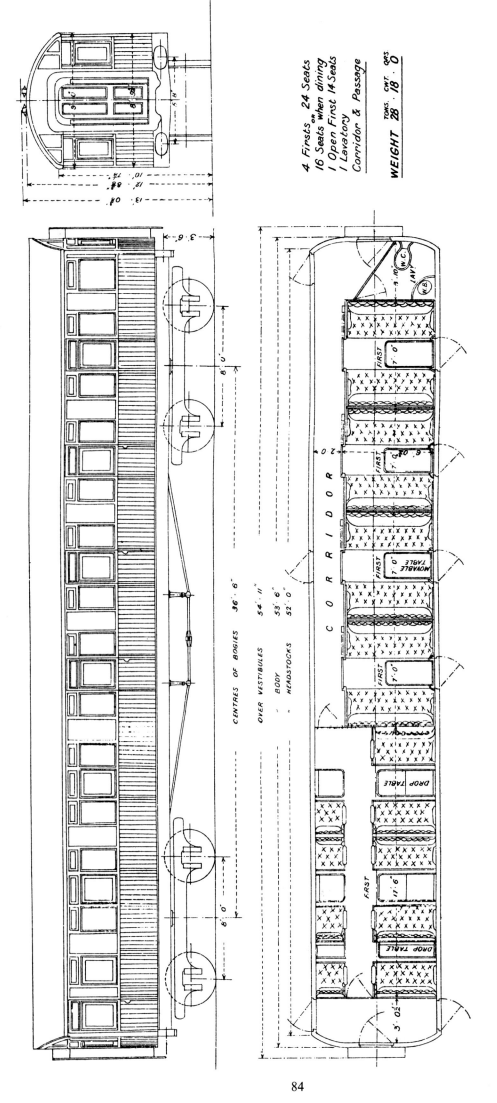

E. C. J. S. SEMI-OPEN FIRST CLASS CARRIAGE.

N.ºs 92. 121.

Built by N.E.Cº December, 1905.

4 Firsts 24 Seats or 16 Seats when dining
1 Open First 14 Seats
1 Lavatory
Corridor & Passage

	TONS.	CWT.	QRS.
WEIGHT	28	18	0

CENTRES OF BOGIES   36´ · 6˝
OVER VESTIBULES   54´ · 11˝
"   BODY   53´ · 6˝
"   HEADSTOCKS   52´ · 0˝

Dgm. 57. There were two 8-wheel Semi-Open 1st class vehicles, 92 and 121, with four 1st class compartments and an open section seating 14. Although the compartments had individual external doors the open section had no doors and access was through the adjacent end doors.

E.C.J.S. First Class Corridor
Nos 92 & 121.

Built by N.E.R.Cº 1905.

Converted from semi open First, Diagram Nº 57. by N.E.R.Cº 1914.

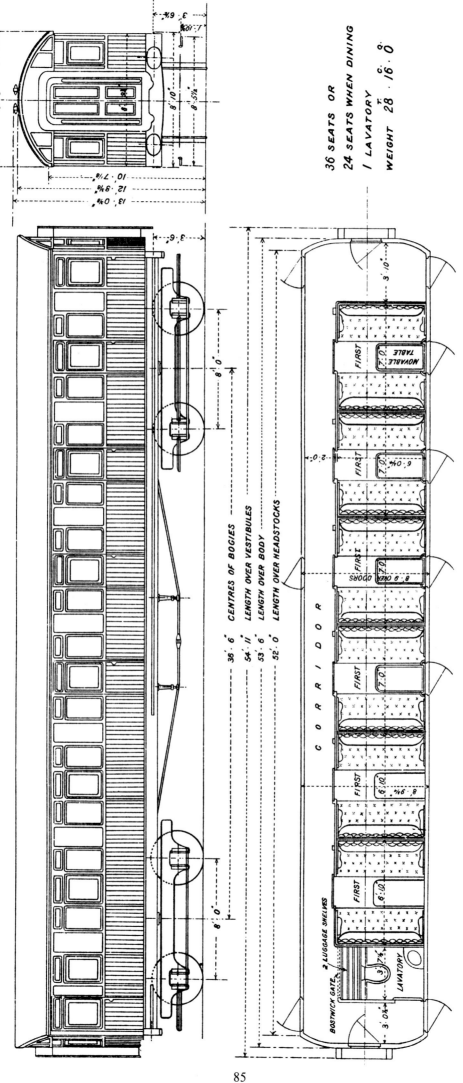

Dgm. 57A. In 1914 both Nos 92 and 121 had their open sections replaced by two compartments and a lavatory; however, the two new compartments were not provided with external doors to correspond with the original four compartments. They became GN Section 4149 and 4150 in 1931.

E.C.J.S. Corridor Third Class Carriage.

Built by N.E.R. Co. Novr. 1906.

Nos. 24. 69. 70. 71. 72. 207. (Built 1907) 356. 357. 358. 359. 360. 361. 362. 363. 364. 365. 366. 367. 368. 369. 370. 371. 372. 373 & 374.

8 Third Class Compartments

48 Seats

Full Corridor

2 Lavatories

Weight 31.15.0

Dgm. 34. This Dgm. and photograph have been chosen to show the new East Coast outline which followed H.N. Gresley's accession at Doncaster, although the vehicle illustrated was actually built at York. It was a normal 8-compartment Corridor 3rd, with a lavatory at both ends and set the pattern for many years. When they were replaced in the 1930s these coaches were distributed to the Great Central, Great Eastern, Northern Scottish and Southern Scottish sections of the LNER. No. 72 (as SS 31061) was slightly damaged in the Castlecary collision of 10th December 1937, and 357 (as SS 31083) was badly damaged in the same collision.

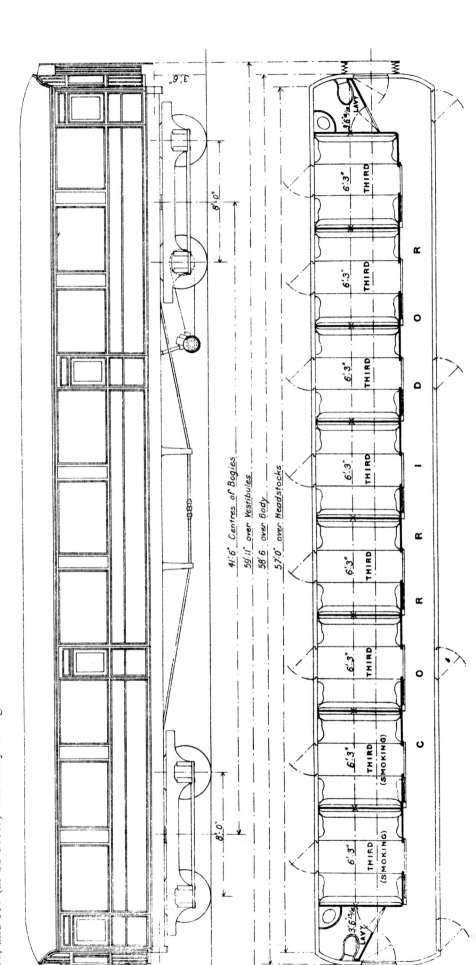

41'6" Centres of Bogies

59'11" over Vestibules

58'6 over Body

57'0" over Headstocks

E. C. J. S. Third Class Brake.

97, 98, 387, 388, 389, 390, 391, 392, 393, 394.

Built at Doncaster, 1908.

6 Third Compts. & 1 Toilet
36 Seats.
WEIGHT   TONS. CWTS. QRS.

Dgm. 49. Some 6-compartment Brake 3rds were built at Doncaster in 1908, and illustrated in No. 97. Some had their side projections ('duckets') removed in 1925/6, and earlier, in 1914, Doncaster had modified 97 and 388 by removing three compartments and using the space made available for extending the van section, increasing its length from 16 ft to 35 ft 0⅜ in. They were sent to other sections of the LNER in 1934–6.

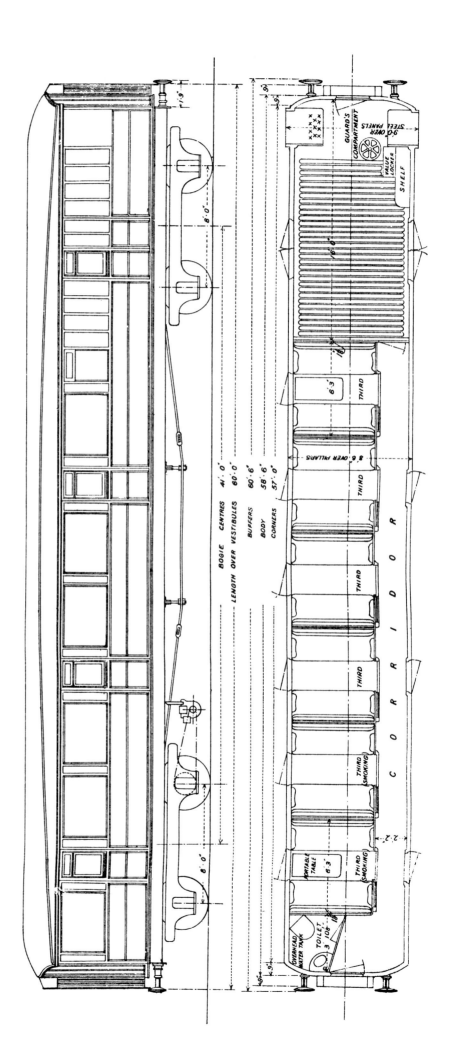

Dgm. 34. 8-wheel 8-compartment 3rd No. 24, built at York in 1906.

Dgm. 49. 6-compartment Brake 3rd No. 97, built at Doncaster in 1908. (*BR*)

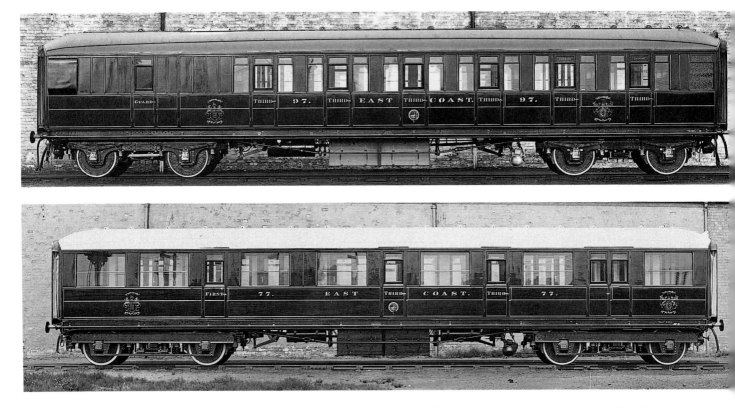

Dgm. 2B. Composite No. 77, built at Doncaster in 1914, corridor side. Two 1st class compartments and 1st class coupé + four 3rd class compartments + luggage. (*BR*)

Dgm. 3A. Composite No. 78, built at Doncaster in 1914. Two 1st class compartments and 1st class coupé + four 3rd class compartments and 3rd class coupé. (*BR*)

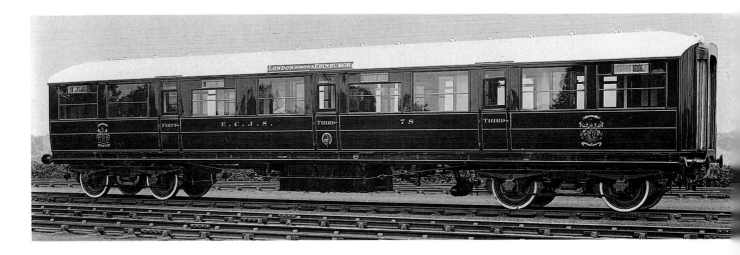

E. C. J. S. Composite Brake.

347.

Built at Doncaster 1911.

2 FIRST COMPT.S 2 THIRD COMPT.S

2 TOILETS & GUARDS COMPT.

SEATS FOR 8 FIRSTS & 12 THIRDS.

WEIGHT 33·2·0

Dgm. 47A. This covered a single vehicle, No. 347, which was built at Doncaster in 1911 to replace an earlier No. 347 destroyed by fire at Wallyford in 1909. Although the original 347 had a clerestory roof, and the replacement had a high roof, the layout was similar, but the new 347 had the van section shortened to accommodate an additional lavatory. The number 347 was an unlucky omen as the 1909 vehicle was damaged in a collision at Retford on 13th February 1923 and it was withdrawn in the following May.

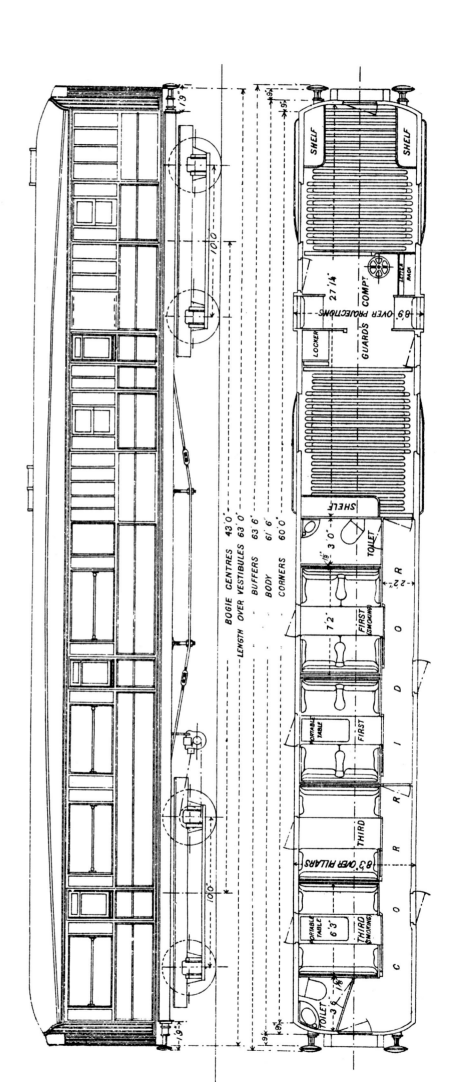

6 Brake Vans

All ECJS vehicles—passenger carrying, brake vans, and Royal Train coaches—were numbered in one series between 1 and 396. However, in October 1925 a start was made on renumbering the brake vans into a separate series, but following the LNER practice of having all East Coast vehicle numbers commencing with the figure 1. They were arranged first in order of Diagram Numbers, and then in numerical order under that Diagram. The task was completed by the end of 1927, except for one vehicle allocated to Royal Train duties, which was not dealt with until May 1929.

Because of the nature of the long-distance traffic on the East Coast route, with passengers taking large amounts of luggage for their sojourn in Scotland or London, a sizeable fleet of brake vans was required. Some 19 ft 6-wheelers dating from the 1880s and 1890s were in use until 1922, and then put in more service on the lines of the partners—largely the Great Northern. By the time they became redundant on the East Coast many had received a letter 'A' suffix. Vans 32 ft long were built in 1893–6 (Dgm. 40 and 41) the first, No. 51, being a replacement for the vehicle lost in the Thirsk accident; it went to the Great Northern in October 1922, and at the same time, Nos 224/5/6/61 went to the North Eastern and Nos 227/57/8/9 to the North British. No. 49 was destroyed at Montrose on 3rd December 1915.

Brake vans were usually built at Doncaster, but 29 ft Nos 214–221 were obtained in 1893 from Cravens for the first East Coast dining car services. All except 220 and 221 finished their days as Great Northern stock, the other two going to the North Eastern in 1919–22.

Cowlairs turned out three 46 ft 6 in bogie brake vans in 1901 (Nos 289/90/1) and a further 16 to a slightly modified design in 1903, and these lasted in East Coast service until the 1920s, except for No. 82 destroyed in the 1906 Grantham accident. From 1925 the survivors were renumbered into the Van List and subsequently dispersed, mainly to the Great Eastern Section.

In August 1905 it was recommended that six 56 ft 6 in vans should be built by the Great Northern and six by the North British, and this was confirmed in March 1906. At the same time it was agreed to adopt 'elliptical roofs curved downwards at the ends, and curved side panels' as the standard for the future, obviously the result of Mr Gresley's ideas. The Cowlairs vans, Nos 19 and 133–7, became Dgm. 35 in the 1909 Diagram Book, and the Doncaster vans, Nos 126/7/8/30/1/2, became Dgm. 39, although they were virtually identical. The Doncaster van was adopted as standard and subsequent additions accounted for Dgms. 39A, 39B, 39C, 39D and 39E.

Bogie brake van No. 7 built at York in 1910 was damaged beyond repair in the Burntisland accident in April 1914, and a new No. 7, but to a different Diagram (39B) was built at York in 1916. Doncaster van No. 128 was destroyed in an accident between Finsbury Park and Holloway on 1st January 1920, and a new van to Dgm. 39C was built in 1922.

As a replacement for the van lost in the Grantham accident a new No. 82 was built at Doncaster in 1908 and this was fitted with a boiler, stove, sink and refrigerator for use in the new East Coast Royal Train. It was renumbered into the Van List in May 1929 and became No. 109; as such it performed its Royal duties both in LNER and British Railways' days, eventually being retired and preserved in the National Railway Museum at York. Doncaster built van No. 132 was also transferred to the Royal Train and was changed from Dgm. 39 to Dgm. 38; it became van No. 114 in July 1926. Also, brake van No. 145, built at Doncaster in 1922, took up Royal Train work in March 1926 after modification from Dgm. 39C to Dgm. 39E and undergoing renumbering to 135. Presumably it replaced van No. 114, which was transferred to the Great Eastern Section in November 1928, where it became No. 6732.

Other 56 ft 6 in vans were Nos 5, 6 and 7, built at York in 1910 to Dgm. 34A. No. 7 was destroyed in the Burntisland accident already mentioned, and 5 and 6 were renumbered into the Van List in 1926 becoming Nos 11 and 12. The body of No. 6 was placed on the fish-belly type of frame from sleeping car No. 120 in August 1923.

Vans 8, 9, 10, 26 and 129 were built at Doncaster in 1910 and were renumbered into the Van List as 115–9, the first four subsequently becoming Great Eastern Section 6733, 6736, 6734 and 6735, whilst 119 became GN 4176. Nos 152–7 from Doncaster, and 44, 158, 160, 161, 164 and 175 from York, were built in 1914 and became 122–7, 121 and 128–32 respectively; No. 121 went to the Scottish Area in April 1936, and the others to the Great Central Section in 1935–7.

The final ECJS vans, 128, 144 and 145 from Doncaster, and 214, 218, 219 and 260 from York, built in 1921/2, became Van Stock 133–9; they were distributed to the GN and GC Sections in the 1930s, except for No. 135 (originally 145) which became a Royal Train vehicle in March 1926, being reclassified Dgm. 39E, whereas the others remained Dgm. 39C. Vans 140–6 appeared in LNER days, but were followed in the renumbering scheme by ECJS 289/90/1 (Cowlairs 1901) to Dgm. 42.

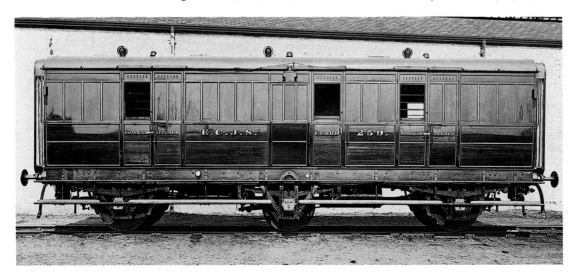

Dgm. 41. 6-wheel Brake No. 259, built at Doncaster in 1896.

E. C. J. S. Luggage Brake Van   (6 Wheels)

Nos 259. 260. 261.   Built at Doncaster 1896

	TONS.	CWTS.	QRS.
WEIGHT	14	3	3

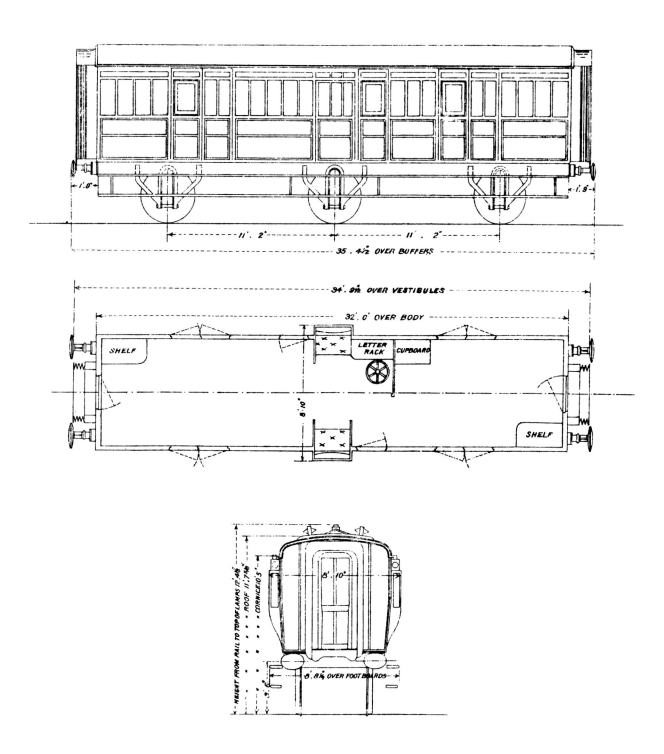

Dgm. 41. Beacuse of the nature of the traffic between London and Scotland large amounts of luggage had to be accommodated and a fleet of vans could be found in the ECJS list. No. 259 was built at Doncaster in 1896 and this vehicle, together with No. 260, passed to the NBR, and No. 261 to the NER just prior to the 1923 Grouping.

E. C. J. S. Luggage Brake Van

Nos 289. 290. 291.

Built at Cowlairs 1901.

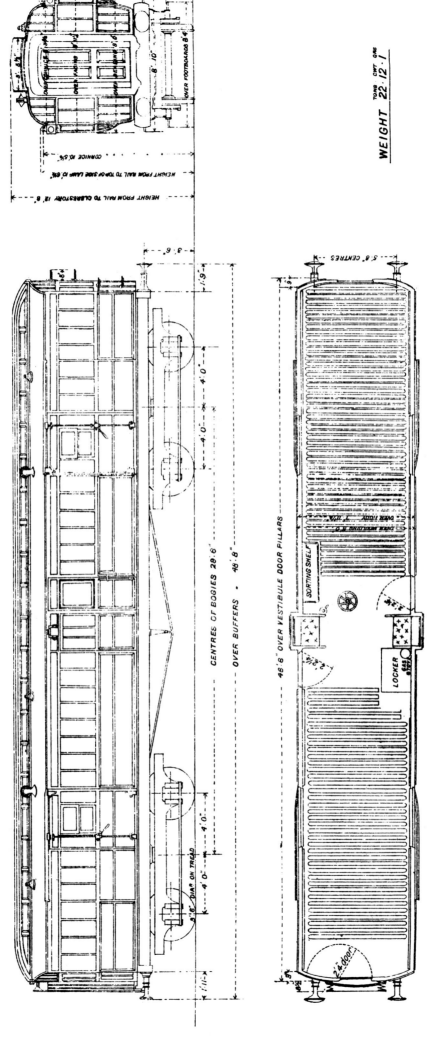

WEIGHT TONS CWT QRS 22.12.1

Dgm. 42. Nos 289/90/1 were three bogie vans built at Cowlairs in 1901. When built they had gangway connections at one end only. No. 289 was renumbered Van 147 in October 1925 and transferred to Great Eastern Section stock in February 1928; No. 290 was condemned in April 1927, and 291 became Van 149.

Dgm. 42. 8-wheel Brake No. 147, built at Cowlairs in 1901—the first vehicle in train hauled by Class C7 4-4-2 No. 719, passing Peases Siding, between Cockburnspath and Reston. (*C. J. L. Romanes*)

Dgm. 39. 8-wheel Brake No. 126, built at Doncaster in 1906. (*BR*)

Dgm. 39B. 8-wheel Brake No. 154, one of six built at Doncaster in 1914, with a further six from York.

E. C. J. S. Luggage Brake Van.

126. 127. 128. 130. 131. 132.

Built at Doncaster, 1906.

WEIGHT 23 . 15 . 0.

Dgm. 39. This was the new standard elliptical roof Brake Van from Doncaster in March 1906. No. 128 of this batch was destroyed in an accident between Finsbury Park and Holloway on 1st January 1920, and the survivors were renumbered into Van Stock as 110–4 in 1925/6.

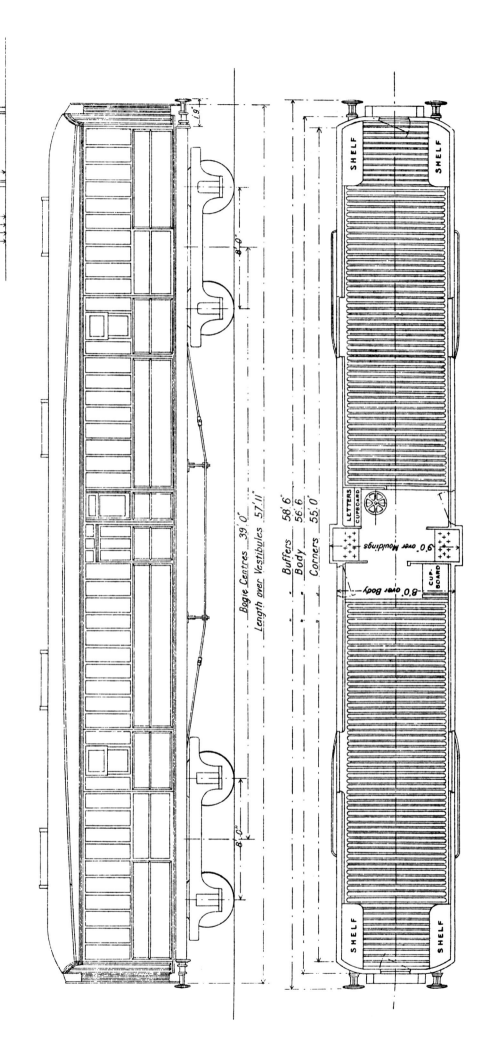

Height from Rail to Top of Torpedoes 13' 3¾"

Roof 12' 8⅝" Cornice 10' 6"

8'0" over Body

8'0" over Stepboards

Bogie Centres 39' 0"

Length over Vestibules 57' 11"

Buffers 58' 6"

Body 56' 6"

Corners 55' 0"

9'0" over Mouldings

8'0" over Body

8' 0"

8'-0"

1'9"

SHELF   SHELF

SHELF   SHELF

LETTERS
CUPBOARD

CUP-
BOARD

Brake Vans – LNER 1925 Renumbering

Van No.	Built	Diagram	Former ECJS No.	Date Renumbered	Transferred To
11	1910	34A	5	9/26	GE 6726 8/28
12	1910	34A	6	9/26	GE 6727 7/28
13	1906	35	19	12/26	GN 4180 3/29
14	1906	35	133	7/26	SS 311 2/28
15	1906	35	134	4/26	GN 4021 7/28
16	1906	35	135	5/26	SS 313 4/28
17	1906	35	136	1/26	GN 4031 12/28
18	1906	35	137	7/26	SS 316 2/28
19	1903	36	52	—	SS 9/26
100	1903	36	53	12/26	Condemned 11/27
101	1903	36	54	—	Condemned 8/25
102	1903	36	83	12/25	GE 6730 5/28
103	1903	36	85	8/27	GE 6737 3/29
104	1903	36	100	12/26	GE 6738 3/29
105	1903	36	101	—	SS 9/26
106	1903	36	102	3/26	GN 4035 4/28
107	1903	36	103	—	Condemned 2/26
108	1903	36	111	3/26	GE 6731 5/28
109	1908	38	82	5/29	Royal Train van
110	1906	39	126	10/25	GN 4037 11/28
111	1906	39	127	12/25	GN 4039 10/28
112	1906	39	130	12/25	GN 4044 6/28
113	1906	39	131	12/25	GN 4075 5/28
114	1906	39	132	7/26	GE 6732 11/28
115	1910	39A	8	9/26	GE 6733 8/28
116	1910	39A	9	—	GE 6736 3/28
117	1910	39A	10	6/26	GE 6734 6/28
118	1910	39A	26	3/26	GE 6735 5/28
119	1910	39A	129	6/26	GN 4176 1/29
120	1916	39B	7	10/25	GE 6728 2/28
121	1914	39B	44	8/26	SS 310 4/36
122	1914	39B	152	5/26	GC 5250 6/36
123	1914	39B	153	7/26	GC 5251 12/35
124	1914	39B	154	7/26	GC 5252 11/35
125	1914	39B	155	10/26	GC 5253 5/36
126	1914	39B	156	2/26	GC 5254 9/36
127	1914	39B	157	10/25	GC 5261 8/37
128	1914	39B	158	5/26	GC 5262 12/37
129	1914	39B	160	2/26	GC 5263 4/37
130	1914	39B	161	10/25	GC 5264 7/37
131	1914	39B	164	1/27	GC 5265 12/37
132	1914	39B	175	10/25	GC 5266 2/36
133	1922	39C	128	6/26	GC 5267 7/37
134	1922	39C	144	5/26	
135	1922	39C	145	3/26	Royal Train van; became Dgm. 39E.
136	1921	39C	214	11/27	GN 4018 5/31
137	1921	39C	218	7/26	GC 5215 4/31
138	1921	39C	219	8/27	GC 5268 4/38
139	1921	39C	260	2/26	GC 5269 12/36
140–146	1924	LNER-Built Dgm. 43			
147	1901	42	289	10/25	GE 6729 2/28
148	1901	42	290		Condemned 4/27
149	1901	42	291	5/26	Condemned 1/27

7 Royal Train Vehicles

Without a doubt the most notable ECJS coaches were the two Royal saloons built in 1908. No. 395, for the use of King Edward VII was built at Doncaster and No. 396 for Queen Alexandra at York. They were originally proposed in 1906 and on 2nd November they were authorised at £7,000 each, to be divided: GNR 40% = £5,600; NER 35% = £4,900; NBR 25% = £3,500. No. 395 was completed in September 1908 and No. 396 in December 1908, although the latter was not taken into stock until 1909.

Both were built on fish-belly underframes, with bodies 67 ft long and 45 ft 6 in between the centres of the 6-wheel bogies, No. 395 to Dgm. 81 and No. 396 to Dgm. 82, weighing 42 tons $6\frac{1}{2}$ cwt and 44 tons 6 cwt respectively. The two Diagrams differed in details, presumably because one was the work of a Doncaster draughtsman, and the other from a Gateshead man. The layout of the two vehicles can be seen from the Dgms. and that for the Queen's saloon illustrates how the sleeping room could be converted to a dining room seating six. Also in No. 396 there was accommodation for Princess Victoria. No. 395 was maintained by the Great Northern and No. 396 by the North Eastern, but with the formation of the LNER No. 396 was transferred to Southern Area stock for maintenance at Doncaster.

The King's vehicle was divided into smoke-room, day saloon, bedroom and dressing room. The smoke-room was 10 ft long in Jacobean style with the walls of oak inlaid with boxwood and dark pollard oak, the furniture consisting of two armchairs and a large settee, upholstered in reindeer plush hide, with fittings of silver. The 17 ft 6 in day saloon in Louis XVI style, had walls of polished sycamore, inlaid with trellis lines of pewter and light mahogany. The furniture, consisting of two armchairs, a large settee and four smaller chairs, was uphol-

stered in silk brocade; there was also a writing table with adjustable electric lights. The day and smoking saloons were lit by rows of tubular electric lamps concealed behind the cornices on each side.

The bedroom, which could be converted to a dining room, was 14 ft long, with the walls enamelled white and panelled; the furniture was mahogany, inlaid with king-wood, and covered in old-rose coloured silk damask, with green silk embroidered cushions. The dressing room, also finished in white enamel, was provided with a toilet and had a cork parquet floor, with the walls of Italian marble! The attendant's compartment at the end of the coach was fitted with electric urns and kettles, and a switchboard for controlling the lighting and heating of the coach. At the opposite end, next to the smoke-room, was an entrance balcony with double doors on each side. Carpeting was with a plain old-rose carpet, and all curtains and blinds were of soft green silk, with white embroidery. The decoration and furnishing were by Messrs Waring & Gillow.

Two large capacity dynamos connected in parallel, and a battery of accumulators, supplied the current for the lighting and heating.

In the day saloon in the Queen's carriage the furniture was upholstered in silk, with hand-painted designs, and the panelling was of rosewood, also hand-painted. The dining room was also upholstered in silk. The bedroom was panelled in cedar wood, with the furniture of satinwood. The attendant's compartment had electric utensils for preparing refreshments, with a silver tea service, and from this compartment there was telephone communication to other parts of the train, and to the guard's van and the engine.

The accommodation for Princess Victoria consisted of a bedroom and a dressing room, both upholstered to match the decoration in the Queen's bedroom.

Dgm. 81. Royal Saloon No. 395 photographed at Scarborough on 8th July 1965, on a trial run from York Carriage Works. The number is visible in small characters on the framing just to the left of the nearest step-board. A window has been replaced by panelling between the sets of three and two windows at the left-hand end.

(K. Hoole)

E. C. J. S. Royal Saloon for H. M. the King

N° 395.

Built at Doncaster, 1908.

WEIGHT   42. 6. 2.
TONS CWTS. QRS.

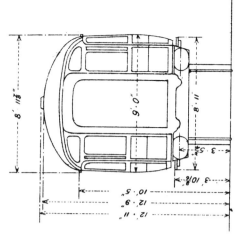

Dgm. 81. No. 395, the Royal Saloon for H.M. The King, built at Doncaster in 1908 and now at the National Railway Museum at York.

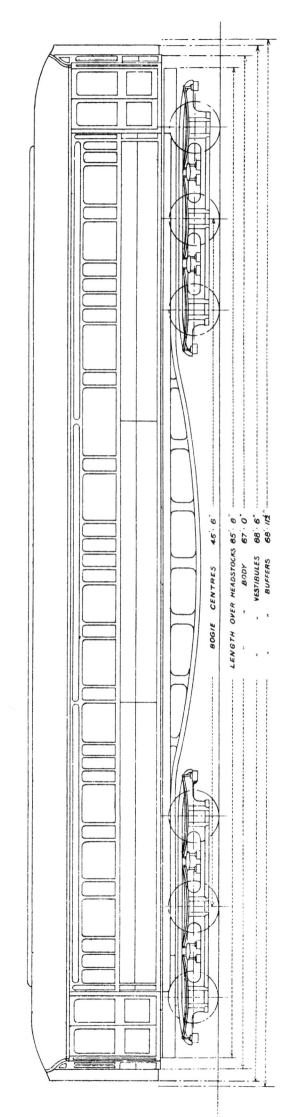

BOGIE CENTRES   45'. 6"

LENGTH OVER HEADSTOCKS	65'. 8"
"	"	BODY	67'. 0"
"	"	VESTIBULES	68'. 6"
"	"	BUFFERS	68'. 11½"

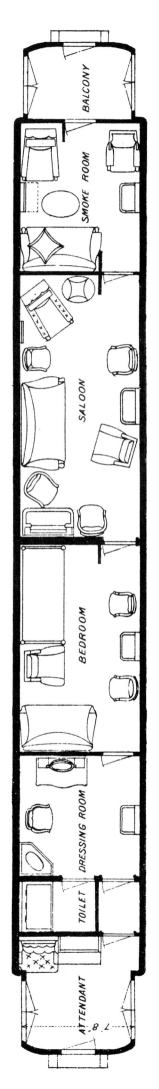

E. C. J. S. Royal Saloon for H.M. the Queen
No. 396.
Built by N.E.R Co 1908.

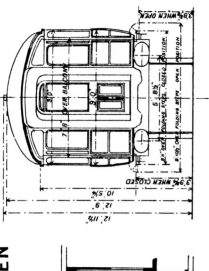

12' 11⅛"
12' 9"
10' 5¾" 3'.9⅞" WHEN CLOSED

7.1⅝" 9'.0" 3.0" OVER BALCONY
8.1⅞" OVER FOLDING STEPS OPEN POSITION 9.10½" OVER FOLDING STEPS CLOSED POSITION
5.8½"
3.8¾" WHEN OPEN

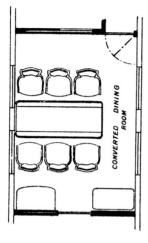

CONVERTED DINING ROOM

BALCONY. Entrance End
H.M. The Queen's. Day Saloon
   "   Convertible Sleeping & Dining Room
   "   Dressing Room
   "   Lavatory
H.R.H. Princess Victoria's.
   "   Lavatory
   "   Dressing Room
   "   Sleeping Room
BALCONY. Attendant's End
ACCOMMODATION H.M. The Queen & Suite (6 Persons)
                     { Dual Brakes
                     { Electric Light
                     { Electric & Patent Warming
                     { & Ventilating System.

              TONS CWTS QRS
WEIGHT   44.   6.   0.

Dgm. 82. No. 396, the Royal Saloon for
H.M. the Queen, built at York in 1908 and
now at Bressingham, Norfolk, although part
of the National Collection.

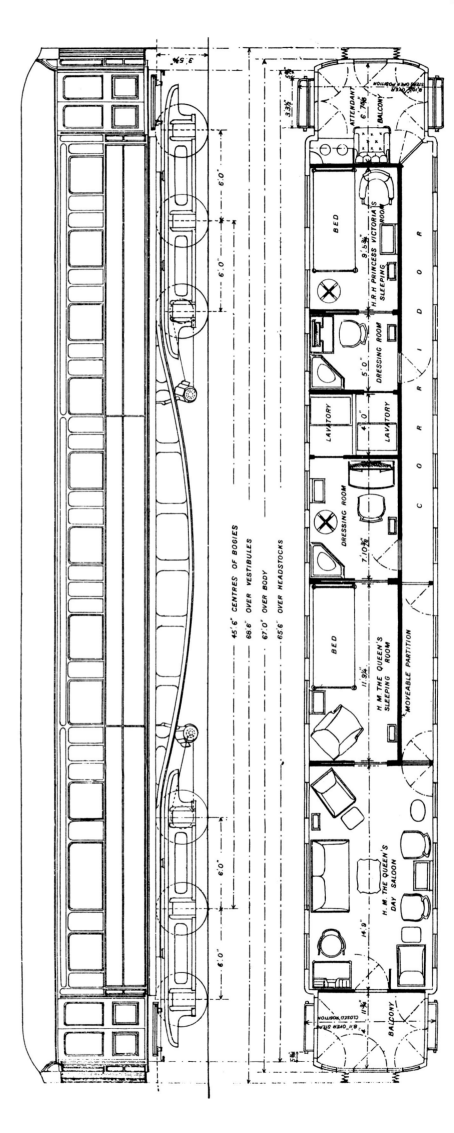

45'.6" CENTRES OF BOGIES
68'.6" OVER VESTIBULES
67'.0" OVER BODY
65'.6" OVER HEADSTOCKS

6'.0"   6'.0"   6'.0"   6'.0"

3'.5½"

ATTENDANT 5½" 6.7⅝" BALCONY 8.10½" OVER STEP OPEN POSITION
3.3½"

BED
H.R.H PRINCESS VICTORIA'S SLEEPING ROOM
DRESSING ROOM 5'.0"
LAVATORY 4'.0" LAVATORY
DRESSING ROOM 7'.10⅜"
CORRIDOR
CORRIDOR

BED 11'.9¾"
H.M. THE QUEEN'S SLEEPING ROOM
MOVEABLE PARTITION

H.M. THE QUEEN'S DAY SALOON 14'.9"

BALCONY 11'9¾" 8'.11" OVER STEP CLOSED POSITION 3'.6"

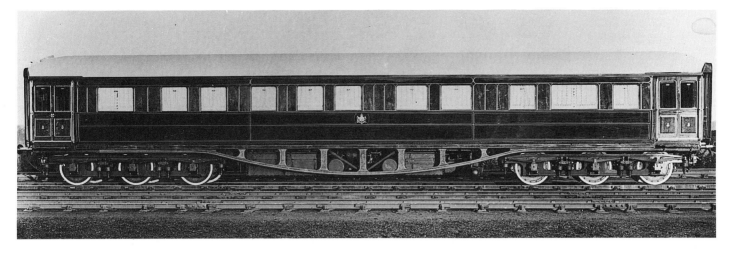

Dgm. 82. Royal Saloon No. 396, as built. (*BR*)

In 1926 the two ECJS vehicles were modified, with No. 395 becoming the Queen's saloon and No. 396 adapted for use by the King and Queen. This resulted in a slight modification to the window arrangement on No. 395. Both vehicles were withdrawn in June 1978, No. 395 the Doncaster-built coach going to the National Railway Museum at York and No. 396, the York-built coach, on loan to Alan Bloom's railway collection at Bressingham. (What a pity the York-built vehicle could not have remained in its birth-place!)

For publicity purposes the NER issued a black leather-backed folder lettered in gold:

NORTH EASTERN RAILWAY
DIAGRAM OF ROYAL TRAIN
East Coast Joint Stock

This contained eight $7\frac{1}{2}$ in $\times$ 5 in linen sheets which folded into the cover, each sheet depicting the elevation and plan of the vehicles forming the East Coast Royal Train. They were:

No. 82	East Coast luggage brake van
No. 1281	GNR 1st class saloon
No. 3100	GNR 1st class saloon
No. 395	East Coast His Majesty's saloon
No. 396	East Coast Her Majesty's saloon
No. 3099	GNR 1st class saloon
No. 1280	GNR 1st class saloon
No. 132	East Coast luggage brake van

8 Pullman Sleeping Cars

The Great Northern and North British companies introduced sleeping cars on East Coast services in 1873, but the introduction of Pullman sleeping cars on the Midland Railway in 1874 made the East Coast companies think again. Although sleepers 'on the Pullman principle' were discussed at the time nothing was done and the matter was allowed to drift. To illustrate the dilatory progress on the East Coast it may be mentioned that the sale of the pioneer GN and NB sleepers to the East Coast companies was first mooted in January 1874 but it was January 1877 before the sale was ratified. New GN-designed sleepers commenced running on 1st July 1877 on the 8.30 pm from King's Cross (to Perth) and the 9.30 pm from King's Cross (to Glasgow).

In October 1877 it was suggested that Mr Oakley, the GN General Manager, should see Mr Pullman again 'and ascertain whether he could propose any form of carriage which would be less weighty and cumbersome than the one proposed', and in August 1878 assent was finally given for a trial of Pullman sleeping cars on the East Coast route, subject to three months' notice of termination of the agreement. Thus from 19th August 1878 a nightly sleeping car service commenced between London and Perth, using the cars *India* and *Germania*; from 14th October the service was altered to run between London and Glasgow. In February 1879 the NER suggested that the Pullman company should provide 'three or four sleeping cars of a shorter and lighter description than those at present in use', and in the following month a new draft agreement was drawn up. In June 1879 it was reported that *India* and *Germania* required renovation.

On 20th April 1880 two further sleeping cars commenced running: these were *Columba* and *Iona*, and although all four cars remained the property of the Pullman company, it was decided in October 1880 that they should be treated as East Coast stock and the cost of repairs paid for by the GN, NE and NB companies in the usual proportions. From 5th July 1881 the Pullman cars were used on the 9 pm from King's Cross and the 6 pm from Glasgow.

In February 1883 it was suggested by the Great Northern that all East Coast sleeping car services should be provided by Pullman cars and the company's solicitor was asked to report on the conditions which could be inserted in the agreement with Mr Pullman. At about this time Mr Pullman was about to supply two 6-wheel sleeping cars for East Coast service—*Balmoral* and *Culross*—but although near agreement was reached in January 1884 the Pullman company wanted sole rights and would not, at first, agree to the continued use of the East Coast's own cars alongside Pullman vehicles. At the same time the Great Northern (negotiating on behalf of the other companies) would not agree to discontinue running the East Coast cars. Eventually it was decided to purchase the Pullman cars and in May 1884 they were valued by Mr Stirling and Mr McDonnell (the new NER Locomotive Superintendent) at:

India	£1,260	(£2,300 asked by Mr Pullman)
Columba	£1,400	(£2,700 asked by Mr Pullman)
Iona	£1,600	(£2,700 asked by Mr Pullman)

The two smaller cars, *Balmoral* and *Culross*, being new, were valued at £2,300 each. *Germania* had left the East Coast, probably in 1880, and had been sent to Italy by the Pullman company, and *Balmoral* and *Culross* were transferred to the Highland Railway in 1885, where the latter was renamed *Dunrobin*. This left bogie cars *India*, *Columba* and *Iona* to maintain the East Coast services. Incidentally, the cars *Balmoral* and *Dunrobin* were eventually returned to the Pullman company at Brighton and subsequently used as the basis of a house at Seaford occupied by Mr F. Marks, the retired Traffic Superintendent of the Pullman Car Co. They were discovered by C. Hamilton Ellis in 1957 and may still be there. (See *Railway Magazine* No. 681, Vol. 104: January 1958).

The purchase of the Pullmans by the East Coast was brought up again in April 1888, leaving negotiations to the Great Northern, but still nothing transpired! The small fleet of three was reduced to to two in November 1892 when *India* was damaged beyond repair in the Manor House (Thirsk) collision, and it was decided to replace it with an East Coast pattern car, with attendant and apparatus for heating. This turned out to be No. 187, ordered from the Lancaster Carriage & Wagon Co. at £1,595; two similar cars from the same contractor were at first numbered 188 and 189 but were renumbered 90 and 106 before being brought into use. In October 1893 it was decided to discontinue running the Pullmans as soon as the three Lancaster cars became available and the date fixed was the end of March 1894, but this was later extended to 30th September, using them on the 8.30 pm to Glasgow and the 9.5 pm return. By December there had been no decision about the continued use of Pullmans on the East Coast, although there was talk of a new 21-year agreement, with additional cars; however, in January 1895 it was reported that *Columba* and *Iona* had been purchased for £3,400 with effect from 1st January. East Coast numbers were allocated later in the month, *Iona* becoming No. 232 and *Columba* No. 233. In February 1895 it was decided that they should be lettered '*EAST COAST (PULLMAN) SLEEPING CAR*'. In the meantime the North Eastern had received a claim from the Pullman company for the value of *India*, lost in the Manor House collision, and agreed to pay £1,700 in compensation.

During 1895 and 1896 discussions were still proceeding with the Pullman company regarding further cars, until in May 1897 Mr Gibb of the NER proposed that the matter be deferred; this was agreed to but the subject came up again in July 1898 and was not finally dropped until October 1898.

The East Coast Pullman cars continued to run between London and Glasgow but in 1901 they were displaced by two York-built sleepers with the same numbers, and thus the Pullmans ended their East Coast days as Nos 232A and 233A. They were withdrawn in December 1901 and 232A, formerly *Iona*, was transferred to Great Northern stock and became 2992; No. 233A, formerly *Columba*, went to the North Eastern and was renumbered 2966. The GN car was fitted with a vestibule connection at one end and provided with a kitchen; it appears to have been used as a buffet car and is believed to have ended its days in October 1925 after service between Nottingham and Skegness. The body was subsequently grounded at Lincoln shed and used as a Mutual Improvement Class meeting and lecture room;

it was not scrapped until BR days.

The North Eastern car was also fitted with a small kitchen and used as a refreshment car, serving breakfasts to West Riding businessmen as they travelled to Leeds from their summer residences at Scarborough, or teas as they travelled home again in the evening. In 1907 it was downgraded to a 3rd saloon and frequently used by Newcastle Football Club when travelling to away matches. It was withdrawn in November 1910.

Interior of Pullman Sleeping Car with the top bunks folded against the ceiling. The lower bunks were used for seating in the daytime. Note that only the lower portions of the windows allowed daylight into the car.

Interior of NER Refreshment Car No. 2966, with top bunks removed.

The body of Pullman Sleeping Car *India* after the rear-end collision at Manor House, near Thirsk, on 2nd November 1892. The car was scrapped and the NER paid the Pullman Car Co. £1,700 in compensation.

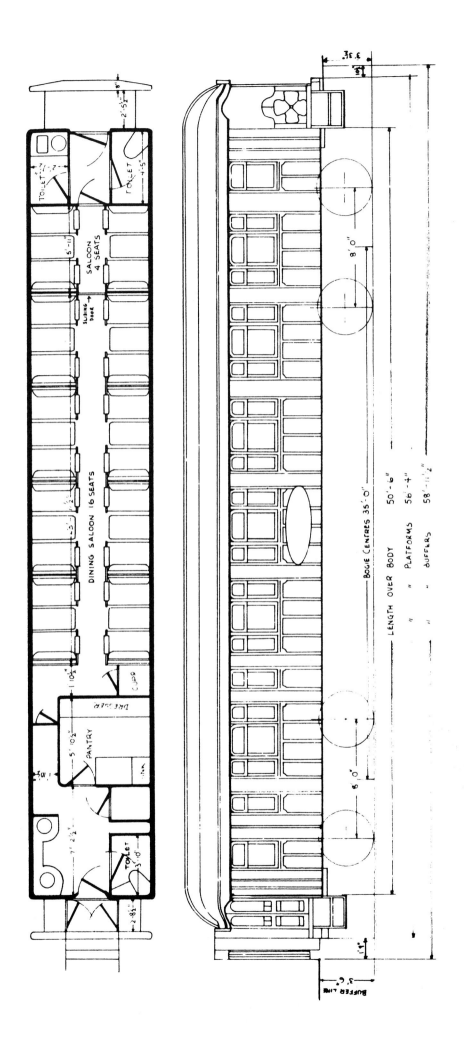

GNR Dining Car No. 2992 (formerly Pullman *Iona*).

Pullman Sleeping Car *Iona* after the Northallerton collision on 4th October 1894. The car was repaired and returned to traffic as the body was not too severely damaged.

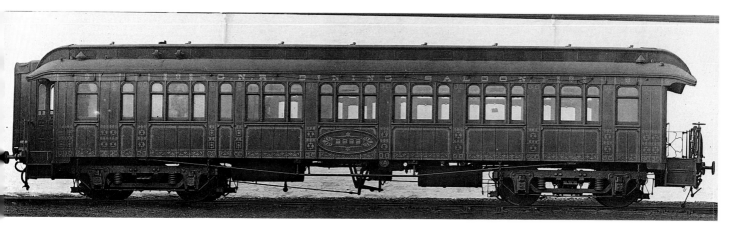

GNR Dining Car No. 2992 (formerly Pullman Car *Iona*), after fitting with a pantry, and gangway connection at one end only. The seating was officially quoted as for twenty passengers. Believed to have been used between Nottingham and Skegness until 1925 and subsequently as a Mutual Improvement classroom at Lincoln. Often wrongly identified as *Prince of Wales*.

NER Refreshment Car No. 2966 (formerly Pullman Car *Columba*) fitted with a kitchen and believed used between Scarborough and Leeds. The seating was quoted as forty, with two seats on each side of the gangway, but there was also a Smoking Compartment seating five, which took the place of the pantry on the GN car. The 40 passengers in the NE car occupied exactly the same space as the 20 passengers on the GN car.

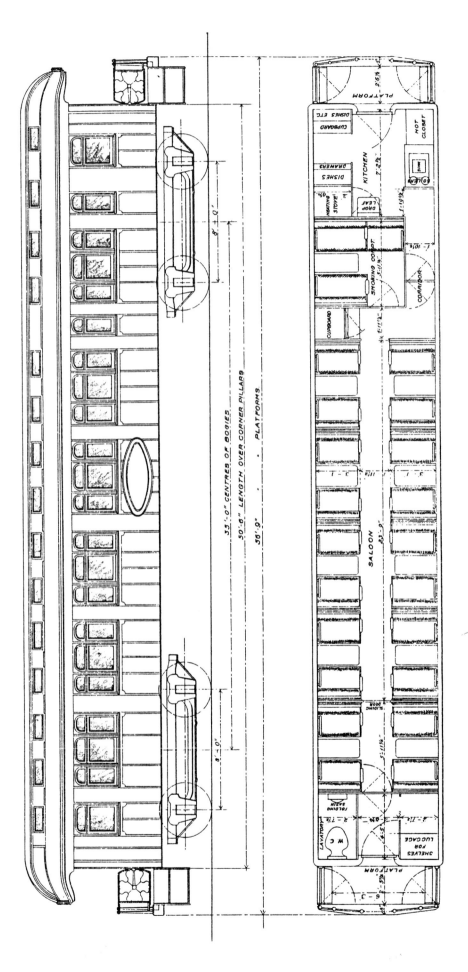

First Class Refreshment Car.

Nº 2966.

NER. DIAGRAM 69.

RECEIVED SECOND-HAND FROM E.C.J.S. AND ALTERED AT YORK, NOVEMBER 1901.

(FORMERLY PULLMAN CAR Nº 233, BUILT IN 1890.)

NER Refreshment Car No. 2966 (formerly Pullman *Columba*).

9 GN & NE Joint Stock

On 9th March 1894 Sir Henry Oakley, the General Manager of the Great Northern Railway, suggested the formation of a Joint Committee of Great Northern and North Eastern directors, to meet occasionally to settle the various matters arising concerning East Coast business. The Great Northern representatives were Sir A. Fairbairn and William Jackson, and the North Eastern appointed Sir M. W. Ridley and Henry Tennant, the chairman and deputy chairman in each case. The first meeting was held on 11th April 1894.

Five years later it was suggested that the time had come to provide separate dining and sleeping cars for the Newcastle traffic, but it was not until 12th January 1903 that it was agreed to run an additional dining car portion for Newcastle on the 6.15 pm from King's Cross to Bradford. Proposals for three composite brake vans, three composite dining cars and three third class brake vans were discussed and it was suggested that the new service should commence on 1st January 1904. In the event two first class dining cars (Nos 1 and 2), two brake thirds (Nos 3 and 4), and two open thirds (Nos 5 and 6) were built, all by the North Eastern at York. Correspondence from the NER Chief Carriage & Wagon Draughtsman, G. F. Groves, reveals that they were to have had clerestory roofs, but after some discussion they were eventually turned out with 'clear sweep' roofs.

The coaches were to be jointly owned and paid for in the proportion of route mileage worked between King's Cross and York and Newcastle, namely:

| | Distance | | Per cent of |
	Miles	chains	total mileage
GNR London–York	188	15	69.25
NER York–Newcastle	83	44	30.75

Maintenance of the stock was to be borne by the two companies in the proportion of ownership, and the profit or loss in catering to be shared in the same proportions.

On 1st October 1903 an additional dining car—an ECJS vehicle—commenced working as far as York with the Newcastle coaches attached to the 6.15 pm from King's Cross, returning the following day as a luncheon car on the 12.20 pm from York. Under this arrangement the Newcastle passengers were not due to reach Tyneside until 12.25 am, and from 1st October 1904 the London–Newcastle service underwent a change; the departure became 5.30 pm from King's Cross (replacing the Nottingham and Sheffield train) and giving a Tyneside arrival at a more respectable hour, namely 10.47 pm. Commencing on 1st July 1905 the 7.40 am from Newcastle was re-timed to leave at 8 am and accelerated so that it arrived at King's Cross at 1.40 pm; it was also made a 'Breakfast and Luncheon Car Express', using the vehicles of the previous day's 5.30 pm 'down'.

The popularity of the trains led to a need for more vehicles and two corridor 3rds (Nos 7 and 8) and two brake 1sts (Nos 9 and 10) were authorised in July 1905. However, the six original vehicles being built at York were still not ready and it was not until 14th December 1905 that the first Great Northern and North Eastern Joint coach was placed in traffic; four further coaches followed two days later, and the second 1st class dining car (No. 2) was ready for use on 16th January 1906.

The delay had largely been due to design problems and differences, with the NER chief draughtsman considering that 6-wheel bogies would be necessary, although 4-wheel bogies were eventually used. The North Eastern was also having clearance problems as it was discovered that when East Coast stock was diverted from the Team Valley line and sent round via 'the old main line' through Washington there was only $2\frac{1}{2}$ in clearance between door handles on 12-wheel coaches near Gateshead East station. Consequently the length of the new coaches was restricted to 53 ft 6 in although later, presumably when the clearances had been increased, some 65 ft 6 in sleeping cars were built.

By the end of 1905 complaints were being made by the North British Railway that East Coast sleeping cars were being used for the London–Newcastle traffic, going

Dgm. 1. 1st class Dining Saloon No. 1. The nearer end housed the kitchen. To GC Section as No. 2001C, April 1925. (*BR*)

against the original concept of the ECJS, and also from the travelling public requiring single-berth cars. Consequently, on 8th June 1906 it was agreed that four GN & NE sleepers should be built, two by the Great Northern (Nos 11 and 12) and two by the North Eastern (Nos 13 and 14). The York-built cars entered service in March 1908, but the Doncaster cars not until June 1909. All had eleven single-berths.

Also in 1906 it was found that the existing fleet did not meet the requirements of the 5.30 pm 'down', the 8 am 'up', and a new working at 10.30 am from Newcastle, so it was agreed that brake 3rd No. 4 should be converted to a full brake, and brake 1st No. 9 to a corridor 1st. In their new guise both were returned to traffic during February 1908. In November 1906 it was reported that a further 21 vehicles were required, and 14 were authorised to be built by the GN and seven by the NER:

By the GN
Brake 3rd No. 15
Open 3rds Nos 21, 22, 23, 24, 25
Dining 3rds Nos 26, 27, 28
Open 1sts Nos 31, 32, 33
Brake 1st No. 34
Brake van No. 35

By the NE
Corridor 3rds Nos 16, 17, 18, 19, 20
Corridor 1sts Nos 29, 30

All the York vehicles were delivered in June 1907, and the Doncaster vehicles between October 1907 and June 1908.

In 1911 brake 1st No. 34 was altered to a corridor 1st, and the final vehicle to appear was brake van No. 36, in July 1912.

In 1922 objections were received from passengers who disliked travelling in sleeping car No. 13, and on 15th March 1922 it exchanged numbers with brake 1st No. 10!

At first the cleaning of the stock was carried out both at King's Cross and at Newcastle, for which no charges were raised, but a special week-end cleaning carried out on Sundays at Newcastle was charged to the joint account. From 1st January 1914, however, the cost of cleaning carried out by both companies was charged to the joint account and the total debit divided between the two partners in ownership proportions. The amounts charged were based on ECJS practice and were:

	s	d
Sleeping cars	3	6
Dining cars-1st class	4	0
Dining cars-3rd class	3	0
Pantry 3rd	3	0
Corridor 1sts	2	6
Corridor 3rd	2	6
Brake 1st	2	6
Brake 3rd	2	6
Brake vans	2	6

Between 1907 and 1915 760 sheets, 514 antimacassars, 3,421 hand towels, 500 roller towels and numerous other items were supplied for use in the GN/NE coaches. Forty East Coast rugs were transferred to the Joint account at a cost of £1 1s each, and in 1908 and 1909 44 new rugs were obtained for the four sleeping cars 11, 12, 13 and 14.

At first the destination boards were made of iron, but in April 1911 it was decided to use wooden boards and 46 were made at Doncaster and 24 at York; they were lettered on one side only LONDON (KINGS CROSS) AND NEWCASTLE. Ten water shields for coaches coupled to the engine were supplied in 1907 and 1908.

From 1st July 1903 an ECJS sleeping car was run on the 11.45 pm from King's Cross to Newcastle, and on the 11.20 pm from Newcastle (Saturdays excepted), and two attendants were appointed at £1 5s per week—one by the GNR and one by the NER. At first the lodging payment was 7s 6d per week, raised in 1913 to 9s per week. An attendant on the day trains worked from the Newcastle end and did the round trip in one day. Because of the long hours involved he was allowed a day off per week, but in January 1914 this was increased to two days a week and 'spare' attendants were appointed by the NER.

Originally the catering staff were under the control of the GN Hotels Department, but from 1st January 1910 the catering on the 8.10 am from Newcastle and the 5.30 pm from King's Cross was taken over by the North Eastern; the conductor received £1 per week, one attendant received 15s a week, and four attendants received 12s a week. The plum job was that of cook and he received £2 7s 6d per week. Great Northern staff worked on the 10.28 am from Newcastle and the 10.35 am from King's Cross and for staying overnight in Newcastle received 3s a week. No doubt they slept in the train! The first ten coaches for the GN/NE Joint services, built at York between December 1905 and May 1906, had straight matchboarded sides as favoured by the North Eastern at that time. At first, Nos 1 and 2, 5 and 6, and 3 and 4, were allocated NER Carriage Diagram numbers 107, 108 and 109 respectively, but soon became GN/NE Joint Diagrams 1, 2 and 3. All were 52 ft over body and 53 ft 6 in over headstocks. Successive vehicles were allocated to Diagrams 4 to 18, two merely as a result of modifications:

	No. 4	No. 9
Type	Brake 3rd	Brake 1st
Original Diagram	3	5
Altered to	Brake van	Corridor 1st
New Diagram	14	15
Date altered	February 1908	February 1908

After the 1923 Grouping the Joint vehicles had 1400 added to their original numbers, but later most of the 36 coaches were dispersed to the various sections forming the LNER and were renumbered in the North Eastern (2xxx), Great Northern (4xxx), Great Central (5xxx), Great Eastern (6xxx) and Great North of Scotland (7xxx) series of Area stock lists. The brake vans were renumbered into the East Coast van stock. Some of the vehicles transferred to North Eastern Area stock were not at first allocated new Diagram Numbers and for a time appeared in the official Registers still with their GN/NE Joint Diagram Numbers; for instance corridor 3rds Nos 1419 and 1420 became 21431 and 21434 and for a time remained as GN/NE Dgm. 7, but later were known as N.E. Area Dgm. 255. Similarly corridor 3rd No. 1409 became 2318 and was at first GN/NE Dgm. 15, later N.E. Dgm. 257; and brake van No. 151 (originally GN/NE No. 4) was renumbered 289, at first known as GN/NE Dgm. 14, and later as N.E. Dgm. 256.

Where space allowed, the sides of the coaches were embellished with the name of the owners and the type of vehicle in full; thus the dining cars had:

GREAT NORTHERN & NORTH EASTERN JOINT STOCK

FIRST CLASS DINING SALOON. 1.

Brake 3rd No. 3, with van and compartment doors, carried only:

3 LUGGAGE G N & N E. J. S. 3

Great Northern and North Eastern Joint Stock

No.	Type	Built by	To Traffic	Dgm.	Disposal		Note
1*	1st dining car	NER	14-12-1905	1	2001C	3/25	
2*	1st dining car	NER	18-1-1906	1	2002C	5/25	
3*	Brake 3rd	NER	16-12-1905	3	288	4/37	
4*	Brake 3rd	NER	16-12-1905	3	289	6/37	1
5*	Pantry 3rd	NER	16-12-1905	2	2005C	6/25	
6*	Pantry 3rd	NER	16-12-1905	2	2006C	6/25	
7*	Corridor 3rd	NER	18-4-1906	4	52057	3/34	
8*	Corridor 3rd	NER	30-5-1906	4	52056	3/34	
9*	Brake 1st	NER	31-5-1906	5	2318	4/36	2
10*	Brake 1st	NER	18-4-1906	5	2319	3/38	3
11	Sleeping car	GNR	30-6-1909	17	COND.	2/36	
12	Sleeping car	GNR	29-6-1909	17	COND.	1/37	
13	Sleeping car	NER	9-3-1908	16	COND.	1/35	4
14	Sleeping car	NER	9-3-1908	16	COND.	2/36	
15	Brake 3rd	GNR	10-1907	8	62086	11/35	
16	Corridor 3rd	NER	6-1907	7	52058	8/33	
17	Corridor 3rd	NER	6-1907	7	52059	11/33	
18	Corridor 3rd	NER	6-1907	7	52060	4/34	
19	Corridor 3rd	NER	6-1907	7	21431	2/34	
20	Corridor 3rd	NER	6-1907	7	21434	5/34	
21	Open 3rd	GNR	10-1907	9	61799	7/33	
22	Open 3rd	GNR	10-1907	9	43133	8/33	
23	Open 3rd	GNR	11-1907	9	43134	8/33	
24	Open 3rd	GNR	6-1908	9	43135	7/33	
25	Open 3rd	GNR	6-1908	9	43136	7/33	
26	3rd dining car	GNR	10-1907	10	COND.	7/60	
27	3rd dining car	GNR	11-1907	10	?	?	
28	3rd dining car	GNR	6-1908	10	COND.	10/59	
29	Corridor 1st	NER	6-1907	6	784	5/36	
30	Corridor 1st	NER	6-1907	6	786	4/36	
31	Open 1st	GNR	10-1907	11	7122	12/40	
32	Open 1st	GNR	10-1907	11	7123	12/40	
33	Open 1st	GNR	12-1907	11	7124	12/40	
34	Brake 1st	GNR	10-1907	12	788	7/37	5
35	Brake van	GNR	10-1907	13	4019	6/28	6
36	Brake van	GNR	7-1912	18	4191	1/29	7

Notes
1 No. 4 converted to brake van Dgm. 14 2-1908. Van 151 11-1925.
2 No. 9 converted to corridor 1st Dgm. 15 2-1908; to corridor 3rd 1935.
3 No. 10 renumbered 13 15-3-1922, but disregarded for disposal details.
4 No. 13 renumbered 10 15-3-1922, but disregarded for disposal details.
5 No. 34 converted to corridor 1st 12-1911.
6 Van 150 5-1926.
7 Van 152 3-1926.
* Matchboarded sides

G.N. and N.E.J.S. Third Class Dining Carriage with Pantry.

Nos. 5. 6.

BUILT DEC. 1905.

DRAWING Nº 795Y

2 OPEN COMPARTMENTS. — 48 THIRD CLASS SEATS.

1 PANTRY.

1 LAVATORY.

CORRIDOR AND PASSAGES.

WEIGHT 31-3. $\frac{T}{C}$

Dgm. 2. 3rd Dining Car with pantry, Nos 5 and 6.

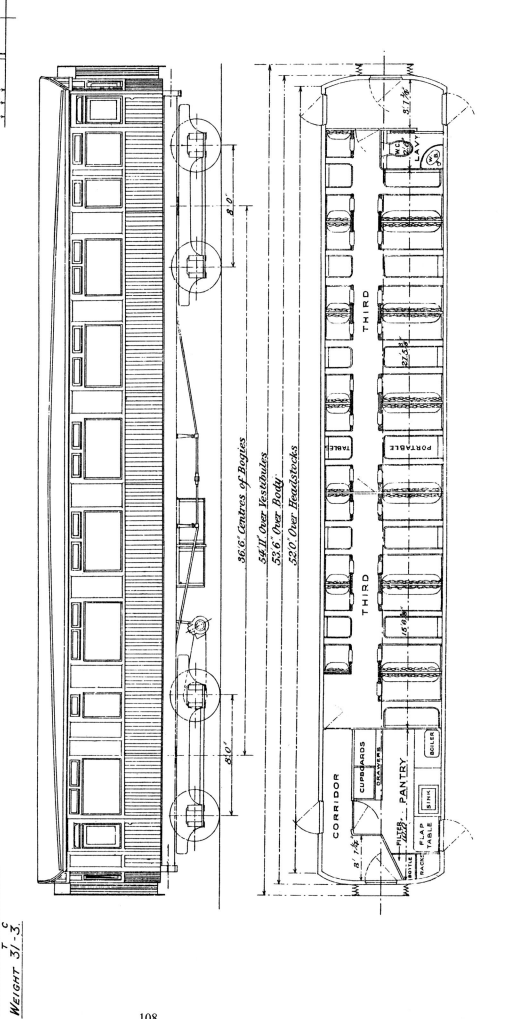

G.N. AND N.E.J.S. THIRD CLASS AND BRAKE VAN.

Nos 3. 4.

BUILT DEC. 1905.

DRAWING Nº 793ʸ

N.E. DIAGRAM 109 3

2 THIRD CLASS COMPARTMENTS - 12 SEATS
or
8 SEATS WHEN DINING

1 LUGGAGE AND BRAKE VAN

1 LAVATORY

CORRIDOR

WEIGHT 27.

Dgm. 3. 3rd Brake Van, Nos 3 and 4. York version.

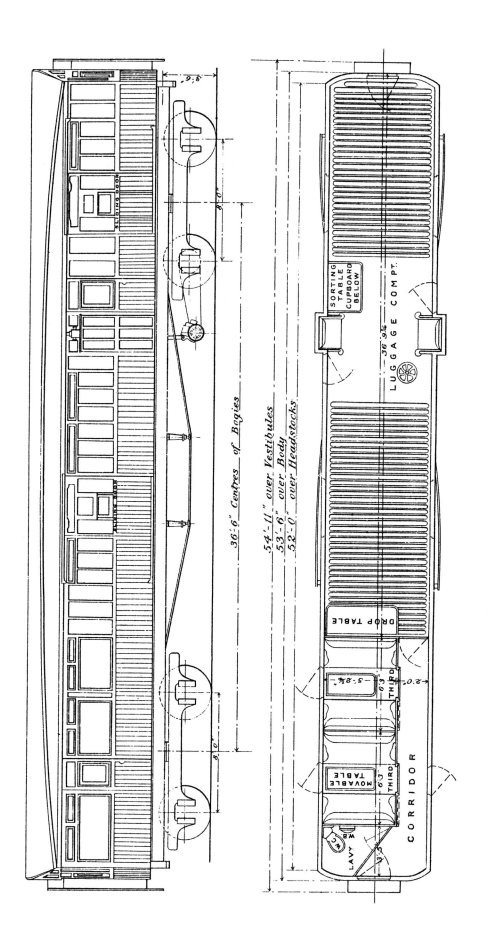

SLIDING DOOR

36'-6" Centres of Bogies

54'-11" over Vestibules
53'-6" over Body
52'-0" over Headstocks

8'-0"

9'-6"

8'-0"

8'-0"

SORTING TABLE CUPBOARD BELOW

LUGGAGE COMPT.

36.9¾

DROP TABLE

THIRD

THIRD

THIRD

MOVABLE TABLE

LAVY

WB

WC

CORRIDOR

6'-3"

6'-3"

5'-3¾"

2'-0"

3'-3"

8'-1½" over Cornices

10'-4⅜"
10'-7½"
12'-8¾"
13'-0⅜"

5'-8"

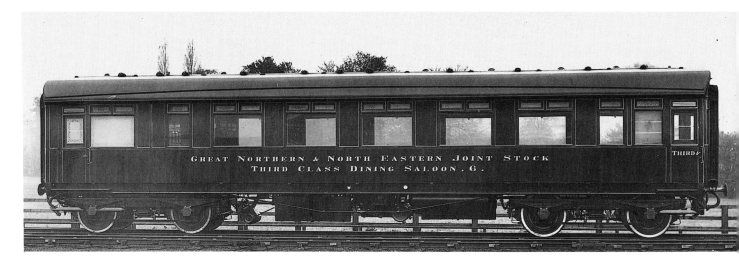

Dgm. 2. 3rd class Dining Saloon No. 6. This had a pantry at the left-hand end. To GC Section as No. 2006C, June 1925. (*BR*)

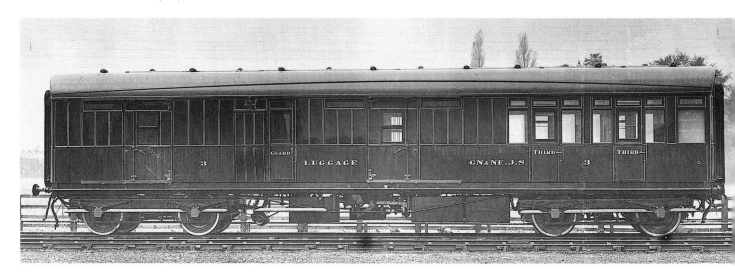

Dgm. 3. 3rd class Brake No. 3. Became LNER No. 1403 and converted to a full van by removing the two compartments. To NE Area 288 Dgm. NE 184 April 1937. (*BR*)

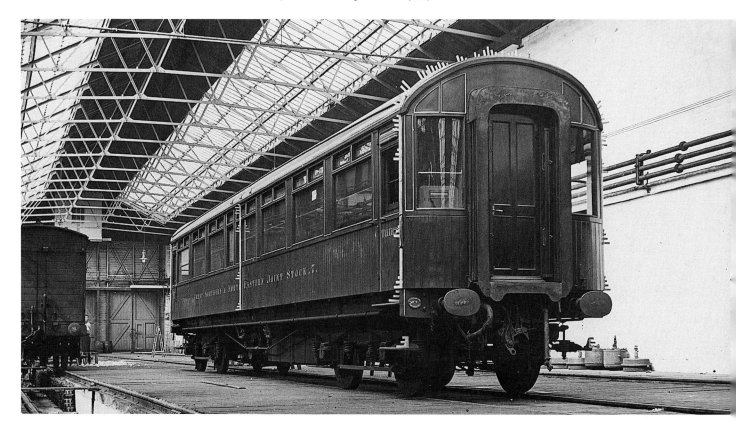

Dgm. 4. Corridor 3rd No. 7. Fitted with gauging 'fingers'. To GC Section as No. 52057, March 1934.

G. N. & N. E. THIRD CLASS BRAKE

Nº 15.

Grenfard

Built at Doncaster 1907

2 Third Compts & 1 Toilet.

12 Seats.

WEIGHT. 26·19·3

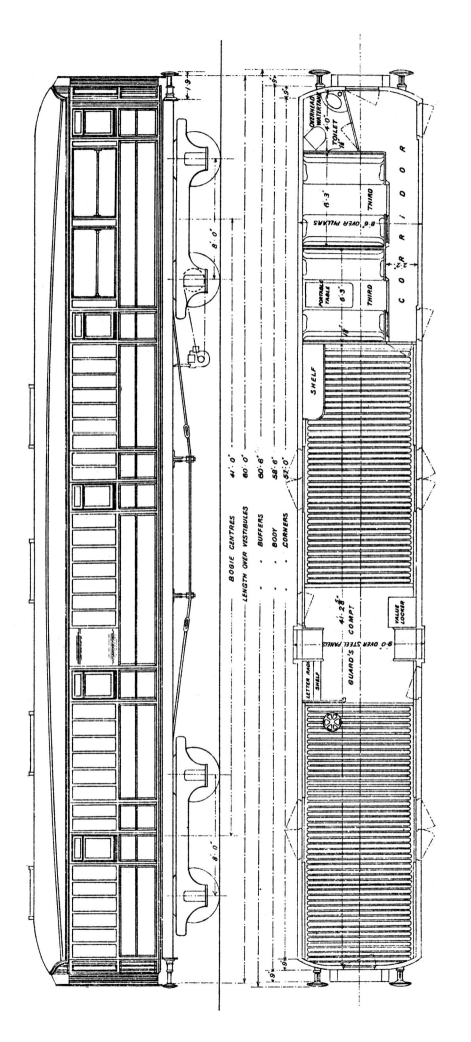

Dgm. 8. 3rd Brake Van, No. 15. Doncaster version.

BOGIE CENTRES	4'. 0"	
LENGTH OVER VESTIBULES	60'. 0"	
BUFFERS	60'. 6"	
BODY	58'. 6"	
CORNERS	57'. 0"	

DRAWING No. 1333Y.

DIAGRAM No. 14.

G.N. & N.E.J.S. VAN.

No. 4.

CONVERTED FEBRUARY, 1908.

ORIGINALLY CORRIDOR VAN THIRD. BUILT DECEMBER, 1905.

(DIAGRAM 3.)

1 VAN COMPARTMENT (TO CARRY 5 TONS).

ELECTRIC LIGHT.
STEAM HEATING.
DUAL BRAKES.

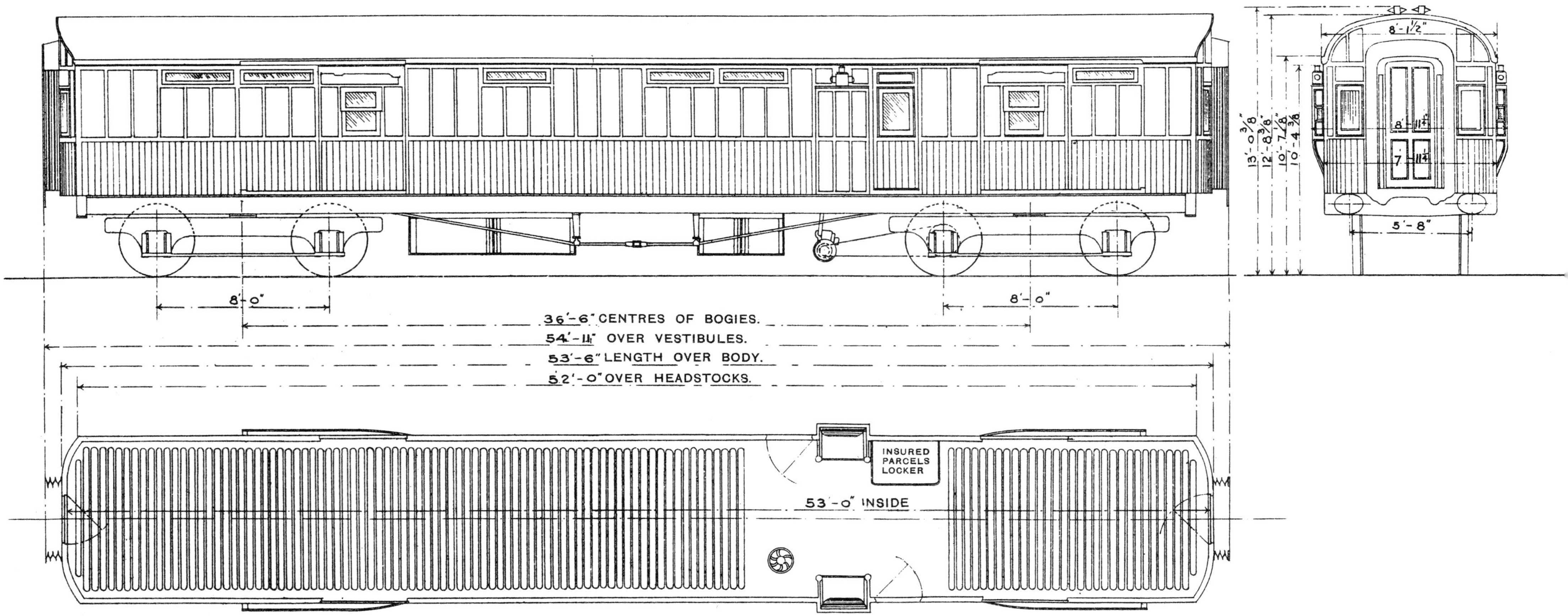

WEIGHT - 25T 5C 1Q

8-1½"
8-11½"
7-11½"
5-8"
10-4⅜"
12-7⅞"
13-0⅜"

36'-6" CENTRES OF BOGIES.
54'-1½" OVER VESTIBULES.
53'-6" LENGTH OVER BODY.
52'-0" OVER HEADSTOCKS.

8'-0"
8'-0"

INSURED PARCELS LOCKER

53'-0" INSIDE

Dgm. 14. Brake Van, No. 4. Converted from 3rd Brake No. 4 (Dgm. 3), February 1908.

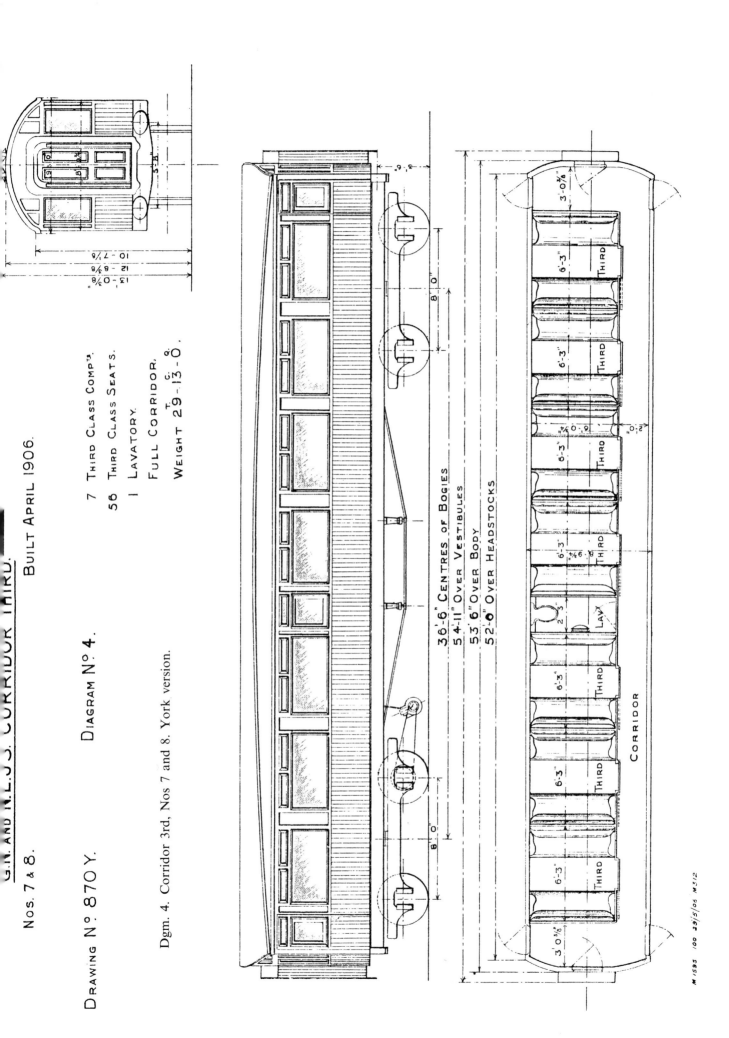

G.N. AND N.E.J.S. CORRIDOR THIRD.

Nos. 7 & 8.

BUILT APRIL 1906.

DRAWING No. 870 Y.

DIAGRAM No. 4.

Dgm. 4. Corridor 3rd, Nos 7 and 8. York version.

7 THIRD CLASS COMPT.S.
56 THIRD CLASS SEATS.
1 LAVATORY.
FULL CORRIDOR.
WEIGHT 29-13-0. T.C.Q.

36'-6" CENTRES OF BOGIES
54-11" OVER VESTIBULES
53'-6" OVER BODY
52'-0" OVER HEADSTOCKS

113

— G.N. & N.E.J.S. CORRIDOR THIRD. —

— Nos. 16, 17, 18, 19, & 20. —

BUILT JUNE, 1907.

DIAGRAM NO. 7.

DRAWING NO. 1340Y.

8 THIRD CLASS COMPARTMENTS. 48 SEATS.
2 LAVATORIES.
CORRIDOR.

WEIGHT - 31 T. 15 C. 0 Q. { ELECTRIC LIGHT.
STEAM HEATING.
DUAL BRAKES.

Dgm. 7. Corridor 3rd, Nos 16–20, built at York.

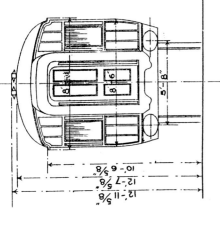

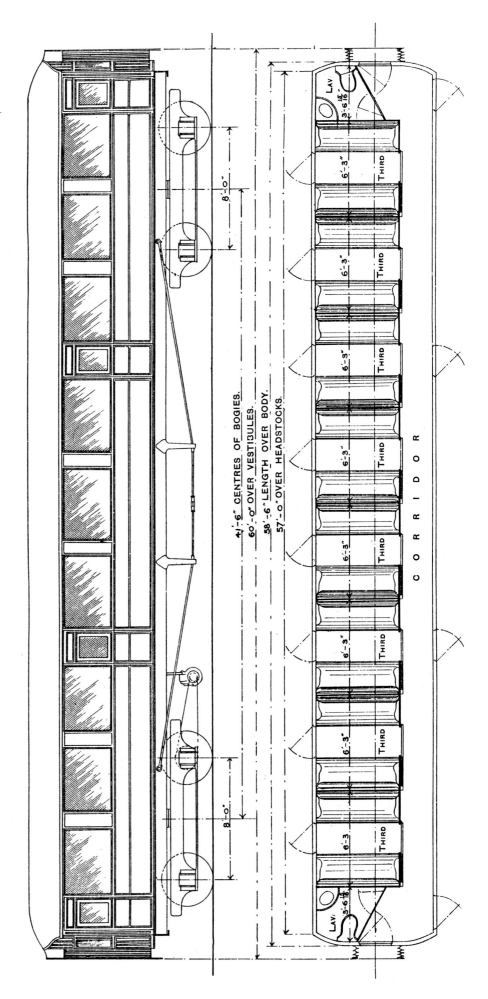

5'-8"

10'-6 5/8"

12'-7 5/8"

12'-11 5/8"

8'-0"

8'-0"

4'-6" CENTRES OF BOGIES.
60'-0" OVER VESTIBULES.
58'-6" LENGTH OVER BODY.
57'-0" OVER HEADSTOCKS.

LAV. 3'-6 15/16"

6'-3" THIRD
6'-3" THIRD
6'-3" THIRD
6'-3" THIRD
6'-3" THIRD
6'-3" THIRD
6'-3" THIRD
6'-3" THIRD

CORRIDOR

LAV. 3'-6 15/16"

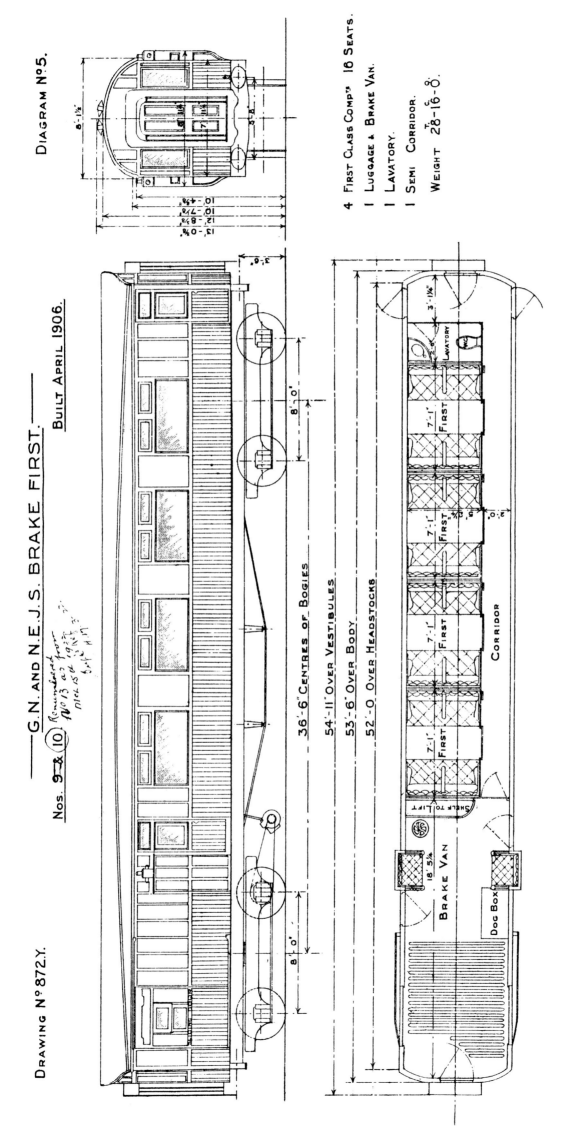

DIAGRAM Nº5.

G.N. AND N.E.J.S. BRAKE FIRST.

BUILT APRIL 1906.

DRAWING Nº 872.Y.

NOS. 9 & 10

4 First Class Comp's 16 Seats.
1 Luggage & Brake Van.
1 Lavatory.
1 Semi Corridor.
Weight 28-16-0.

Dgm. 5. Brake 1st, Nos 9 and 10.

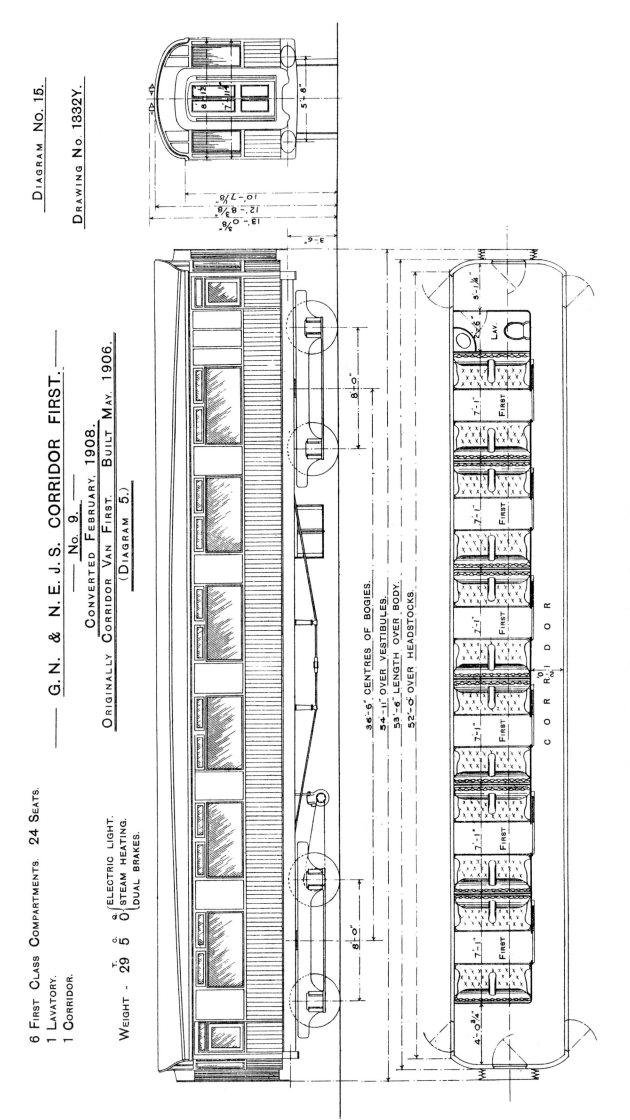

DRAWING NO. 1832Y.

G.N. & N.E.J.S. CORRIDOR FIRST.

No. 9.

CONVERTED FEBRUARY, 1908. BUILT MAY, 1906.

ORIGINALLY CORRIDOR VAN FIRST.

(DIAGRAM 5.)

6 FIRST CLASS COMPARTMENTS. 24 SEATS.
1 LAVATORY.
1 CORRIDOR.

WEIGHT - 29 5 0 { ELECTRIC LIGHT. STEAM HEATING. DUAL BRAKES.

36'-6" CENTRES OF BOGIES.
54'-11" OVER VESTIBULES.
53'-6" LENGTH OVER BODY.
52'-0" OVER HEADSTOCKS.

Dgm. 15. Corridor 1st, No. 9. Converted from Brake 1st No. 9 (Dgm. 5) February 1908.

Dgm. 6. Corridor 1st No. 29. Destination board reads 'NEWCASTLE AND KING'S CROSS'. To GNS Section as No. 784, May 1936. (*BR*)

Dgm. 7. Corridor 3rd No. 17. LNER No. 1417. To GC Section as No. 52059, November 1933.

Dgm. 16. Sleeping Car No. 13. Eleven single berths. Renumbered 10 from 15th March 1922 after complaints from passengers. LNER No. 1410, withdrawn January 1935. (*BR*)

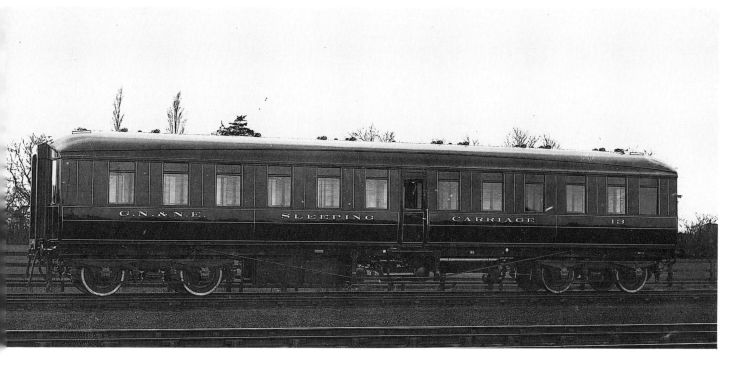

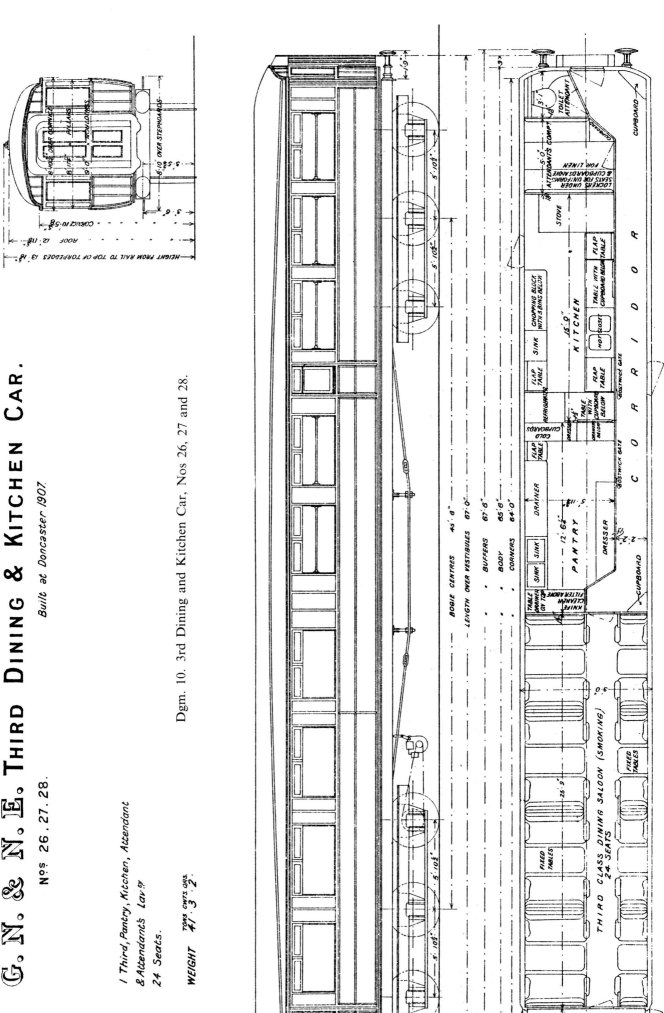

G. N. & N. E. THIRD DINING & KITCHEN CAR.

Built at Doncaster 1907.

Nos. 26. 27. 28.

1 Third, Pantry, Kitchen, Attendant
& Attendant's Lav.y
24 Seats.

WEIGHT 41.3.2. TONS CWTS QRS.

Dgm. 10. 3rd Dining and Kitchen Car, Nos 26, 27 and 28.

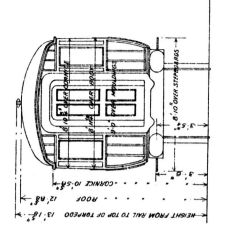

G. N. & N. E. OPEN FIRST CLASS.

Nos. 31, 32, 33.

Built at Doncaster 1907.

2 OPEN FIRSTS & 1 TOILET.

26 SEATS.

WEIGHT 28 · 10 · 2 TONS CWTS QRS

Dgm. 11. Open 1st, Nos 31, 32 and 33.

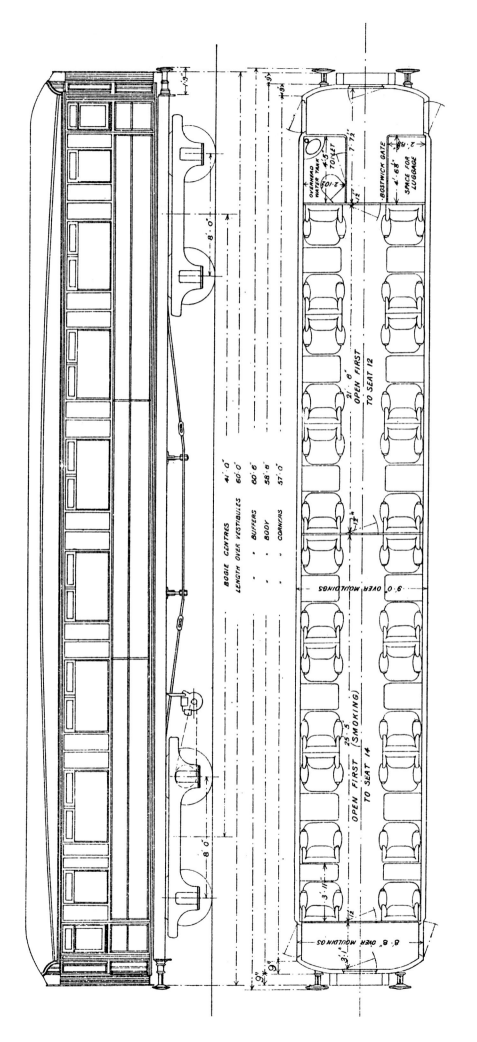

BOGIE CENTRES	41' 0"
LENGTH OVER VESTIBULES	60' 0"
" " BUFFERS	60' 6"
" " BODY	58' 8"
" " CORNERS	57' 0"

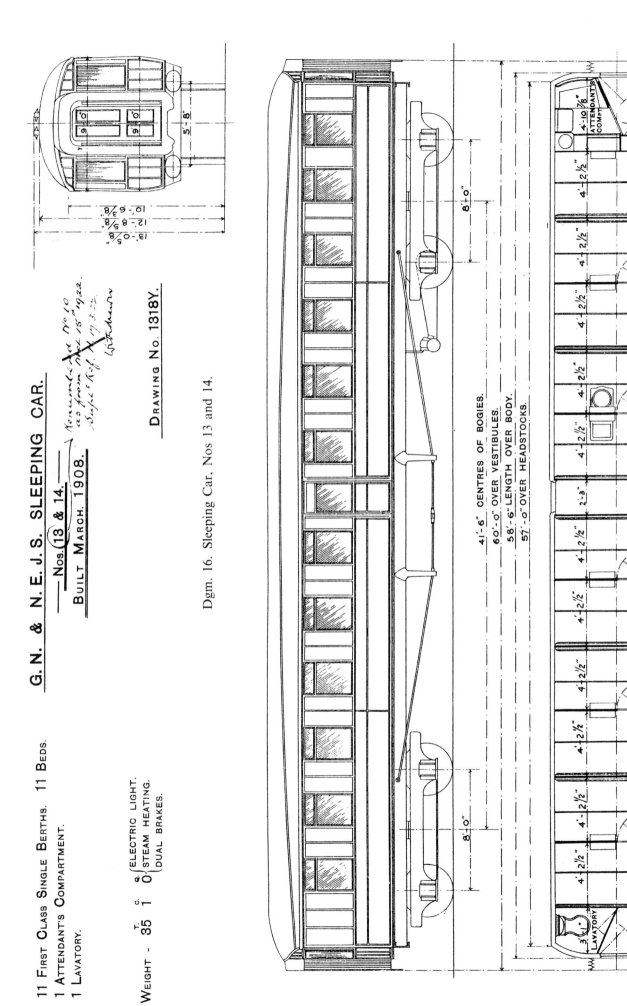

G.N. & N.E.J.S. SLEEPING CAR.

Nos. (13 & 14.)

BUILT MARCH 1908.

Renumbered No 10 as from Nov 15 1922. Supt 5 R-f X 17.3.22. (signature)

DRAWING No. 1318Y.

11 FIRST CLASS SINGLE BERTHS. 11 BEDS.
1 ATTENDANT'S COMPARTMENT.
1 LAVATORY.

WEIGHT – 35 T. 1 C. 0 Q. { ELECTRIC LIGHT. STEAM HEATING. DUAL BRAKES. }

5'-8"
10'-6⅝"
12'-8⅝"
13'-0⅝"

8'-0"
8'-0"

41'-6" CENTRES OF BOGIES.
60'-0" OVER VESTIBULES.
58'-6" LENGTH OVER BODY.
57'-0" OVER HEADSTOCKS.

ATTENDANTS COMPT
4'-10⅞"

SINGLE BERTH 4'-2½"
SINGLE BERTH 4'-2½"
SINGLE BERTH 4'-2½"
SINGLE BERTH 4'-2½"
SINGLE BERTH 4'-2½"
SINGLE BERTH 4'-2½"

2'-3"

SINGLE BERTH 4'-2½"
SINGLE BERTH 4'-2½"
SINGLE BERTH 4'-2½"
SINGLE BERTH 4'-2½"
SINGLE BERTH 4'-2½"

LAVATORY 3'-1"

CORRIDOR

Dgm. 16. Sleeping Car, Nos 13 and 14.

120

10 Locomotive and Train Working

As early as September 1854 North Eastern engines were working between Berwick and Edinburgh, but via Kelso, and it was not until May 1862 that an Agreement was signed between the North Eastern and the North British. This included the section 'The NER and the NBR shall maintain and work in full efficiency in every respect the East Coast route via Berwick, and grant Running Powers to the NER between Berwick and Edinburgh, contingent upon the passing of the North Eastern and Newcastle & Carlisle Amalgamation Bill'.

However, nothing was done at that time and it was not until March 1869 that the general managers of the North British and the North Eastern inspected the line between Berwick and Edinburgh with a view to through working of East Coast trains, using North Eastern engines between Newcastle and Edinburgh, to commence on 1st May 1869. Whether this decision was spurred by the introduction of Joint coaches is unclear. However, Tomlinson records that North Eastern engines actually started working through on 1st June 1869, but a contemporary report quotes Thursday 1st July as the date of commencement. Certainly the first appearance of such trains was in the NER Working Timetable for 1st June 1869.

On 7th August 1869 the North British agreed to provide accommodation for the NER engines based at Edinburgh, and it was decided to erect a shed at St Margarets, with the North Eastern paying $6\frac{1}{2}$% interest on the capital for seven years, plus £25 per engine—but with free water! No. 1 coal was to be supplied at 9s 6d per ton.

Things appear to have run smoothly until after 20 years the North British felt that it should play a part in the East Coast workings, and on 18th January 1894 the company gave notice to the NER that NE locomotive workings should cease from 30th April 1894; later extended to 31st December 1894. However, the North Eastern engines continued working through until 14th January 1897 because the English company would not accept the North British decision. From January 1897 engines were changed at Berwick.

In the meantime the dispute had been referred to the Railway Commissioners and hearing began on 20th May 1897; when their decision was given on 9th February 1898 it was that the North British should receive 75% of the gross receipts between Berwick and Edinburgh, and that the North Eastern should work five trains in each direction daily between Berwick and Edinburgh; this coming into operation on 1st March 1898. The matter then went to arbitration on 4th May 1898 and the North Eastern was allowed to continue working the five trains, with the engines of other East Coast trains being changed at Berwick. However, in 1904 the North British decided to ask the North Eastern to work all the East Coast trains and this commenced on 1st September.

It was about this time that it was decided to house the NE engines at Haymarket instead of St Margarets, still at a charge of £25 per year per engine, with water at 1s 0d per tender and a charge of 6d for a boiler washout; lighting up from the NB furnace was 1s 0d per engine.

Fortunately many types of North Eastern engines were photographed at Edinburgh, of which a number were taken by Dr Budden; they ranged from Fletcher and Tennant 2-4-0s to Raven Pacifics, but the most commonly photographed were the 4-4-0s of Classes M and R, and the Atlantics of Classes V, Z and Z1. At Grouping on 1st January 1923 four Raven Atlantics were stationed at Haymarket and used solely on trains to Newcastle, manned by North Eastern men outstationed from Tweedmouth.

One result of the Grouping was the LNER's policy to integrate engines stationed away from their home shed into the stock of the host Area; thus the ex-North Eastern engines at Haymarket were transferred to the Southern Scottish Area stock and for the first time became available for use on routes other than the Newcastle line.

A similar rationalisation took place with the former North Eastern men stationed at Haymarket to work the East Coast trains, but they were given the option of moving to the North Eastern Area or being assimilated into the 'links' at Haymarket. Thus the reconstituted workings at Haymarket brought former North British crews on to East Coast expresses, and for a time ex-North British and ex-North Eastern Atlantics could be seen arriving at Newcastle from the north. Later, of course, the Gresley Pacifics, 'Deltics' and High Speed Trains maintained the tradition set up by North Eastern engines and men in 1869.

When the service between Edinburgh and Berwick first appeared in the North Eastern working timetable from 1st June 1869 four 'up' trains were listed but for two of them, the 11.55 am and 12.2 am from Berwick to Newcastle, no departure time was quoted from Edinburgh, although they were referred to as "Day Express" and "Night Express" respectively. However, the other two through trains did have departure times from Edinburgh, namely the 2.50 pm "Night Mail" and the 7 pm Day Mail. In the opposite direction only the 6.13 am "Night Mail" and the 11.45 am "Express" from Newcastle had Edinburgh arrival times, although the 5.10 am "Night Express" and the 5.5 pm "Day Express" obviously ran through to Edinburgh.

The July 1869 issue of the WTT had, for the first time, instructions to NER drivers and guards working between Berwick and Edinburgh. In the August issue the 11.55 am and 12.2 am Berwick to Newcastle had become the 10.20 am and 10.15 pm from Edinburgh respectively, and in the 'down' direction the 4.53 am (formerly 5.10 am) and the 5.5 pm from Newcastle acquired Edinburgh arrival times of 8.20 am and 8.50 pm respectively. For the first time the heading "East Coast Express" was used for the new 2.50 am Newcastle to Edinburgh which, with a five-minute stop at Berwick, was due in Edinburgh at 6.5 am. The same description was not given to any train in the 'up' direction.

Once the East Coast Joint Stock coaches had been introduced the following notice began to appear in NER public timetables:

'Passengers by the through trains between London (King's Cross Station) and Scotland, are conveyed in through carriages of the most improved description, the joint property of the Companies forming the East Coast route, and especially constructed for the accommodation of this traffic. These carriages are used for the fast trains leaving King's Cross at 9.0, 10.0 and 10.10 am, and 8.30 and 9.15 pm for Scotland, and for those arriving at King's Cross at 6.45, 9.40 am, and 8.25 and 9.30 pm from Scotland. The carriages run to and from the North of Scotland, via Stirling. Saloon and Family Carriages have also been constructed for the conveyance of Families or Invalids and their servants, the charge for which can be ascertained on application.'

In the summer of 1872 there were only four trains from London to Edinburgh, at 10 am ("Scotch Express"), 10.10 am ("Express"), 8.30 pm ("Scotch Night Express"), and 9.15 pm ("Express"), arriving at Edinburgh at 7.30 pm, 8.40 pm, 6 am and 8.15 am. The 'up' trains left Edinburgh at 10.25 am, 10.45 am, 7.30 pm and 10.15 pm. The fare from London to Edinburgh was Single: 1st class 70s 0d; 2nd class 51s 0d; 3rd class 33s 0d. Return: 1st class 116s 9d; 2nd class 85s 0d.

Even after 30 years there was not a great change in the timetable, although there was an increase in the number of night trains, according to the Summer 1902 timetable:

		am	am	am
King's Cross	dep.	5.15	10.0	10.10
Edinburgh	arr.	3.0	6.15	6.25
		am	am	pm
King's Cross	dep.	10.35	11.25	2.20
Edinburgh	arr.	8.40	7.55	10.45
		pm	pm	pm
King's Cross	dep.	7.45	8.15	8.45
Edinburgh	arr.	3.30	4.0	5.55
		pm	pm	pm
King's Cross	dep.	11.30	11.45	10.30
Edinburgh	arr.	7.15	7.30	8.58

The 10 am, 10.10 am, 11.25 am, and 2.20 pm were all shown as "Dining Car Express"; the 11.25 am ran via Harrogate. All the night trains were shown as conveying sleeping cars to various destinations in Scotland—Perth, Aberdeen, Inverness, Glasgow and Fort William, and most of them were specially noted as, 'Corridor Sleeping Carriage with transverse berths, accompanied by an attendant who provides tea, coffee, &c'.

The corresponding 'up' trains left Edinburgh at 10 am, 10.10 am, 10.20 am, 12.20 pm, 2.20 pm, 7.45 pm, 9.40 pm, 10.50 pm and 11.15 pm.

Only passengers for beyond Edinburgh were conveyed by the 10 am from King's Cross. Tea or coffee, with bread and butter, could be obtained at any time except during the service of breakfast, lunch or dinner and the cost—6d! Breakfast was 2s 6d; luncheon 1st class 2s 6d, 3rd class 2s 0d; dinner 1st class 3s 6d, 3rd class 2s 6d. Luncheon baskets (hot or cold) could be obtained at York, Darlington, or Newcastle at a charge of 3s 0d, or without wine, ale, stout, or aerated water, 2s 6d each. Telegrams ordering luncheon baskets could be sent free of charge from any of the principal stations en route.

In 1922, the last year of the true ECJS, the service had not fully recovered after World War I and departures from King's Cross for Edinburgh and beyond were at 9.50 am, 10 am, 1.20 pm, 7.30 pm, 9.25 pm, 10.20 pm and 10.30 pm. One notable change was that East Coast trains were being utilised to convey through coaches for destinations other than London and Edinburgh. Thus the 10 am from Edinburgh conveyed a through coach between Edinburgh and Oxford; the 10.15 am from Edinburgh conveyed a through coach from Newcastle to Hull (Riverside Quay) on Wednesdays and Saturdays and a through coach from Glasgow to Southampton daily; and the 1.30 pm from Edinburgh conveyed the Aberdeen to Penzance coach. All these were detached at York and went their separate ways.

Great Northern Railway. The leading vehicle is ECJS No. 245, a Composite Brake, altered from Corridor Composite with Luggage Locker in 1906. It was condemned in January 1926. The engine is GNR Class C1 4-4-2 No. 1442, the 'Royal' engine.

Great Central Section. The leading vehicle is No. 52024, ex-ECJS No. 288, a Brake 3rd built at Cowlairs in 1901. Transferred to the GC Section in May 1927 it is seen near Woodhead hauled by D11 class 4-4-0 No. 5510 *Princess Mary*. (*H. Gordon Tidey*)

North Eastern Railway. Fletcher 2-4-0 No. 153 on the 'up' "Scotsman" in 1882 passing Low Fell.

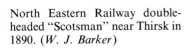

North Eastern Railway double-headed "Scotsman" near Thirsk in 1890. (*W. J. Barker*)

North Eastern Railway Q class 4-4-0 No. 1902 near Northallerton on the 'up' "Scotsman" in 1897.

North Eastern Railway R class 4-4-0 No. 2014 near Portobello in 1900.

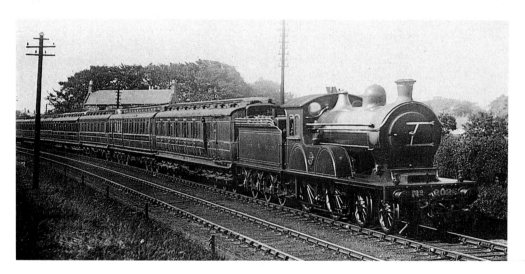

North Eastern Railway R class 4-4-0 No. 2026 near Benton c1904.

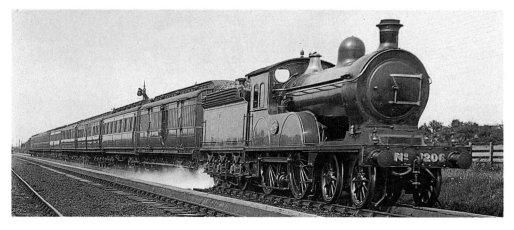

North Eastern Railway R class 4-4-0 No. 1206 on Wiske Moor troughs c1910. (*F. E. Mackay*)

The 10am from King's Cross heading north at Benton Quarry c1910. The engines are No. 1753, a Class V Atlantic, and an unidentified Class M1 4-4-0. (*R. J. Purves*)

Great Northern Railway Stirling 'Single' Class G 4-2-2 No. 1 with a special train for the RCTS, using the ECJS replica train, photographed at Peterborough on 11th September 1938. (*C. L. Turner*)

One of the 6-wheel composite coaches in the ECJS replica train assembled to mark the introduction of new coaches for the "Flying Scotsman" service in 1938.

11 A Chapter of Accidents

Strange as it may seem one of the most dangerous places to travel on a British railway was aboard an East Coast sleeping car train, running between London and Edinburgh, particularly in the final 30 years of the 19th century! This was because these trains were involved in numerous collisions and derailments, often leading to loss of life and destruction of ECJS vehicles. Particularly prone to disaster were the 8.30 pm from King's Cross, the 7.30 pm from Edinburgh, and the 10.20/10.30 or 10.40 pm from Edinburgh. The 8.30 pm 'down' suffered at least seven incidents between 1872 and 1884 (followed by the Grantham derailment in 1906), and in the opposite direction the 7.30 pm 'up' suffered six accidents between 1872 and 1876. The late evening departure was involved in five mishaps between 1874 and 1894.

On one occasion, (10th December 1891) the 6.50 pm Aberdeen–Edinburgh, conveying through coaches (including sleeper) for attaching to the 10.40 pm to King's Cross at Edinburgh, collided with a mineral train at Kinghorn and three East Coast vehicles were damaged. The passengers were worked forward to Edinburgh and sent south on a hastily made up special of East Coast stock, including another sleeper, behind NBR 4-4-0 No. 637. This left Waverley station at 1.43 am—two hours behind the main train—but it ran into trouble at Berwick at 2.51 am when it collided with a shunting goods train. I wonder when those unfortunate passengers did reach King's Cross? Another incident north of Edinburgh happended on 3rd October 1893 when the 4.30 am Edinburgh–Aberdeen, conveying East Coast coaches (including sleeping car) from London, was involved in a collision at Inverkeithing.

An unusual accident happened at Selby on 9th August 1890 when an 'up' East Coast sleeping car train made a booked stop in the station, where the 'up' platform is served by a loop which diverges from the 'up' main immediately south of Selby swing bridge. Because the train was too long for the loop the engine was foul of the main line at the front (south) end, and the brake van was foul at the back (north) end, but amply protected by signals—or so it seemed! However, the driver of NER 0-6-0 No. 306, working a Hull-York goods, passed several signals at danger and was all set to run into the rear of the stationary East Coast train when the signalman, warned by an alarm whistle from the engine on a Leeds-Hull passenger train, managed to reverse the points, thus diverting the runaway along the 'up' main. As it ran forward the engine demolished the rear off-side corner of the van standing foul, passed the standing coaches without doing any damage, but then struck the tender of the Great Northern engine at the head of the train. It separated the GN engine (No. 670) from its tender and pushed the engine forward (leaving the tender behind), eventually coming to rest on its side, with the GN engine ahead of it and the GN tender behind it!

The East Coast train at the platform included a Pullman sleeping car, which was undamaged, but not all the Pullmans running in East Coast service were so fortunate as they suffered on a number of occasions:

Date	Location	Accident	Vehicle involved
11-8-1881	Abbey Hill (Edinburgh) (NBR)	Break-away on gradient	Unidentified Pullman
11-12-1882	Essendine (GNR)	Collision	Pullman *Columba*
9-8-1884	Portobello (NBR)	Collision	Unidentified Pullman
9-8-1890	Selby (NER)	Collision	Unidentified Pullman
2-11-1892	Manor House (NER)	Collision	Pullman *India*—destroyed
4-10-1894	Northallerton (NER)	Collision	Pullman *Iona*
10-11-1895	St Neots (GNR)	Derailment and collision	Pullman *Iona*

Accidents Between London and Edinburgh Involving East Coast Night Expresses 1872–1916

Date	Location	Accident	Train	Remarks
3-8-1872	Near Durham	Derailment	8.30 pm down	
16-4-1872	Darlington	Collision	7.30 pm up	
17-9-1872	Newcastle	Collision	9.15 pm down	2 engines, 18 vehicles
24-9-1873	Reston	Collision	8.30 pm down	
6-11-1873	Durham	Collision	8.30 pm down	Court of Inquiry held
21-10-1873	Ferryhill-Bradbury	Collision	7.30 pm up	
11-4-1874	Christon Bank	Derailment	10.40 pm up	Incl. sleeping car
22-7-1874	Chathill	Derailment	7.30 pm up	
1-1-1875	Thirsk	Double collision	7.30 pm up and 8.30 pm down	

Date	Location	Accident	Train	Remarks
17-2-1876	Drem	Derailment	7.30 pm up	
14-4-1876	Corby	Collision	7.30 pm up	
25-3-1877	Morpeth	Derailment	10.30 pm up	NE eng. 901
4-1-1878	Hatfield	Collision	8.30 pm down	Incl. sleeping car
11-8-1881	Edinburgh	Collision	8.30 pm down	2 engines 17 vehicles
11-12-1882	Essendine	Collision	10.20 pm up	
9-8-1884	Portobello	Collision	8.30 pm down	NE engs. 367 and 53
9-8-1890	Selby	Collision	3.30 am up ex-York	NE engs. 306. GN eng. 670
11-12-1891	Berwick	Collision	1.43 am up special	NB eng. 637
2-11-1892	Manor House	Collision	10.30 pm up (2nd part)	NE eng. 178
4-10-1894	Northallerton	Collision	10.40 pm up	NE engs. 905 and 1622
10-11-1895	St Neots	Derailment and collision	11.30 pm down	GN eng. 1007
11-11-1902	Morpeth	Collision	7.45 pm up	NE eng. 2015
20-12-1902	Manors	Derailment	10.50 pm up	NE eng. 2111
19-9-1906	Grantham	Derailment	8.45 pm down	GN eng. 276
9-4-1909	Ouston Junc.	Derailment	11.30 pm down	
13-9-1913	Chevington	Derailment	11.45 pm down	
19-5-1916	Scremerston	Derailment	11.30 pm down	

Not that the daytime trains were accident free! On 14th February 1879 an axle broke on ECJS 4-wheel composite coach No. 17 at Bawtry on the 'up' "Flying Scotchman" (sic). The train was made up of three 6-wheel and five 4-wheel vehicles and the coach concerned cost £25 to repair! Fortunately only one passenger was injured.

At the Board of Trade enquiry Mr Cockshoot, the Superintendent of the Great Northern Railway, stated that the 4-wheel stock was being replaced by 'carriages of the most modern design, and with all the recent improvements', and that this transition would be completed 'within the next few days'. The engine was GNR No. 215.

The Marshall Meadows (near Berwick) derailment on 10th August 1880 also involved the 10 am from Edinburgh, when three ECJS vehicles were 'broken up' and three were 'much damaged'. The value of the destroyed coaches ranged from £289 for a van to £382 for a 1st class, but one vehicle cost only £3 to repair as it suffered only two broken footboards. The engine was NER 2-4-0 No. 178.

At Essendine on 19th January 1881 the 10.15 am from Edinburgh headed by GN 'single' No. 4 ran into the rear of an engine propelling a snowplough. Six ECJS vehicles were damaged but none severely.

In addition to the Marshall Meadows accident the North British suffered a rear-end collision at Kinghorn on 10th December 1891, when the 6.50 pm express from Aberdeen ran into the rear of a mineral train. The passenger train included four East Coast vehicles, of which three were damaged, including a sleeping car No. 153; all were 6-wheel coaches. The engine was North British 4-4-0 No. 642.

Another collision occurred on 3rd October 1893, this time at Inverkeithing, when the 4.30 am from Edinburgh to Aberdeen ran into a goods train which was being shunted out of its way. The passenger train, headed by 4-4-0 No. 37, included three East Coast vehicles, and once again a sleeping car was involved, this time No. 185. However, the most damage was sustained by van No. 145.

A North Eastern engine was involved in the sidelong collision at East Fortune on 1st November 1906, when the 2.20 pm from King's Cross to Edinburgh came into contact with derailed wagons forming part of an 'up' North British goods. The engine was Class R 4-4-0 No. 592, and although it was damaged on its right-hand side, it was the East Coast coaches which suffered most as four had their 'side completely destroyed', and a fifth had its 'side panels damaged'.

Accidents did not cease with the formation of the LNER and the end of the separate East Coast Joint Stock fleet: on 13th February 1923 a high-speed rear-end collision at Retford; on 10th May 1926 a deliberate derailment at Cramlington, and on 25th November 1926 another rear-end collision, this time at Finsbury Park, all involving former ECJS vehicles. The Cramlington and Finsbury Park incidents both involved the 10 am from Edinburgh to King's Cross!

Brake 3rd No. 41 was built at Doncaster in 1920 as a replacement for corridor 3rd No. 41 destroyed in the Burntisland collision on 14th April 1914, but the 1920 vehicle was also destroyed in an accident, this time at Welwyn Garden City on 15th June 1935.

Vehicles which had passed out of East Coast stock and into the various LNER Areas also suffered! In the Castlecary collision on 10th December 1937 corridor 3rd; 31061 (ex-ECJS 72), slightly damaged; 31083 (ex-ECJS 357) was badly damaged and 31090 (ex-ECJS 383) was destroyed.

127

12 Miscellaneous Details

Brakes

In September 1876 discussions took place regarding the fitting of some form of continuous brake to East Coast vehicles and the Smith vacuum brake was favoured by the Great Northern, although the North Eastern said that, 'the subject will require further consideration before the Directors of this Company will decide on its adoption'. In April 1877 the NER agreed to the fitting of sufficient East Coast carriages with this form of brake to work two trains daily between London and Edinburgh, and at the same time called for a report from T. E. Harrison, the company's engineer, on the 'Westinghouse Automatic Pressure Brake' which was to be tried on its own express trains on lines where there was little interchange with other companies. However, within three months it was reported that Mr Stirling (of the Great Northern) was rapidly fitting East Coast stock with the vacuum brake 'with the latest improvements'.

In 1878 Mr Harrison recommended the North Eastern to adopt the Westinghouse brake and this was accepted, 'subject to the necessary use of Smith's vacuum brake for the through Scotch traffic run in connection with the Great Northern Railway, so long as that company continues to use that system'. By the middle of February 1879 138 East Coast vehicles had been fitted with the continuous vacuum brake.

Mr Harrison submitted a lengthy report, again favouring the Westinghouse brake, in April 1879, and mentioned the various improvements he and Mr Westinghouse had made to the equipment during the trials on the North Eastern. His report concluded, 'every day's experience further confirms my views, and I am confident that there is no brake which will beat it in stopping power, in economy of first cost and maintenance, or in certainty of action'.

In June 1880, with the failure to get the Great Northern to accept the Westinghouse brake, T. E. Harrison put forward a plan for fitting coaches with a combined vacuum and Westinghouse brake and his suggestions were sent to the Great Northern for consideration for fitting the gear to all East Coast vehicles. However, it transpired that while the East Coast coaches were being fitted with vacuum brake gear they were receiving only pipes for the Westinghouse brake, so that when North Eastern engines were in charge between York and Edinburgh the Westinghouse brake could only be applied by the driver on the engine or by the guard in his van, with the brake acting only on the engine itself. Consequently when North Eastern engines were in charge the trains had to be worked on the inferior vacuum brake, as they were when Great Northern engines were in charge south of York.

At this time the North British also requested that the East Coast stock should be fitted with the Westinghouse brake, not just piped, and in view of the two-against-one situation it was agreed that this should be done 'if the (GN) Locomotive Engineer is of the opinion that the proposal is practicable'. Note that there is no mention of Mr Harrison's design! In 1882 Mr Stirling submitted his design for dual brakes but nothing was done until November 1883, when Mr Walker of the North British wrote to Mr Oakley, General Manager of the Great Northern, pointing out that the West Coast stock was being fitted with the Westinghouse brake, 'and if the East Coast stock be not fitted with the same brake, I think there can be no question that the Caledonian Company will seize that as another opportunity for delaying the East Coast trains, as Caledonian engines have no other brake'.

In November 1883 it was pointed out that Mr Stirling was prepared to go ahead with fitting the Westinghouse brake as soon as he received the necessary authority to spend approximately £3,000 on equipping about 120 East Coast vehicles, and 17 GN saloons used on East Coast trains, and this was given on 7th December.

In March 1887 it was agreed that a change should be made to the automatic vacuum brake and this was then used side by side with the Westinghouse for 24 years, until in February 1911 it was decided to use only the vacuum brake and a start was made on removing the Westinghouse gear, although it was eventually decided (in February 1913) to retain the air brake on 78 East Coast vehicles of various types (including four Royal Train saloons and vans). In January 1915 it was reported that the Westinghouse brake had been removed from 113 vehicles and that 165 remained to be stripped; of course stock built after the 1911 decision was turned out only with the vacuum brake.

The unsatisfactory state of the braking equipment led to a number of accidents, notably on 11th August 1881 at Abbey Hill Junction (Edinburgh) and on 9th August 1884 at Portobello. In the former the 8.30 pm King's Cross-Edinburgh was being run with the vacuum brake but at Berwick an assistant engine was attached next to the train, so that the engine which had worked the train from Newcastle was then leading. However, the driver of the leading engine could not operate the train brake, which was now under the control of the driver on the second engine. Also at Berwick an unfitted and unpiped fish truck was attached 'inside' the rear van, so that the guard lost control of the vacuum brake. After restarting from a signal check at the west end of Calton Hill Tunnel the rear four vehicles broke away and ran back to collide with a following train; the handbrake in the rear van and another on the Pullman sleeping car were insufficient to bring the vehicles to a stand. The Smith pattern brake, being non-automatic, did not bring the vehicles to a stand when they broke away although, of course, it actually operated on only two of the four vehicles.

At Portobello three years later once again the driver on the leading engine (2-4-0 No. 367) on the 8.30 pm from King's Cross could operate only the brake on his engine, leaving the brakes on the train to be applied by the driver of the assistant engine (2-4-0 No. 53). The driver of No. 367 saw from some 130 yards away a North British engine was about to cross his path and he made every effort to stop, but the driver of the second engine did not see the danger and although he intended to stop at the signal protecting the conflicting movement he misjudged his speed and braking power and over-ran the signal to collide with the North British engine at about 4 mph. Permitting a movement across the path of an approaching train was allowed under the NBR Rules, but it was pointed out at the Board of Trade enquiry that signalmen rarely allowed such a movement to take place because they realised the danger—well illustrated in this case, where the train was booked and signalled to stop for ticket examination and collection. The Inspecting

Officer pressed the North British to alter their Rules so that such a move was expressly forbidden.

The NER and the Straight-sided Stock

J. D. Twinberrow was appointed NER Chief Carriage & Wagon Draughtsman at the end of 1904 and it seems safe to assume that he was largely responsible for the design of the straight-sided stock introduced in the following year for North Eastern, East Coast Joint, and Great Northern & North Eastern Joint services.

Straight-sided matchboard stock had first made its appearance on the NER in 1903 with the Tyneside electric vehicles and the design was also used on the two petrol-electric railcars built in 1903; however, the East Coast coaches were the first to be built for locomotive haulage.

A total of 43 vehicles were built to five different designs for the NER; nine of three different designs for the ECJS; and ten of five different designs for the GN/GE stock. The ECJS coaches were: Corridor brake composites 80, 81, 142, 143, 12-wheel, York, Oct. 1905; Semi-open 1sts, 92, 121, 8-wheel, York, Dec. 1905; Composite sleeping cars, 90, 106, 187, 8-wheel, York, Dec. 1905.

Even before the first matchboard vehicle for the ECJS appeared the Great Northern expressed its disapproval of the design, although this was mainly because of the absence of a sloping roof at the ends.

The brake composites were magnificent vehicles, with a 1st class lavatory next to the brake van, then two 1st class compartments, three 3rd class compartments and a 3rd lavatory at the end. External doors were provided to each compartment and there were three doors on the corridor side. The body was 65 ft 6 in long, with two 12 ft bogies at 44 ft 6 in centres.

These coaches were the first to break the monopoly of clerestory roofs on East Coast bogie vehicles as the Gresley pattern roof did not appear until the following year.

East Coast Rugs and Pillows

Passengers travelling by ordinary and excursion trains, by day or by night, on the East Coast route could hire a rug and/or a pillow at 6d per item, and these could be obtained at the main stations between King's Cross and Edinburgh, and also at Glasgow, Perth, Dundee and Aberdeen.

The pillows collected at the end of a journey could be reissued, using a clean pillow-slip, and the used pillow-slips sent to King's Cross for washing, whereas rugs had to be returned immediately to the issuing station. If a rug had not been returned to the station marked on it within three days 'steps must be taken to trace it, and if not found within a reasonable time a report had to be sent to the District Superintendent'.

Hampers for the conveyance of pillows, pillow-slips and rugs were carried on the 8.45 pm King's Cross–Glasgow; 11.30 pm King's Cross–Aberdeen, 11.45 pm King's Cross–Newcastle, 11.19 pm Newcastle–King's Cross, 10.20 am Edinburgh–King's Cross, 7.35 pm Aberdeen–King's Cross, 9.15 pm Perth–King's Cross and the 9.35 pm Glasgow–King's Cross.

The above instructions were issued in 1905, and when re-issued in 1922 the charge had been increased to 1s 0d per item.

Cost of Constructing Sleeping Car No. 183 at York, 1902

		£	s	d
Materials	Timber	230	8	1
	Iron work	328	18	6
	Springs	47	15	7
	Sundries	616	12	7
	Paints	42	19	4
Special Fittings	Brakes	48	17	3
	Electric bells	9	13	0
	Gas fittings	102	11	8
	Heating apparatus	36	8	7
	Vestibules	91	5	0
Wheels	6 pairs @ £26 1s 6d	156	9	0
	Total Materials	1,711	18	7
Wages	Timber, setting out	6	10	0
	Timber, machining	49	3	8
	Timber, Carrying	9	0	0
	Ironwork, smithing	2	5	11
	Ironwork, machining	8	14	1
	Ironwork, fitting	28	5	8
	Brass work, finishing	8	12	9
	Building	80	15	1
	Finishing compartments	206	19	5
	Kitchen	3	5	6
	Lavatories	21	13	8
	Trimming	29	9	6
	Painting	90	19	7
Special Fittings	Brakes	4	18	11
	Electric bell	1	6	9
	Gas fittings	7	0	0
	Heating apparatus	5	5	10
	Vestibules	4	0	0
	Wood carving	2	0	0
	Total Wages	561	15	4 (sic)
Shop Expenses = 50% Wages		280	17	8
	Total Cost in Carriage Works	2,554	11	7

Painting Specifications

Vehicles built for the ECJS differed in minor details according to the works where they were built. For instance on a series of brake vans built at Doncaster and York in 1914 the GN built vehicles had 3 ft 7 in wheels and the NE built ones had 3 ft 6 in; the GN springs were 4 ft 6 in long, with eight 4 in × $\frac{1}{2}$ in plates, whereas the NE springs were 5 ft long, with an unspecified number of plates $3\frac{1}{2}$ in × $\frac{1}{2}$ in.

However, it was in the field of preparation and painting that there were the most differences due, no doubt, to the long established practices at the two works:

Roof Boards – GN Build To have one coat of lead colour, all screw holes to be filled up with white lead putty, then to have a layer of thick white lead and boiled oil applied with a stiff brush. The raw canvas to be placed on this, tightly stretched, nailed down all round, to be well sleekered down to work the lead through the canvas, and then to be left 14 days to dry hard.

Roof Boards – NE Build To have one coat of slate colour (zinc), all screw holes to be filled up with ordinary oil putty, and another coat of slate colour put on. One coat of stiff jointing paste put on, and the raw canvas placed on this, tightly stretched, nailed on and well rubbed down. Two or three days afterwards to have one coat of jointing paste thinned down with turpentine, then allowed to stand until brought into the Paint Shop.

Painting Body The same painting specification applied at both works. The body to be finished varnished teak. To be given one coat of Japan gold size and one coat of preparing varnish before outside mouldings are fixed. The mouldings to be painted on back, fixed on the body, and then to be given one coat of Japan gold size, and one coat of preparing varnish. A second coat of preparing varnish to be given, and whilst wet to be well rubbed into the grain of the wood with rock pumice stone. When dry a third coat of preparing varnish to be given all over, but the sides only to be rubbed in wet as before.

All holes to be stopped up and sand papered. A fourth coat of preparing varnish to be given. When thoroughly hard to be faced down with rock pumice stone. The screw holes in door hinges and sill plates to be puttied up and painted teak colour. The undersides of pitch pine cant rails in doorways to be stained teak. The mouldings to be picked out with size, coloured with lemon chrome, and gilded with ribbon gold leaf. The gold to be pencil varnished, and when dry, fine lined with vermilion on both edges. The transfers and lettering to be put on. The whole to be given two coats of preparing varnish, and two coats of finished body varnish. When dry to be flattened down with two coats of finishing body varnish.
Bogies – GN Build To be well cleaned off, and given one coat of lead colour, and one coat of oil black.
Bogies – NE Build To be well cleaned off and given one coat of red anti-corrosive paint on the inside, and one coat of oil black, and one of black Japan outside.
Roof Outside – GN Build When canvas is hard to be given one coat of white lead paint, and left to get thoroughly dry.
Roof Outside – NE Build To have two coats of white zinc paint. When thoroughly dry to be well sandpapered down and given another coat of white zinc paint, and lastly one coat of white protective paint.
Roof Inside – GN Build All knots to have one coat of knotting, to be given one coat of white lead paint. All holes to be then puttied up and given two coats of light blue paint, including the three lining boards below the cant rail.
Roof Inside – NE Build All knots to have one coat of knotting, and roof to be given one coat of zinc white paint. All holes to be then puttied up, and the roof given another coat of zinc white paint, and one finishing coat of Kingston flat white.
Interior – GN Build All knots to have one coat of knotting, then one coat of white lead paint. All holes to be then puttied up and given two coats of fawn colour. Brake wheel and column to have one coat of lead colour and one coat of black Japan. Heaters to have one coat of black.
Interior – NE Build All knots to have one coat of knotting, and then one coat of white zinc paint. All holes to be then puttied up, and two coats of fawn colour put on. Brake wheel and column to have one coat black colour and one coat of black Japan. Heaters to have one coat of silverette galvanising paint.

Automatic Couplers

The automatic coupler was developed in America in the 1880s and a multitude of compatible variations appeared, usually differing only in the means of securing and/or releasing the movable knuckle. Thus the release mechanism could be operated from above, from the side, or from below, using chains or levers. The Great Northern and the East Coast (and later the North Eastern) at first favoured the Gould coupler, manufactured by the Gould Coupler Co. of Depew, New York, and couplers of this pattern were included in the designs of the new stock for the 10 am trains submitted by Mr Howlden on 29th July 1895.

It has not been possible to establish how many vehicles were fitted initially but confirmation that these couplers were in use comes from instructions dated 1st January 1898:

Instructions for Working New East Coast Bogie Stock

"This stock is fitted with Gould's vestibules and couplings, and movable side buffers. The Gould couplings with the vestibules are made to act both as buffers and couplers. The couplings will engage and couple automatically on being pushed together. They are released by pulling one of the chains which lead from the side of each coupling. This frees the catch and allows the jaws of the coupler to open. Before coupling together two of these carriages by means of the centre couplings the side buffers must be in the fixed short position.

To couple, it is only necessary to push the vehicles together, when the couplings and vestibules will connect automatically. The brake pipes, heating pipes &c must be connected afterwards. Before putting back to couple together, the centre coupling of one of the carriages required to be coupled together must have the coupling open, the coupling on the other carriage being closed.

To uncouple, disconnect the brake pipes, heating pipes, electric and cord communication, then pull the handle or lever which is attached to the chain near the buffer in order to disconnect the centre coupling. The handle must be put back as soon as the coupling has been disconnected and the split pin put in its place to secure it. The handle must not be touched except when required to free the couplings. If the handle or lever will not move, extra force must not be used, but the driver requested to back slightly. This will enable the lever to be drawn back without difficulty."

Instructions dated October 1901 varied slightly with regard to the Gould coupler, and by then both the Gould and buckeye were in use:

1: Automatic couplers will not join when the coaches are standing on an 'S' curve.
2: When joining two Gould couplers both should be open.
3: When joining a Gould coupling to a buckeye the Gould should be closed and the buckeye open.
4: When joining two buckeye couplings one should be closed and the other open.

Instructions for using the Gould couplings last appeared in 1908, presumably by which time they had almost all been replaced by the buckeye pattern.

As is well known the buckeye coupling became the East Coast, and later LNER main line, standard and it has proved its worth in many accidents, holding coaches in line and preventing coaches from over-riding one another.

The Pullman type gangways on East Coast vehicles could, of course, only be used on stock fitted with buckeye couplings as there was no actual means of connecting together the two gangways. They were held together under the compression obtained when the two vehicles were brought close enough together to actuate the buckeye coupler. The faceplates were larger than on the British Standard gangways used on screw-coupled stock, where the two gangways were physically fastened together, and although Pullman and British Standard gangways were compatible this could only be achieved by an adaptor which allowed the two types to be locked together.

Seating Arrangements

East Coast open vehicles were designed to seat three passengers on one side of the gangway and one on the other, arranged in bays seating eight. However, in 1907 a general instruction reduced this to 2 + 1, making bays of six seats.

Carriage diagrams often included a figure for the normal seating capacity and a lesser figure 'when dining'. This applied to 3rd class compartment stock with three-a-side seating, where the folding tables could accommodate only the window seat and centre seat passengers, and not the corridor seat travellers. Thus a 7-compartment corridor 3rd would normally accommodate 42 passengers, but only 28 when dining.

Seating in 1st class 6-wheel non-corridor stock was three-a-side, with two intermediate arm-rests, and in corridor compartments two-a-side with centre arm-rests. However, on corridor composite 1st and open 3rds 301/2/3 the 1st class seating in the compartments was three on each side, but with only one arm-rest per side, dividing the seats into 2 + 1.

Ambulance Trains

In 1917 two ambulance trains were sent to Dover for transporting the injured to hospitals throughout the country; these were made up of GN and ECJS vehicles, the latter being:

Ambulance Train No. 24: twin compo 204 + 204A; 6-wheel kitchen car No. 198; 6-wheel 3rd No. 210.

Ambulance Train No. 25: twin compo 205 + 205A; 6-wheel kitchen car No. 201; 6-wheel 3rds 172, 173, 179 and 209.

All the vehicles were returned to the Great Northern and the East Coast vehicles were reinstated in the ECJS fleet; however, the 6-wheel coaches were disposed of in September to October 1922, and the articulated twins eventually passed to the Great Northern Section of the newly formed LNER.

In the later stages of World War I dining car services were withdrawn and in December 1917 the four 1914 dining cars 190–3 were stored at Battersby (North Yorkshire) in the 3-road locomotive shed which had not been used for some 20 years.

Fish-Belly Underframes

Three NER 8-wheel designs were fitted with substantial 'fish-belly' girder underframes carrying 56 ft 6 in bodies: Dgm. 64 Sleeping cars 165–170, built York 1906; Dgm. 63 Sleeping car 120, built York June 1907; Dgm. 74 Composite sleeping car 231, built York December 1907.

In 1924/5 these frames were replaced by plain underframes to Drawing 11594, but there is an unexplained discrepancy; in August 1923, according to one copy of the Diagram Book, the body of sleeping car No. 120 was placed on the frame of brake van No. 6, and the body from the van placed on the frame of No. 120. However,

a subsequent entry states that the fish-belly underframe of 120 was replaced by a normal frame in September 1924—and yet the old frame is recorded as having gone to brake van 6 a year earlier.

The two 12-wheel Royal Saloons, one built at York and one at Doncaster, both had fish-belly underframes, which they have retained to the present day.

From 1911 8 ft 6 in wheel base compound bolster bogies were used on East Coast vehicles, and later most of the elliptical roof passenger stock built between 1906 and 1910 and their 8 ft bogies replaced by the new pattern. Most of these were changed between 1923 and 1927, although a few were not changed until the 1930s.

Carriage Roster

A carriage roster headed EAST COAST RAILWAYS: THROUGH CARRIAGE WORKING was issued at intervals and this dealt with all ECJS coaches working between London and Edinburgh, but did not normally include the GN/NE Joint coaches on London to Newcastle workings. However, where GN/NE stock was included in the make-up of a train conveying London to Edinburgh vehicles then the GN/NE coaches did appear. This gave rise to an odd situation on the 10.36 am King's Cross to Edinburgh and Glasgow, which conveyed a GN/NE pantry 3rd and a GN/NE kitchen 1st between London and Newcastle, but these were replaced by a NE composite dining car and a NE brake composite from Newcastle to Edinburgh. This same train left King's Cross with two GN non-vestibule coaches for Cromer (detached at Peterborough), picked up three Midland coaches from Bristol for the York-Newcastle section, and collected two NE vehicles for Alnmouth at Newcastle. The detaching and attaching operations at Newcastle required a 25-minute stop.

An unexpected entry in the Working book is the 8.55 am Leeds to Glasgow which, in British Railways days was christened "The North Briton"; this was made up of seven NE corridor coaches, and its inclusion was due to the fact that from York it conveyed a single London-Edinburgh brake van, which had left King's Cross at 5.5 am.

In the Carriage Working Book the types of ECJS vehicles to be used were denoted by 'Class'. For instance the 10.50 pm from Edinburgh comprised nine ECJS vehicles and a NB brake van:

Class in Carriage Working Book	Page in Diagram Book	Accommodation Seats 1st	3rd	Berths
45	36	–	–	–
98	49	–	36	–
73	22	–	48	–
347	47A	8	12	–
165	64	–	–	10
146	70A	–	12	6
90	69	–	12	6
246	6	12	24	–
262	50	–	24	–
		20	168	22

The tare weight of the train was 306 tons 12 cwt, giving the weight per passenger of 1.46 tons! The practice of denoting the type of vehicle by 'Class' was continued by the LNER and was still in use in 1939.

1938 Publicity

In 1938, in connection with the introduction of new sets of coaches for the "Flying Scotsman" trains, the LNER, as a publicity move, restored to working order the GN Stirling 'single' No. 1. For years this engine was stored at King's Cross shed, until it ran under its own steam in the Stockton & Darlington Centenary Procession held on 2nd July 1925, followed by static display at Stooperdale. It then became available for the Railway Museum at York, where it remained undisturbed until 13th June 1938, when it was taken out of the Museum and towed to Doncaster Works for a hurried overhaul, ready for working a special Press special from King's Cross to Stevenage on 30th June. There the invited passengers transferred to a modern East Coast train headed by A4 Pacific No. 4498 *Sir Nigel Gresley*.

To accompany No. 1 a set of 6-wheel coaches was formed and repainted in ECJS livery. One of these was No. 92, originally a 4-compartment 1st with two lavatories, built at Doncaster in 1884 and Dgm. 41 in the 1903 Diagram Book. It was taken over by the GNR in 1905, when it became No. 3027, and it was subsequently used on branch line services.

For the remainder of 1938 the engine and its vintage train of coaches was put on display at stations on the LNER system, as far north as Edinburgh. They also worked public excursions, until the engine was returned to York Museum in January 1939. Unfortunately none of the coaches survived.

Survivors

In the 1970s a determined effort was made by the NER Coach Group to identify a number of ECJS bodies 'grounded' in Yorkshire; most were derelict after being neglected for some 50 years, but one at Easingwold was still lived in until 1977. This was No. 107, a Dgm. 70 composite sleeping car, with six berths and two 3rd class compartments; it had been condemned in July 1927. When vacated it was purchased for preservation but its present whereabouts are unknown to me.

However, one vehicle that has already received attention is No. 189, a Dgm. 25 dining saloon and one of the four hurriedly built at Doncaster in 1894 to replace the 'too good' cars designed by the NER for the first East Coast dining car trains. No. 189 was condemned in February 1927 and after more than 50 years it was purchased by Mr M. Ford of Holme-on-Spalding-Moor, who has managed to keep it under cover so that restoration work could go ahead. At the time of writing this is well in hand and almost complete. The same enthusiast also has the body, alas in two parts, of one of the 'too good' cars replaced by No. 189 above. This is No. 194. When East Coast Nos 194–7 were sold to the North Eastern in November 1896 196 and 197 were rebuilt at York as 1st class saloons, provided with pantries, fitted with clerestory roofs, and renumbered 2647 and 2646. When they were returned to the East Coast fleet in May 1898 they became EC 194 and 195.

The roofs of both 189 and 194 deserve mention; the former was built in the period when the standard East Coast clerestory was just evolving, and on this vehicle the clerestory does not slope down at the ends. On 194 the roof was originally a low curved type, and the clerestory with which it is now fitted was added during the period when the coach was owned by the North Eastern in 1896–8.

Also, there are the three former Royal Train vehicles, already mentioned: King's Saloon No. 395, Queen's Saloon No. 396 and brake van No. 109 (ex-82), all in the National Collection, as is 3rd class No. 12, while No. 377, another 3rd, is at the Colne Valley Railway, Essex.

No. 12. A 3rd class vehicle of 1898 undergoing restoration at the Steamtown Railway Centre, Carnforth in June 1985, on behalf of the National Railway Museum, York.

(Courtesy NRM, York)

13 Diagram Books and Stock Lists

A printed stock list of East Coast vehicles was issued at irregular intervals, usually as a result of a request for a new issue at an East Coast committee meeting; this gave the vehicle number, type of accommodation, arrangement of compartments, maker and year built. Amendments between printed lists were circulated by duplicated notices. Stock lists known are dated November 1881, 13th October 1891, August 1893, 1st March 1895, and September 1913, and similar details can be obtained from the 1st April 1903 and 1st January 1909 Diagram Books.

An 'Album of Plans of East Coast Stock' was in use in the 1890s but the date of issue is not known. On 1st April 1903 a large hardback Diagram Book was issued, containing 59 diagrams each 24 in × 12½ in, covering 19 types of 6-wheel, 14 types of 8-wheel, and 26 types of 12-wheel coaches and vans, drawn to a scale of ¼ in = 1 ft. At first amendments were issued on similar size sheets, utilising the page numbers between 1 and 59 with a letter 'A' suffix, but supplementary sheets issued from 1906 were 16½ in × 9 in and mostly drawn to a scale of $\frac{3}{16}$ in = 1 ft. There were exceptions, however, notably page 28A covering the two coaches returned from the NER in 1906, Nos 354 and 355; for some reason this drawing is to an indeterminate scale—and the horizontal and vertical scales differ, producing an odd-looking vehicle which appears as if it has been compressed lengthways!

The 1909 Diagram Book, another hardback volume, used the $\frac{3}{16}$ in scale drawings throughout and contained pages 1 to 82, although pages 81 and 82 covered the two Royal saloons 395 and 396 and were not issued generally. Only in a few instances did the same type of vehicle appear on the same page in the two books; usually there was no relationship between the two. Supplementary sheets were issued for new and modified vehicles, usually with a suffix letter (as far as 'E' for page 39) but occasionally blank numbers were re-used (i.e. 59 and 68, two new designs first produced in 1922). However, it must be stressed that it was not ECJS practice to refer to vehicles by their Diagram Number; usually they were referred to by the page number in the Diagram Book, and at other times by the lowest number in a series of coaches of the same type. In this work, for ease of reference, the Diagram Book page number has usually been quoted as the Diagram Number.

In the 1909 Diagram Book the various types of vehicles were grouped together under page numbers:

Pages 1–13	Composites
Pages 14–34	Thirds
Pages 35–42	Brake vans
Page 43	Brake first
Pages 44–47	Brake composites
Pages 48–55	Brake thirds
Pages 56–61	Firsts
Pages 62–68	Sleeping cars
Pages 69–74	Sleeping composites
Pages 75–77	Dining saloons
Pages 78 & 79	Dining composites
Page 80	Kitchen cars
Pages 81 & 82	Royal saloons

The subsequent designs, or modifications to existing designs, were denoted by a letter suffix and comprised:

Page	Type	Built	Rebuilt	
2A	Composite	1911	—	
2B	Composite	1914	—	
3A	Composite	1914	—	
11A	Open third	1900	1913	From p. 11
19A	Third	1903	1913	From p. 19
29A	Dining saloon	1914	—	
31A	Third	1921	—	
34A	Brake van	1910	—	
39A	Brake van	1910	—	
39B	Brake van	1914	—	
39C	Brake van	1921	—	
43A	First	1900	1913	From p. 43 See Note
47A	Brake composite site	1911	—	
49A	Brake third	1908	1914	From p. 49
49B	Brake third	1920	—	
56A	First	1903	1914	From p. 56
57A	First	1905	1914	From p. 57
63A	Sleeping car	1910	1921	From p. 70A See Note
64A	Sleeping car	1905	1921	From p. 69
70A	Sleeping composite	1910	1921	To p. 63A See Note
75A	Dining saloon	1914	—	
76A	Dining first	1900	1914	From p. 76
77A	Dining first	1902	1914	From p. 77
80A	Kitchen car	1914	—	

Note

Some vehicles differed between the heading on the actual page in the Diagram Book and the description in the Index. For instance p. 25 was headed Dining Saloon and thus should have been included in the pages numbered in the seventies, but in the Index these vehicles were treated as 3rds and correctly allocated a page number in the twenties.

When the three p. 43 brake 1sts were altered to full 1sts in 1913 they became p. 43A and thus were out of place in their new form. However, a later change of type was allocated a new page number in its correct series; this covered the four sleeping composites built in 1910 (70A) which, when altered to full sleepers in 1921, became p. 63A in their correct series.

In some examples only one of a series of vehicles was modified, but in others all the vehicles were altered and in the latter case the page number became blank. For instance the two Dgm. 57 vehicles built in 1905 were altered to Dgm. 57A in 1914 and p. 57 became blank.

East Coast Joint Stock Diagrams (1903 and 1909)

Diagram No. 1909	1903	Type	Wheels	Length	Roof	Numbers	Built		Remarks
1	1	Semi-corridor composite	6	37'6"	—	1–10, 26, 129	Doncaster	1893	Note 1
2	2	Corridor composite	8	53'6"	Clerestory	17, 18, 20, 21, 22 25, 28	York	1898–1900	Note 1
2A	—	Corridor composite	8	58'6"	Elliptical	1, 2, 3, 4	Doncaster	1911	Originally Dgm. 2B
2B	—	Corridor composite	8	61'6"	Elliptical	76, 77	Doncaster	1914	
3	5	Corridor composite	6	37'2"	—	60	Doncaster	1893	Note 1
3A	—	Corridor composite	8	58'6"	Elliptical	78, 79	York	1914	
4	7	Corridor composite	6	37'0"	—	87, 122, 123	Doncaster	1883/4	Note 2
5	—	Articulated twin compo.	12	76'1"	—	202 + 202A, 203 + 203A, 204 + 204A, 205 + 205A	Doncaster	Rebuilt 1907	Note 3
6	11, 12	Corridor composite	12	65'6"	Clerestory	246–50	Doncaster	1896	
6A	8	Corridor composite	12	65'6"	Clerestory	247	Doncaster	1896	Converted from Dgm. 6
—	8	Composite	6	36'0"	—	126/7/8/30–7	Doncaster	1888	
—	9	Composite	12	64'0"	Clerestory	196 & 197	York	1902	Note 4
10	14	Corridor composite	12	65'0"	Clerestory	292, 293, 294	York	1900	
11	15	Open composite	12	65'2"	Clerestory	296 & 297	York	1900	Also 295 destroyed in Grantham accident 1906
11A	—	Open third	12	65'2"	Clerestory	296 & 297	York	1900	From Dgm. 11
12	16	Corridor composite	12	65'6"	Clerestory	298, 299, 300	York	1900	
13	17	Corridor composite	12	65'2"	Clerestory	301, 302, 303	York	1900	
14	18	Corridor third	8	55'0"	Clerestory	11, 12, 13	York	1898	
15	17	Open third	8	55'0"	Clerestory	14, 15, 16, 67, 68 270, 271, 272	York	1898–1902	Note 5
16	17A	Corridor third	8	53'6"	Elliptical	27 & 29	York	1906	
17	18B	Corridor third	8	53'6"	Elliptical	30–33	Doncaster	1906	
18	18C	Corridor third	8	53'6"	Elliptical	34–37	Doncaster	1906	
19	19A	Corridor third	8	53'6"	Clerestory	38–43, 55–59	Doncaster	1903	Note 6
19A	—	Corridor third	8	53'6"	Clerestory	58	Doncaster	1903	Reb. from Dgm. 19 (Enlarged lavatory)
20	20	Corridor third	6	37'2"	—	44, 155–164, 174–178, 180	Doncaster	1889–91	Note 7
21	29	Corridor third	12	63'5¼"	Clerestory	319, 320, 321	Doncaster	1900	
22	22A	Corridor third	8	58'6"	Elliptical	73, 74, 75, 96, 375–386	Doncaster	1907	Note 8
23	21A	Corridor third	8	53'6"	Clerestory	93, 94, 99, 114, 116, 138–141	York	1903	
24	24	Corridor third	6	37'2"	—	63, 163, 171, 172, 173, 179	Doncaster	1891–1894	Note 9
25	57	Dining saloon (third)	8	52'6"	Clerestory	188, 189, 222, 223	Doncaster	1894	Modified 1909 (Seating reduced and pantry added) 211 & 212 later became part of articulated twin
26	25	Corridor third	6	37'6"	—	208–212	Oldbury C&W	1893	
27	26	Corridor third	12	63'5¼"	Clerestory	251, 253, 255	Doncaster	1896	
28	27	Open third	12	65'5¼"	Clerestory	252, 254, 256	Doncaster	1896	
29	28	Open third with pantry	12	65'6"	Clerestory	304, 305, 306	York	1900	
29A	—	Dining saloon (third)	8	58'6"	Elliptical	192, 193	Doncaster	1914	Relettered RESTAURANT CAR, and eventually reclassified Open 3rd
30	58	Dining saloon (third)	12	64'5¾"	Clerestory	313, 314, 315	Doncaster	1900	
31	23	Open third with pantry	8	55'0"	Clerestory	64, 65, 66, 95, 273, 274, 275	York	1899–1902	Note 10

Notes

1: Nos 26, 60 and 129 replaced vehicles destroyed in Thirsk accident 2nd November 1892.

2: Proposal to convert Nos 87 and 123 to articulated twin deferred.

3: 6-wheel 1sts 202, 203, 204 and 205 were paired with 6-wheel 3rds 206, 211, 212 and 213. Originally each portion retained its own number but they later became 202 + 202A, 203 + 203A, 204 + 204A, and 205 + 205A.

4: To NER 3498 and 3499 in Nov. 1904 but returned to ECJS in February 1906 as 354 and 355 (Dgm. 33).

5: GN Section 41805 restored as ECJS 12 for King's Cross Centenary Exhibition October 1952.

6: No. 41 damaged beyond repair at Burntisland 14th April 1914 and replaced by Brake 3rd No. 41 to Dgm. 49B.

7: No. 163 destroyed in Thirsk accident 2nd November 1892 and replaced by No. 163 to Dgm. 24.

8: No 383 (as Southern Scottish Area 31090) destroyed in Castlecary accident 10th December 1937.

9: No. 163 replaced vehicle with same number destroyed in Thirsk accident 2nd November 1892.

10: Originally with full width attendant's compartment restricting through access but modified with pantry allowing side corridor.

Dia.		Type	No. of Compts.	Length	Roof	Running Nos.	Built at	Date	Remarks
32	—	Corridor third	8	53'6"	Elliptical	165, 171, 177, 178, 180, 206	York	1921	
33	28A	Open third	12	65'6"	Clerestory	336–341	York	1903	
34	18A	Corridor third	8	58'6"	Clerestory	354 & 355	York	1902	Note 11
34A	—	Brake van	8	56'6"	Elliptical	24, 69–72, 207, 356–374	York	1906/7	207 replacement for six wheel 207 destroyed in Grantham accident
35	32A	Brake van	8	56'6"	Elliptical	5, 6, 7	York	1910	Note 12.
36	30A	Brake van	8	56'6"	Clerestory	19, 133–137	Cowlairs	1905/6	Originally Dgm. 34B
37	30	Brake van	6	29'0"	—	45–48, 50, 52, 53, 54, 82, 83, 85, 100–103, 111	Cowlairs	1903	Note 13
38	32B	Brake van	8	56'6"	Elliptical	See Note 15	Doncaster	1883–1890	Notes 13 and 14
39		Brake van	8	56'6"	Elliptical	82	Doncaster	1908	Note 16
39A	—	Brake van	8	56'6"	Elliptical	126, 127, 128, 130, 131, 132	Doncaster	1906–8	Note 13. Used in Royal train
39B	—	Brake van	8	56'6"	Elliptical	8, 9, 10, 26, 129	Doncaster	1910	Notes 13 & 17. No. 132 to Dgm. 38 for Royal Train
39C	—	Brake van	8	56'6"	Elliptical	152–157	York	1914	Note 13. Originally Dgm. 39B
39E	—	Brake van	8	56'6"	Elliptical	7, 44, 158, 160, 161, 164, 175	York	1914–16	Note 13
40	31	Brake van	6	32'0"	—	214, 218, 219, 128, 144, 145	Doncaster	1921	Note 13
41	32	Brake van	6	32'0"	Clerestory	145	Doncaster	1922	Note 13
42	33	Brake van	8	46'6"	Elliptical	51, 224–7, 257, 258	Doncaster	1922	Note 13. From Dgm. 39C for Royal Train
43	34	Corridor brake first	12	61'0"	Clerestory	295, 260, 261	York	1893–6	No. 51 replacement for No. 51 lost at Thirsk.
43A	40B	Corridor first	12	61'0"	Clerestory	289, 290, 291	Cowlairs	1896	Note 13
44	40C	Corridor composite brake	12	65'4 1/4"	Clerestory	307, 308, 309	York	1901	Altered to Dgm. 43A
45	10, 12	Corridor composite brake	12	65'6"	Elliptical	307, 308, 309	York	1900	Matchboard sides
46	40A	Corridor composite brake	12	65'6"	Clerestory	23	Doncaster	1900	Originally corridor composite with luggage locker.
47	—	Corridor composite brake	12	61'0"	Clerestory	80, 81, 142, 143	Doncaster	1903	Note 18. Rebuilt from brake 3rd.
47A	—	Corridor composite brake	8	61'6"	Elliptical	239–245	Doncaster	1911	Replacement. Damaged at Retford 13-2-1923 and Condemned 5-23.
48	34A	Brake third	6	33'10 1/2"	—	342–351	Doncaster	1883	
49	—	Brake third	8	58'6"	Elliptical	347	Doncaster	1908/9	6 compartments.
49A	—	Brake third	8	58'6"	Elliptical	76, 77, 78, 79, 80, 81, 142, 143	Doncaster	1908/9	From Dgm. 49. 3 compts.
49B	—	Brake third	8	58'6"	Elliptical	97, 98, 387–394	Doncaster	1920	Replacement for No. 41 destroyed at Burntisland 14-4-1914. Dgm. 19
50	35	Brake third	12	61'1 5/8"	Clerestory	97, 388	Doncaster	1896/7	Corridor on opposite side from that shown in Dgm.
51	36	Brake third	12	61'1 5/8"	Clerestory	41	Doncaster	1897	
52	37	Brake third	12	61'0"	Clerestory	262, 263, 264	Cowlairs	1900/2	
53	38	Brake third	12	61'0"	Clerestory	265, 266, 267, 280, 281, 282	Cowlairs	1901/2	
54	39	Brake third	12	61'1 5/8"	Clerestory	328, 329 / 283–8, 330, 331 / 322, 324, 326	Doncaster	1902	

11: Originally ECJS Nos 196 and 197 (Dgm. 9 in 1903 Dgm. Book) but to NER in 1904 and returned 1906 as ECJS 354 & 355. See Note 4.

12: Nos 5 and 6 renumbered 11 and 12 in Van stock. No. 7 destroyed in Burntisland accident 14th April 1914 and replacement built to Dgm. 39B.

13: See Table of van renumberings.

14: No. 82 destroyed at Grantham 19th September 1906.

15: Nos 46A, 47A, 48A, 49, 50A, 51, 52A, 53A, 54A, 82, 83A, 84, 85A, 100A, 101A, 102A, 110, 112, 144, 145, and 214–221 built Craven 1893.

16: No. 51 destroyed at Thirsk 2 November 1892 and No. 49 destroyed at Montrose 3rd December 1892. No. 82 destroyed at Grantham 19th September 1906.

17: No. 128 destroyed in accident between Finsbury Park and Holloway 1st January 1920.

18: No. 347 destroyed by fire at Inveresk Junction, Wallyford, 6th May 1909 and replacement built to Dgm. 47A.

Diagram No. 1909	1903	Type	Wheels	Length	Roof	Numbers	Built		Remarks
55	40	Brake third	12	61'1⅝"	Clerestory	323, 325, 327	Doncaster	1902	Reb. to Dgm. 56A 1914
56	41A	Semi-open first	8	53'6"	Clerestory	86, 88, 89, 91	York	1903	From Dgm. 56
56A	—	Corridor first	8	53'6"	Clerestory	86, 88, 89, 91	York	1903	Matchboard sides
57	41B	Semi-open first	8	53'6"	Elliptical	92 and 121	York	1905	From Dgm. 57 1914
57A	—	Corridor first	8	53'6"	Elliptical	92 and 121	York	1905	Note 19
58	—	Corridor first	8	58'6"	Elliptical	122 and 295	Doncaster	1908	
59	51	Dining car first	8	46'0"	—	190, 191, 193	Lancaster C&W	1893	
59	—	Corridor first	8	61'6"	Elliptical	49, 60, 87, 123 196, 353	Doncaster	1922	Nos. 196 and 353 replaced vehicles sold to NBR in 1913. Note 20.
60	52	Dining car first	8	46'0"	—	192	Lancaster C&W	1893	To articulated twin
61	42	Corridor first	6	37'6"	—	203, 204	Gloucester C&W	1893	
62	44	Sleeping car	12	53'6"	Clerestory	104/5/9/17/20/4/5 183–6, 232/3, 276–9	York	1899–1901	Note 21
63	—	Sleeping car	8	56'6"	Elliptical	120	York	1907	Note 22
63A	47B	Sleeping car	8	56'6"	Elliptical	146, 148, 150, 151	York	1910	From Dgm. 70A 1921
64	—	Sleeping car	8	56'6"	Elliptical	165–70	York	1906	From Dgm. 69 1921
64A	—	Sleeping car	8	55'0"	Elliptical	187	York	1905	Matchboard sides.
65	45	Sleeping car	8	52'0"	Clerestory	234	York	1895	First ECJS vehicle built at York
66	46	Sleeping car	8	53'6"	Clerestory	235–8	York	1896	
67	47	Sleeping car	8	55'0"	Clerestory	268 and 269	York	1897	
68	43	Sleeping car	8	44'0"	—	90A, 106A, 187A	Lancaster C&W	1893	
68	—	Sleeping car	12	113'6"	Elliptical	181 and 181A	Doncaster	1922	Later No. 1181 and 1182 Matchboard sides. No. 187 converted to Dgm. 64A 1921
69	47A	Sleeping car composite	8	55'0"	Elliptical	90, 106, 187	York	1905	
70	48	Sleeping car composite	12	55'0"	Clerestory	107 and 108	York	1901	To Dgm. 63A 1921
70A	—	Sleeping car	8	56'6"	Elliptical	146, 148, 150, 151	York	1910	
71	49	Sleeping car	6	36'5"	—	146, 148, 150–4, 181, 182	Doncaster	1889–1892	
72	50	Sleeping car composite	8	53'6"	Clerestory	147 and 149	York	1897	Note 23
73	50A	Sleeping car composite	12	55'0"	Clerestory	228, 229, 230, 231	York	1903	Note 24
74	—	Sleeping car composite	8	56'6"	Elliptical	231	York	1907	Note 25
75	53	Dining saloon & kitchen	8	46'0"	Clerestory	194 and 195	Oldbury C&W	1893	Note 26
75A	—	Dining saloon first	8	58'6"	Elliptical	190 and 191	Doncaster	1914	
76	54	Dining saloon first	12	62'0½"	Clerestory	310, 311, 312	Doncaster	1900	Conv. to Dgm. 76A
76A	—	Dining saloon first	12	62'0½"	Clerestory	310, 311, 312	Doncaster	1900	Conv. from Dgm. 76 by adding 2 seats.
77	55	Dining saloon first	12	62'0½"	Clerestory	332–5	Doncaster	1902	Conv. to Dgm. 77A
77A	—	Dining saloon first	12	62'0½"	Clerestory	332–5	Doncaster	1902	Conv. from Dgm. 77 by adding 2 seats.
78	55A	Dining car composite	12	64'2½"	Clerestory	196, 197, 352, 353	Doncaster	1905	196 and 353 sold to NBR 1913
79	56	Dining car composite	12	63'8½"	Clerestory	316, 317, 318	Doncaster	1900	
80	59	Kitchen car	6	34'0"		198, 199, 200, 201	Birmingham C&W	1893	For first East Coast dining car trains
80A	—	Kitchen car	8	53'6"	Elliptical	211, 212, 213	York	1914	
81	—	Royal saloon	12	67'0"	Elliptical	395	Doncaster	1908	

19: Both replacements for vehicles lost in Grantham accident 19th September 1906.

20: No. 49 (as 149) damaged in deliberate derailment at Cramlington 10th May 1926.

21: No. 120 destroyed in Grantham accident 19th September 1906.

22: Replacement for above.

23: Replacement for Nos 147 and 149 destroyed at St Neots in November 1895.

24: No. 231 destroyed in Grantham accident 19th September 1906.

25: Replacement for above.

26: Originally ECJS but sold to NER 1896 and returned (fitted with clerestory roof) in 1897.

Composite Stock List

No.	Dgm.	Built		Type	Wheels	Roof	Cond.	To Section or Area		Re-No.	Note
1	1	Don	1893	Semi-corr. compo	6	–					
1	2B/2A	Don	1911	Composite	8	E	–	NE	3/37	2315	
2	1	Don	1893	Semi-corr. compo	6	–					
2	2B/2A	Don	1911	Composite	8	E	–	SS	3/36	31152	
3	1	Don	1893	Semi-corr. compo	6	–					
3	2B/2A	Don	1911	Composite	8	E	–	SS	4/37	31153	
4	1	Don	1893	Semi-corr. compo	6	–					
4	2B/2A	Don	1911	Composite	8	E	–	SS	10/36	31155	
5	1	Don	1893	Semi-corr. compo	6	–					
5	34B/34A	York	1910	Brake van	8	E	–	GE	8/28	6726	
6	1	Don	1893	Semi-corr. compo	6	–	–	NE	5/10	3760	
6	34B/34A	York	1910	Brake van	8	E	–	GE	7/28	6727	
7	1	Don	1893	Semi-corr. compo	6	–	–	NE	5/10	3761	
7	34B/34A	York	1910	Brake van	8	E	4/14	–	–	–	1
7	39B	York	1916	Brake van	8	E	–	GE	10/25	6728	
8	1	Don	1893	Semi-corr. compo	6	–	–	NE	5/10	3762	
8	39B/39A	Don	1910	Brake van	8	E	–	GE	8/28	6733	
9	1	Don	1893	Semi-corr. compo	6	–	–	NE	5/10	3763	
9	39B/39A	Don	1910	Brake van	8	E	–	GE	3/28	6736	
10	1	Don	1893	Semi-corr. compo	6	–					
10	39B/39A	Don	1910	Brake van	8	E	–	GE	6/28	6734	
11	14	York	1898	Third	8	C	–	GN	3/26	41802	
12	14	York	1898	Third	8	C	–	GN	11/25	41805	2
13	14	York	1898	Third	8	C	–	GN	11/25	41810	
14	15	York	1898	Open third	8	C	–	NE	3/25	874Y	
15	15	York	1898	Open third	8	C	–	NE	3/25	2185Y	
16	15	York	1898	Open third	8	C	–	GE	7/26	41830	
17	2	York	1898	Composite	8	C	10/27	–	–	–	
18	2	York	1898	Composite	8	C	1/28	–	–	–	
19	35	Cow	1906	Brake van	8	E	–	GN	3/29	4180	
20	2	York	1898	Composite	8	C	–	GE	12/26	63804	
21	2	York	1898	Composite	8	C	2/26	–	–	–	
22	2	York	1898	Composite	8	C	11/27	–	–	–	
23	44	Don	1905	Composite brake	12	C	–	NS	2/35	7772	
24	34	York	1906	Third	8	E	–	SS	6/34	31049	
25	2	York	1898	Composite	8	C	2/27	–	–	–	
26	1	Don	1893	Semi-corr. compo	6	–					3
26	39B/39A	Don	1910	Brake van	8	E	–	GE	5/28	6735	
27	16	York	1906	Third	8	E	–	NE	8/29	22339	
28	2	York	1900	Composite	8	C	6/29	–	–	–	
29	16	York	1906	Third	8	E	–	NE	8/29	22142	
30	17	Don	1906	Third	8	E	–	GC	7/29	52031	
31	17	Don	1906	Third	8	E	–	GC	7/29	52032	4
32	17	Don	1906	Third	8	E	–	SS	11/29	3626	
33	17	Don	1906	Third	8	E	–	GC	7/29	52033	
34	18	Don	1906	Third	8	E	–	GE	4/34	61794	
35	18	Don	1906	Third	8	E	–	GE	11/33	61798	
36	18	Don	1906	Third	8	E	–	GC	11/34	52052	
37	18	Don	1906	Third	8	E	–	SS	7/34	31051	
38	19	Don	1903	Third	8	C	–	GN	12/25	41627	
39	19	Don	1903	Third	8	C	–	GN	12/25	41630	
40	19	Don	1903	Third	8	C	–	GN	9/25	41633	
41	19	Don	1903	Third	8	C	4/14	–	–	–	5
41	49B	Don	1920	Brake third	8	E	8/35	–	–	–	6
42	19	Don	1903	Third	8	C	–	GN	5/25	41634	
43	19	Don	1903	Third	8	C	–	GN	10/25	41638	
44	20	Don	1889	Third	6	–	–	NE	/12	3772	
44	39B	York	1914	Brake van	8	E	–	SS	4/36	310	
45	36	Cow	1903	Brake van	8	C	12/24	–	–	–	
46A	37	Don	1883	Brake van	6	–					
46	36	Cow	1903	Brake van	8	C	12/24	–	–	–	
47A	37	Don	1883	Brake van	6	–					
47	36	Cow	1903	Brake van	8	C					

137

No.	Dgm.	Built	Type	Wheels	Roof	Cond.	To Section or Area	Re-No.	Note
48A	37	Don 1883	Brake van	6	–				
48	36	Cow 1903	Brake van	8	C	11/23	–	–	–
49	37	Don 1890	Brake van	6	–				7
49	59	Don 1922	First	8	E	–	GC 11/33	52049	8
50A	37	Don 1883	Brake van	6	–				
50	36	Cow 1903	Brake van	8	C	12/24	–	–	–
51	40	Don 1893	Brake van	6	–	–	GN 11/22		9
52A	37	Don 1883	Brake van	6	–	5/11	–	–	–
52	36	Cow 1903	Brake van	8	C	–	SS 9/26	38 or 39	
53A	37	Don 1883	Brake van	6	–				
53	36	Cow 1903	Brake van	8	C	11/27	–	–	–
54A	37	Don 1883	Brake van	6	–	5/11	–	–	–
54	36	Cow 1903	Brake van	8	C	8/25	–	–	–
55	19	Don 1903	Third	8	C	–	GN 8/25	41639	
56	19	Don 1903	Third	8	C	–	GN 3/25	41658	
57	19	Don 1903	Third	8	C	–	GN 7/25	41712	
58	19	Don 1903	Third	8	C	–	GN 8/25	41694	
59	19	Don 1903	Third	8	C	–	GN 7/26	41713	
60	3	Don 1893	Composite	6	–				10
60	59	Don 1922	First	8	E	–	GC 9/34	52050	
61	19	Don 1903	Third	8	C	–	GN 2/26	41737	
62	19	Don 1903	Third	8	C	–	GN 12/25	41738	
63	24	Don 1894	Third	6	–	–	NE 11/22		
64	31	York 1902	Open third	8	C	11/37	–	–	–
65	31	York 1902	Open third	8	C	7/36	–	–	–
66	31	York 1902	Open third	8	C	1/38	–	–	–
67	15	York 1902	Open third	8	C	–	GN 7/26	41832	
68	15	York 1902	Open third	8	C	–	GN 7/26	41833	
69	34	York 1906	Third	8	E	–	SS 10/33	31052	
70	34	York 1906	Third	8	E	–	SS 10/33	31054	
71	34	York 1906	Third	8	E	–	SS 8/33	31057	
72	34	York 1906	Third	8	E	–	SS 10/33	31061	
73	22	Don 1907	Third	8	E	–	SS 12/33	31081	
74	22	Don 1907	Third	8	E	–	SS 8/33	31082	
75	22	Don 1907	Third	8	E	–	GC 7/29	52034	
76	48	Don 1883	Brake third	6	–	–	NB /13		
76	2B	Don 1914	Composite	8	E	–	SS 11/35	3367	
77	48	Don 1883	Brake third	6	–	–	NB /13		
77	2B	Don 1914	Composite	8	E	–	GN 1/36	42515	
78	48	Don 1883	Brake third	6	E	–	NB /13		
78	3A	York 1914	Composite	8	E	–	NS 12/36	7819	
79	48	Don 1893	Brake third	6	–	–	NB /13		
79	3A	York 1915	Composite	8	E	–	NS 11/36	7820	
80	45	York 1905	Brake composite	12	E	–	NE 9/36	2321	
81	45	York 1905	Brake composite	12	E	–	NE 11/36	2322	
82A	37	Don 1883	Brake van	6	–				
82	38	Don 1908	Brake van	8	E	–	–	–	11
83A	37	Don 1883	Brake van	6	–				
83	36	Cow 1903	Brake van	8	C	–	GE 5/28	6730	
84	37	Don 1890	Brake van	6	–	–	GN 10/22		
85A	37	Don 1883	Brake van	6	–	–	/13		
85	36	Cow 1903	Brake van	8	C	–	GE 3/29	6737	
86	56	York 1903	Semi-open first	8	C	12/24	–	–	12
87	4	Don 1883	Composite	6	–	–	NE 5/13	3781	13
87	59	Don 1922	First	8	E	–	SS 2/35	31936	
88	56	York 1903	Semi-open first	8	C	1/25	–	–	12
89	56	York 1903	Semi-open first	8	C	12/24	–	–	12
90A	68	Lan 1893	Sleeping car	8	E	–	GN /10	3187	14
90	69	York 1905	Composite sleeping car	8	E	12/33	–	–	15
91	56	York 1903	Semi-open first	8	C	12/24	–	–	12
92	57	York 1905	Semi-open first	8	E	–	GN 8/31	4149	16
93	23	York 1903	Third	9	C	–	GC 12/29	52035	
94	23	York 1903	Third	8	C	–	GN 3/26	41817	
95	31	York 1901	Open third	8	C	4/38	–	–	–
96	22	Don 1907	Third	8	E	–	GE 8/33	61795	
97	49	Don 1908	Brake third	8	E	–	GC 10/35	52092	17
98	49	Don 1908	Brake third	8	E	–	GC 1/35	52061	
99	23	York 1903	Third	8	C	–	GN 3/26	41823	
100A	37	Don 1883	Brake van	6	–	12/12	–	–	–
100	36	Cow 1903	Brake van	8	C	–	GE 3/29	6738	

No.	Dgm.	Built		Type	Wheels	Roof	Cond.	To Section or Area		Re-No.	Note
101A	37	Don	1883	Brake van	6	–	5/11				
101	36	Cow	1903	Brake van	8	C	–	SS	9/26	39 or 38	
102A	37	Don	1883	Brake van	6	–	6/13				
102	36	Cow	1903	Brake van	8	C	–	GN	4/28	4035	
103	36	Cow	1903	Brake van	8	C	2/26	–	–	–	
104	62	York	1901	Sleeping car	12	C	7/26	–	–	–	
105	62	York	1901	Sleeping car	12	C	11/25	–	–	–	
106A	68	Lan	1893	Sleeping car	8	E	–	NE	5/10	3758	
106	69	York	1905	Sleeping car	8	E	12/33	–	–	–	18
107	70	York	1901	Composite sleeping car	12	C	7/27	–	–	–	
108	70	York	1901	Composite sleeping car	12	C	1/27	–	–	–	
109	62	York	1901	Sleeping car	12	C	4/26	–	–	–	
110	37	Don	1890	Brake van	6	–	–	GN	/22		
111	36	Cow	1903	Brake van	8	C	–	GE	5/28	6731	
112	37	Don	1890	Brake van	6	–	–	GN	10/22		
113	19	Don	1903	Third	8	C	–	GN	4/25	41744	
114	23	York	1903	Third	8	C	–	NE	1/26	21016	
115	19	York	1903	Third	8	C	–	GN	7/25	41746	
116	23	York	1903	Third	8	C	–	GC	10/26	52009	
117	62	York	1901	Sleeping car	12	C	1/27	–	–	–	
118	62	York	1901	Sleeping car	12	C	9/27	–	–	–	
119	62	York	1901	Sleeping car	12	C	1/26	–	–	–	
120	63	York	1907	Sleeping car	8	E	11/37	–	–	–	19
121	57	York	1905	Semi-open first	8	E	–	GN	2/31	4150	20
122	58	Don	1908	First	8	E	–	GN	4/35	4194	21
123	4	Don	1884	Composite	6	–	–	NE	5/13	3782	
123	59	Don	1922	First	8	E	–	GN	4/37	4145	
124	62	York	1901	Sleeping car	12	C	6/26	–	–	–	
125	62	York	1901	Sleeping car	12	C	9/25	–	–	–	
126	39	Don	1906	Brake van	8	E	–	GN	11/28	4037	
127	39	Don	1906	Brake van	8	E	–	GN	11/28	4039	
128	39	Don	1906	Brake van	8	E	1920	–	–	–	22
128	39C	Don	1922	Brake van	8	E	–	GC	7/37	5267	
129	1	Don	1893	Composite	6	–					23
129	39B/39A	Don	1910	Brake van	8	E	–	GN	1/29	4176	
130	39	Don	1906	Brake van	8	E	–	GN	6/28	4044	
131	39	Don	1906	Brake van	8	E	–	GN	5/28	4075	
132	39	Don	1906	Brake van	8	E	–	GE	11/28	6732	
133	35	Cow	1906	Brake van	8	E	–	SS	2/28	311	
134	35	Cow	1906	Brake van	8	E	–	GN	7/28	4021	
135	35	Cow	1906	Brake van	8	E	–	SS	4/28	313	
136	35	Cow	1906	Brake van	8	E	–	GN	12/28	4031	
137	35	Cow	1906	Brake van	8	E	–	SS	2/28	316	
138	23	York	1903	Third	8	C	–	NE	10/25	21507	
139	23	York	1903	Third	8	C	–	GN	3/26	41824	
140	23	York	1903	Third	8	C	–	GC	2/30	52036	
141	23	York	1903	Third	8	C	–	SS	10/29	3617	
142	45	York	1905	Brake composite	12	E	–	NE	12/36	2327	
143	45	York	1905	Brake composite	12	E	3/37	–	–	–	
144	37	Don	1888	Brake van	6	–	–	GN	4/19		
144	39C	Don	1922	Brake van	8	E					
145	37	Don	1888	Brake van	6	–	12/19				
145	39C	Don	1922	Brake van	8	E	–				24
146	71	Don	1889	Sleeping car	6	–					
146	70B/70A/63A	York	1910	Composite sleeping car	8	E	1/35	–	–	–	25
147	72	York	1897	Composite sleeping car	8	C	2/25	–	–	–	26
148	71	Don	1889	Sleeping car	6	–					
148	70B/70A/63A	York	1910	Sleeping car	8	E	1/35	–	–	–	25
149	72	York	1897	Composite sleeping car	8	C	1/25	–	–	–	27
150	71	Don	1889	Sleeping car	6	–					
150	70B/70A/63A	York	1910	Composite sleeping car	8	E	2/36	–	–	–	25
151	71	Don	1889	Sleeping car	6	–					
151	70B/70A/63A	York	1910	Sleeping car	8	E	1/35	–	–	–	25
152	71	Don	1889	Sleeping car	6	–					
152	39B	Don	1914	Brake van	8	E	–	GC	6/36	5250	
153	71	Don	1889	Sleeping composite	6	–					
153	39B	Don	1914	Brake van	8	E	–	GC	12/35	5251	
154	71	Don	1889	Sleeping car	6	–					
154	39B	Don	1914	Brake van	8	E	–	GC	11/35	5252	
155	20	Don	1889	Third	6	–		NE	1/11	3764	

No.	Dgm.	Built		Type	Wheels	Roof	Cond.	To Section or Area		Re-No.	Note
155	39B	Don	1914	Brake van	8	–	–	GC	5/36	5253	
156	20	Don	1889	Third	6	–	–	NE	1/11	3765	
156	39B	Don	1914	Brake van	8	E	–	GC	4/36	5254	
157	20	Don	1889	Third	6	–	–	NE	1/11	3766	
157	39B	Don	1914	Brake van	8	E	–	GC	8/37	5261	
158	20	Don	1889	Third	6	–	–	NE	1/11	3767	
158	39B	York	1914	Brake van	8	E	–	GC	12/37	5262	
159	20	Don	1889	Third	6	–	–	NB	9/22		
160	20	Don	1890	Third	6	–	–	NE	6/12	3773	
160	39B	York	1914	Brake van	8	E	–	GC	4/37	5263	
161	20	Don	1890	Third	6	–	–	NE	6/12	3774	
161	39B	York	1914	Brake van	8	E	–	GC	7/37	5264	
162	20	Don	1890	Third	6	–	–	GN	9/22		
163	24	Don	1893	Third	6	–	–	GN	4/19		28
163	31A	York	1921	Third	8	E	–	GC	5/35	52077	
164	20	Don	1890	Third	6	–	–	NE	6/12	3775	
164	39B	York	1914	Brake van	8	E	–	GC	12/37	5265	
165	64	York	1906	Sleeping car	8	E	11/31	–	–	–	
166	64	York	1906	Sleeping car	8	E	4/31	–	–	–	
167	64	York	1906	Sleeping car	8	E	11/31	–	–	–	
168	64	York	1906	Sleeping car	8	E	11/31	–	–	–	
169	64	York	1906	Sleeping car	8	E	11/32	–	–	–	
170	64	York	1906	Sleeping car	8	E	12/31	–	–	–	
171	24	Don	1891	Third	6	–	–	GN	4/19		
171	31A	York	1921	Third	8	E	–	GC	12/35	52078	
172	24	Don	1891	Third	6	–	–	GN	10/22		
173	24	Don	1891	Third	6	–	–	GN	10/22		
174	20	Don	1891	Third	6	–	–	GN	9/22		
175	20	Don	1891	Third	6	–	–	NE	6/12	3776	
175	39B	York	1914	Brake van	8	E	–	GC	2/36	5266	
176	20	Don	1891	Third	6	–	–	GN	9/22		
177	20	Don	1891	Third	6	–	–	NE	6/12	3777	
177	31A	York	1921	Third	8	E	–	GC	2/36	52079	
178	20	Don	1891	Third	6	–	–	NE	6/12	3778	
178	31A	York	1921	Third	8	E	–	GC	5/35	52080	
179	24	Don	1891	Third	6	–	–	GN	11/22		
180	20	Don	1891	Third	6	–	–	NE	6/12	3779	
180	31A	York	1921	Third	8	E	–	GC	1/36	52081	
181	71	Don	1892	Sleeping car	6	–	–	GN	9/22		
181	68	Don	1922	Sleeping car	Artic.	E	–				
181A	68	Don	1922	Sleeping car	Artic.	E	–				29
182	71	Don	1892	Sleeping composite	6	–	–	GN	9/22		
183	62	York	1902	Sleeping car	12	C	9/25	–	–	–	
184	62	York	1902	Sleeping car	12	C	4/27	–	–	–	
185	62	York	1902	Sleeping car	12	C	12/25	–	–	–	
186	62	York	1902	Sleeping car	12	C	1/26	–	–	–	
187A	68	Lan	1893	Sleeping car	8	–	–	NE	5/10	3758	
187	64A	York	1905	Sleeping car	8	E	11/31	–	–	–	
188	25	Don	1894	Dining third	8	C	2/26	–	–	–	
189	25	Don	1894	Dining third	8	C	2/27	–	–	–	
190	59	Lan	1893	Dining first	8	–	–	GN	/10	3185	
190	75A	Don	1914	Dining	8	E	–	GC	1/36	52103	
191	59	Lan	1893	Dining first	8	E	–	GN	/10	3186	
191	75A	Don	1914	Dining	8	E	–	GC			
192	60	Lan	1893	Dining first	8	–	–	NE	5/10	3756	30
192	29A	Don	1914	Dining third	8	E	–	SS	7/35	3925	
193	59	Lan	1893	Dining first	8	–	–	NB	/10		
193	29A	Don	1914	Dining third	8	E	–	SS	7/35	3927	
194	75	Old	1893	Dining	8	C	5/23	–	–	–	31
195	75	Old	1893	Dining	8	C	5/23	–	–	–	32
196	78	Don	1905	Dining composite	12	C	–	NB	7/13	162	33
196	59	Don	1922	First	8	E	–	GC	9/37	52102	
197	78	Don	1905	Dining composite	12	C	–	SS	11/28	32452	
198	80	Bhm	1893	Kitchen car	6	–	–	GN	/22		
199	80	Bhm	1893	Kitchen car	6	–	–	GN	/22		
200	80	Bhm	1893	Kitchen car	6	–	–	GN	/22		
201	80	Bhm	1893	Kitchen car	6	–	–	NB	/22		
202	5	Glo	1893	First	Artic.	–	–	GN	8/25		34
203	5	Glo	1893	First	Artic.	–	–	GN	3/25		34
204	5	Glo	1893	First	Artic.	–	–	GN	9/25		34

No.	Dgm.	Built	Type	Wheels	Roof	Cond.	To Section or Area	Re-No.	Note
205	5	Glo 1893	First	Artic.	–	–	GN 12/24		34
206	31A	York 1921	Third	8	E	–	GC 12/35	52082	
207	34	York 1906	Third	8	E	–	GE 2/34	61796	35
208	26	Old 1893	Third	6	–	–	NE 10/22		
209	26	Old 1893	Third	6	–	–	NB 10/22		
210	26	Old 1893	Third	6	–	–	NB 10/22		
211	80A	York 1914	Kitchen car	8	E	–	GC 2/30	52039	
212	80A	York 1914	Kitchen car	8	E	–	GN 11/29	42182	
213	80A	York 1914	Kitchen car	8	E	–	GN 7/29	42183	
214	37	Crn 1893	Brake van	6	–	12/19	–	–	–
214	39C	York 1921	Brake van	8	E	–	GN 5/31	4018	
215	37	Crn 1893	Brake van	6	–	–	GN 10/22		
216	37	Crn 1893	Brake van	6	–	–	GN 10/22		
217	37	Crn 1893	Brake van	6	–	–	GN 10/22		
218	37	Crn 1893	Brake van	6	–	–	GN 4/19		
218	39C	York 1921	Brake van	8	E	–	GC 4/31	5215	
219	37	Crn 1893	Brake van	6	–	–	GN 4/19		
219	39C	York 1921	Brake van	8	E	–	GC 4/38	5268	
220	37	Crn 1893	Brake van	6	–	–	NE 10/22		
221	37	Crn 1893	Brake van	6	–	–	NE 10/22		
222	25	Don 1894	Dining third	8	C	2/26	–	–	–
223	25	Don 1894	Dining third	8	C	2/26	–	–	–
224	40	Don 1894	Brake van	6	–	–	NE 10/22		
225	40	Don 1894	Brake van	6	–	–	NE 10/22		
226	40	Don 1894	Brake van	6	–	–	NE 10/22		
227	40	Don 1894	Brake van	6	–	–	NB 10/22		
228	73	York 1903	Sleeping composite	12	C	7/25	–	–	–
229	73	York 1903	Sleeping composite	12	C	4/27	–	–	–
230	73	York 1903	Sleeping car	12	C	4/27	–	–	–
231	74	York 1907	Sleeping composite	8	E	12/32	–	–	–	36
232	62	York 1901	Sleeping car	12	C	1/27	–	–	–
233	62	York 1901	Sleeping car	12	C	8/25	–	–	–
234	65	York 1895	Sleeping car	8	C	10/25	–	–	–	37
235	66	York 1896	Sleeping car	8	C	4/23	–	–	–
236	66	York 1896	Sleeping car	8	C	7/25	–	–	–
237	66	York 1896	Sleeping car	8	C	4/23	–	–	–
238	66	York 1896	Sleeping car	8	C	4/23	–	–	–
239	46	Don 1896	Brake composite	12	C	11/27	–	–	–	38
240	46	Don 1896	Brake composite	12	C	11/36	–	–	–	38
241	46	Don 1896	Brake composite	12	C	2/25	–	–	–	38
242	46	Don 1896	Brake composite	12	C	–	GN 5/27	457	38
243	46	Don 1896	Brake composite	12	C	11/25	–	–	–	38
244	46	Don 1896	Brake composite	12	C	2/36	–	–	–	38
245	46	Don 1896	Brake composite	12	C	1/26	–	–	–	38
246	6	Don 1896	Composite	12	C	–	GC 4/27	52014	
247	6	Don 1896	Composite	12	C	–	GC 12/26	52015	
248	6	Don 1896	Composite	12	C	–	GN 2/25	41653	
249	6	Don 1896	Composite	12	C	–	GN 1/26	41654	
250	6	Don 1896	Composite	12	C	–	GN 6/26	41655	39
251	27	Don 1896	Third	12	C	–	GN 1/27	420	
252	28	Don 1896	Open third	12	C	10/26	–	–	–
253	27	Don 1896	Third	12	C	–	GN 4/27	435	
254	28	Don 1896	Open third	12	C	1/27	–	–	–
255	27	Don 1896	Third	12	C	–	GN 2/27	429	
256	28	Don 1896	Open third	12	C	8/26	–	–	–
257	40	Don 1896	Brake van	6	–	–	NB 10/22		
258	40	Don 1896	Brake van	6	–	–	NB 10/22		
259	41	Don 1896	Brake van	6	–	–	NB 10/22		
260	41	Don 1896	Brake van	6	–	–	NB 4/19		
260	39C	York 1921	Brake van	8	E	–	GC 12/36	5269	
261	41	Don 1896	Brake van	6	–	–	NE 10/22		
262	50	Don 1896	Brake third	12	C	5/26	–	–	–
263	50	Don 1896	Brake third	12	C	–	GN 6/27	489	
264	50	Don 1897	Brake third	12	C	–	GN 5/27	465	
265	51	Don 1897	Brake third	12	C	–	GC 11/26	52011	
266	51	Don 1897	Brake third	12	C	–	GC 4/27	52022	
267	51	Don 1897	Brake third	12	C	–	GC 11/26	52023	
268	67	York 1897	Sleeping car	8	C	11/24	–	–	–
269	67	York 1897	Sleeping car	8	C	4/23	–	–	–
270	15	York 1899	Open third	8	C	–	GN 11/25	41839	

No.	Dgm.	Built		Type	Wheels	Roof	Cond.	To Section or Area		Re-No.	Note
271	15	York	1899	Open third	8	C	–	GN	11/25	41842	
272	15	York	1900	Open third	8	C	–	NE	3/25	934Y	
273	31	York	1900	Open third	8	C	1/32	–	–	–	
274	31	York	1899	Open third	8	C	9/32	–	–	–	
275	31	York	1900	Open third	8	C	2/34	–	–	–	
276	62	York	1900	Sleeping car	12	C	10/27	–	–	–	
277	62	York	1900	Sleeping car	12	C	7/26	–	–	–	
278	62	York	1899	Sleeping car	12	C	11/25	–	–	–	
279	62	York	1899	Sleeping car	12	C	10/25	–	–	–	
280	52	Cow	1900	Brake third	12	C	6/27	–	–	–	
281	52	Cow	1900	Brake third	12	C	7/27	–	–	–	
282	52	Cow	1900	Brake third	12	C	9/27	–	–	–	
283	53	Cow	1901	Brake third	12	C	–	GE	4/27	62593	
284	53	Cow	1901	Brake third	12	C	–	GE	12/26	62594	
285	53	Cow	1901	Brake third	12	C	–	GE	6/27	62595	
286	53	Cow	1901	Brake third	12	C	–	GE	4/27	62596	
287	53	Cow	1901	Brake third	12	C	–	GE	5/28	62597	
288	53	Cow	1901	Brake third	12	C	–	GC	5/27	52024	
289	42	Cow	1901	Brake van	8	C	–	GE	2/28	6729	
290	42	Cow	1901	Brake van	8	C	4/27	–	–	–	
291	42	Cow	1901	Brake van	8	C	1/27	–	–	–	
292	10	York	1900	Composite	12	C	–	GC	10/26	52016	40
293	10	York	1900	Composite	12	C	–	GC	3/27	52017	
294	10	York	1900	Composite	12	C	–	GE	6/27	63805	
295	58	Don	1908	First	8	E	–	NS	7/36	785	41
296	11	York	1900	Open composite	12	C	–	GC	3/25	2007C	42
297	11	York	1900	Open composite	12	C	–	GC	3/25	2008C	42
298	12	York	1900	Composite	12	C	–	GC	11/26	52018	
299	12	York	1900	Composite	12	C	–	GE	11/26	63806	
300	12	York	1900	Composite	12	C	–	GC	5/27	52019	
301	13	York	1900	Composite	12	C	–	GE	8/27	63807	
302	13	York	1900	Composite	12	C	–	GE	2/27	63808	
303	13	York	1900	Composite	12	C	–	GE	4/27	63809	
304	29	York	1900	Open third	12	C	–	NE	8/29	22239	
305	29	York	1900	Open third	12	C	–	SS	10/29	3652	
306	29	York	1900	Open third	12	C	–	GN	11/29	42181	
307	43	York	1900	Brake first	12	C	3/37	–	–	–	43
308	43	York	1900	Brake first	12	C	–	GC	7/27	52012	43
309	43	York	1900	Brake first	12	C	–	GC	7/27	52013	43
310	76	Don	1900	Dining first	12	C	–	GN	10/29	43246	44
311	76	Don	1900	Dining first	12	C	–	GN	11/29	43247	44
312	76	Don	1900	Dining first	12	C	3/35	–	–	–	44
313	30	Don	1900	Dining third	12	C	–	GN	11/29	43248	
314	30	Don	1900	Dining third	12	C	–	GN	11/29	43249	
315	30	Don	1900	Dining third	12	C	–	GC	11/29	52026	
316	79	Don	1900	Dining composite	12	C	–	GC	3/25	52003	
317	79	Don	1900	Dining composite	12	C	–	GC	3/25	52004	
318	79	Don	1900	Dining composite	12	C	–	NE	3/25	446Y	
319	21	Don	1900	Third	12	C	–	GN	12/25	41750	
320	21	Don	1900	Third	12	C	–	GN	7/26	41752	
321	21	Don	1900	Third	12	C	–	GN	7/26	41754	
322	54	Don	1902	Brake third	12	C	–	GC	9/26	52025	
323	55	Don	1902	Brake third	12	C	–	GC	5/27	52021	
324	54	Don	1902	Brake third	12	C	12/33	–	–	–	
325	55	Don	1902	Brake third	12	C	12/33	–	–	–	
326	54	Don	1902	Brake third	12	C	6/34	–	–	–	
327	55	Don	1902	Brake third	12	C	–	GC	8/26	52020	
328	52	Cow	1902	Brake third	12	C	–	GE	5/27	62591	
329	52	Cow	1902	Brake third	12	C	–	GE	11/26	62592	
330	53	Cow	1902	Brake third	12	C	–	NE	12/28	22244	
331	53	Cow	1902	Brake third	12	C	–	NE'	5/25	969Y	
332	77	Don	1902	Dining first	12	C	9/37	–	–	–	45
333	77	Don	1902	Dining first	12	C	3/35	–	–	–	45
334	77	Don	1902	Dining first	12	C	9/37	–	–	–	45
335	77	Don	1902	Dining first	12	C	8/35	–	–	–	45
336	32	York	1903	Third	8	C	–	NE	2/26	21224	46
337	32	York	1903	Third	8	C	–	NE	10/25	22050	
338	32	York	1903	Third	8	C	–	NE	8/25	21174	
339	32	York	1903	Third	8	C	–	GC	9/26	52010	
340	32	York	1903	Third	8	C	–	NE	9/25	21096	

No.	Dgm.	Built	Type	Wheels	Roof	Cond.	To Section or Area	Re-No.	Note
341	32	York 1903	Third	8	C	–	SS 12/29	3620	
342	47	Don 1903	Brake composite	12	C	2/26	– –	–	47
343	47	Don 1903	Brake composite	12	C	–	GN 7/27	424	47
344	47	Don 1903	Brake composite	12	C	2/26	– –	–	47
345	47	Don 1903	Brake composite	12	C	9/35	– –	–	47
346	47	Don 1903	Brake composite	12	C	2/25	– –	–	47
347	47	Don 1903	Brake composite	12	C	5/09	– –	–	48
347	47B/47A	Don 1911	Brake composite	8	E	5/23	– –	–	49
348	47	Don 1903	Brake composite	12	C	–	GN 8/27	419	47
349	47	Don 1903	Brake composite	12	C	3/25	– –	–	47
350	47	Don 1903	Brake composite	12	C	2/26	– –	–	47
351	47	Don 1903	Brake composite	12	C	–	GN 3/27	437	47
352	78	Don 1905	Dining composite	12	C	–	SS 1/29	32453	
353	78	Don 1905	Dining composite	12	C	–	NB 1913		50
353	59	Don 1922	First	8	E	–	SS 3/37	31925	
354	33	York 1902	Open third	12	C	–	NE 3/25	159Y	51
355	33	York 1902	Open third	12	C	–	GN 9/25	41747	52
356	34	York 1907	Third	8	E	–	NS 3/35	752	
357	34	York 1907	Third	8	E	–	SS 12/34	31083	53
358	34	York 1907	Third	8	E	–	SS 8/35	3902	
359	34	York 1907	Third	8	E	–	SS 7/35	3910	
360	34	York 1907	Third	8	E	–	SS 5/35	3918	
361	34	York 1907	Third	8	E	–	SS 9/35	3920	
362	34	York 1907	Third	8	E	–	GE 2/34	61797	
363	34	York 1907	Third	8	E	–	SS 7/35	3923	
364	34	York 1907	Third	8	E	–	GC 7/35	52065	
365	34	York 1907	Third	8	E	–	GC 1/36	52066	
366	34	York 1907	Third	8	E	–	GC 5/35	52067	
367	34	York 1907	Third	8	E	–	GC 5/36	52068	
368	34	York 1907	Third	8	E	–	GC 5/35	52069	
369	34	York 1907	Third	8	E	–	GC 8/35	52070	
370	34	York 1907	Third	8	E	–	GC 3/36	52071	
371	34	York 1907	Third	8	E	–	GC 4/36	52072	
372	34	York 1907	Third	8	E	–	GC 12/35	52073	
373	34	York 1907	Third	8	E	–	GC 8/35	52074	
374	34	York 1907	Third	8	E	–	GC 6/35	52075	
375	22	Don 1907	Third	8	E	–	GC 12/34	52053	
376	22	Don 1907	Third	8	E	–	GC 11/34	52054	
377	22	Don 1907	Third	8	E	–	GC 10/34	52055	
378	22	Don 1907	Third	8	E	–	GC 11/29	52037	
379	22	Don 1907	Third	8	E	–	SS 12/34	31084	
380	22	Don 1907	Third	8	E	–	SS 1/35	31087	
381	22	Don 1907	Third	8	E	–	SS 12/34	31088	
382	22	Don 1907	Third	8	E	–	SS 1/35	31089	
383	22	Don 1907	Third	8	E	–	SS 8/34	31090	54
384	22	Don 1907	Third	8	E	–	GC 7/29	52038	
385	22	Don 1907	Third	8	E	–	NE 6/34	21433	
386	22	Don 1907	Third	8	E	–	GC 4/35	52076	
387	49	Don 1908	Brake third	8	E	–	GC 9/35	52087	
388	49	Don 1908	Brake third	8	E	–	GE 1/34	62650	55
389	49	Don 1908	Brake third	8	E	–	GC 9/35	52088	
390	49	Don 1908	Brake third	8	E	–	GC 8/35	52089	
391	49	Don 1908	Brake third	8	E	–	GC 3/36	52090	
392	49	Don 1908	Brake third	8	E	–	GE 9/35	62666	
393	49	Don 1908	Brake third	8	E	–	GE 9/35	62667	
394	49	Don 1908	Brake third	8	E	–	SS 6/35	3937	
395	81	Don 1908	Royal saloon	12	E				56
396	82	York 1908	Royal saloon	12	E				56

Notes

Bhm—Birmingham Railway Carriage & Wagon Co.
Cow—Cowlairs Works (NBR)
Crn—Craven Bros Ltd
Don—Doncaster Works (GNR)
Glo—Gloucester Railway Carriage & Wagon Co.
Lan—Lancaster Carriage & Wagon Co.
Old—Oldbury Carriage & Wagon Co.
York—York Works (NER)

1: No. 7 damaged beyond repair at Burntisland 14th April 1914 and new vehicle built as replacement to Dgm. 39B.
2: No. 41805 restored as ECJS No. 12 for King's Cross Centenary October 1952. Preserved in the National Collection.
3: No. 26 was replacement for vehicle destroyed in the Thirsk accident 2nd November 1892.
4: Badly damaged at Retford 13th February 1923.
5: No. 41 destroyed in Burntisland accident 14th April 1914 and new No. 41 built to Dgm. 39B 1920.

6: Replacement No. 41 condemned August 1935 after Welwyn Garden City accident 15th June 1935.
7: Destroyed at Montrose 3rd December 1915.
8: No. 49 (as 149) damaged in deliberate derailment at Cramlington 10th May 1926 during General Strike.
9: Replacement for No. 51 destroyed in Thirsk accident 2nd November 1892.
10: Replacement for No. 60 destroyed in Thirsk accident 2nd November 1892.
11: Replacement for No. 82 (Dgm. 30A in 1903 book and Dgm. 36 in 1909 book) destroyed in Grantham accident 19th September 1906. No. 82 of 1908 to Royal Train. Preserved in National Railway Museum collection as Van 109.
12: Nos 86, 88, 89 and 91 to Corridor First Dgm. 56A 1914.
13: No. 87 was the first East Coast corridor vehicle. Built as First and converted to Composite April 1898.
14: No. 90A originally No. 188. Replaced and placed on 'A' list 1905.
15: No. 90 reinstated as Touring Camping Coach No. 66 (NE Dgm. 45) 1935.
16: No. 92 converted to Corridor First (Dgm. 57A) 1914.
17: No. 97 number of third class compartments reduced from six to three and reclassified Dgm. 49A 1914.
18: Reinstated by North Eastern Area and became Travelling Signalling School: allocated No. 2100 and Dgm. 43.
19: Replacement for No. 120, Dgm. 62, destroyed in Grantham accident 19th September 1906.
20: Open section replaced by two compartments and lavatory 1914 and became Dgm. 57A.
21: Replacement for 6-wheel No. 122 destroyed in Grantham accident 19th September 1906.
22: Destroyed in accident between Finsbury Park and Holloway 1st January 1920.
23: Replaced vehicle destroyed in Thirsk accident 2nd November 1892.
24: Fitted lavatory and renumbered Van No. 135 March 1926: used for Royal Train. Reclassified Dgm. 39E.
25: Altered to 10-berth sleeping car 1921 and reclassified Dgm. 63A.
26: Replacement for 6-wheel sleeping car destroyed in St Neots accident November 1895.
27: Replacement for 6-wheel sleeping car destroyed in St Neots accident November 1895.
28: Replacement for vehicle destroyed in Thirsk accident 2nd November 1892.
29: Subsequently renumbered (1) 182 as part of articulated set with 181.

30: Modified version of Dgm. 59, with altered seating arrangement.
31: Originally ECJS 196. Sold to NER 1896 but returned to ECJS 1897 and became No. 195.
32: Originally ECJS 197. Sold to NER 1896 but returned to ECJS 1897 and became No. 194.
33: Sold to NBR 1913 for use in Scotland.
34: Paired with 6-wheel Thirds 206, 211, 212 and 213 (by Oldbury 1893) to form articulated units.
35: Replacement for No. 207 destroyed in Grantham accident 19th September 1906.
36: Replacement for 12-wheel sleeping composite No. 231 destroyed in Grantham accident 19th September 1906.
37: First ECJS coach built at York. Started work 10th December 1895.
38: Formerly composite with luggage compartment. Altered 1906 and passenger accommodation reduced by three third class compartments and lavatory.
39: Damaged in Grantham accident 19th September 1906. Frames strengthened May 1918.
40: To Camping Coach No. 119.
41: Replacement for 12-wheel open composite of 1900 destroyed in Grantham accident 19th September 1906.
42: Converted to Open Third at York December 1913 and became Dgm. 11A.
43: Converted to First at York 1913 and became Dgm. 43A.
44: Two additional seats fitted 1914 and became Dgm. 76A.
45: Two additional seats fitted 1914 and became Dgm. 77A.
46: Involved in Eaglescliffe collision 6th May 1933.
47: Altered from Brake Third 1904.
48: Altered from Brake Third 1904. Damaged in Grantham accident 19th September 1906 and destroyed by fire at Wallyford (near Inveresk Junction) 6th May 1909. Replaced by No. 347 to Dgm. 47A.
49: Replacement for 347 destroyed by fire at Wallyford. Damaged at Retford 13th February 1923 and condemned May 1923.
50: Sold to NBR 1913 for use in Scotland.
51: Originally ECJS Open Composite No. 196. To NER 1904 but returned to ECJS 1906.
52: Originally ECJS Open Composite 197. To NER 1904 but returned to ECJS 1906.
53: Badly damaged in Castlecary collision 10th December 1937.
54: Destroyed in Castlecary collision 10th December 1937.
55: To Dgm. 49A 1914 by reducing compartments from six to three, and extending van from 16 ft to 35 ft $0\frac{3}{8}$ in.
56: Preserved in the National Collection.